# THE
# 12-WEEK
# MBA

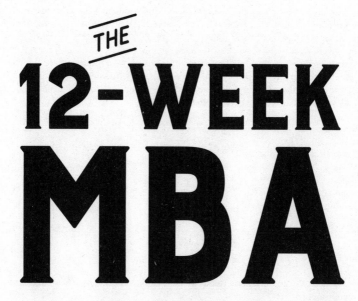

# THE 12-WEEK MBA

## LEARN THE SKILLS YOU NEED TO LEAD IN BUSINESS TODAY

BJORN BILLHARDT *AND* NATHAN KRACKLAUER

hachette
BOOKS

NEW YORK

Cover design by Amanda Kain
Cover copyright © 2024 by Hachette Book Group, Inc.

Hachette Go, an imprint of Hachette Books
Hachette Book Group
1290 Avenue of the Americas
New York, NY 10104
HachetteGo.com
Facebook.com/HachetteGo
Instagram.com/HachetteGo

First Edition: February 2024

Hachette Books is a division of Hachette Book Group, Inc.

The Hachette Go and Hachette Books name and logos are trademarks of Hachette Book Group, Inc.

The Hachette Speakers Bureau provides a wide range of authors for speaking events. To find out more, go to hachettespeakersbureau.com or email HachetteSpeakers@hbgusa.com.

Hachette Go books may be purchased in bulk for business, educational, or promotional use. For information, please contact your local bookseller or email the Hachette Book Group Special Markets Department at Special.Markets@hbgusa.com.

The publisher is not responsible for websites (or their content) that are not owned by the publisher.

Print book interior design by Sheryl Kober

Library of Congress Cataloging-in-Publication Data
Names: Billhardt, Bjorn, author. | Kracklauer, Nathan, author.
Title: The 12-week MBA: learn the skills you need to lead in business today / Nathan Kracklauer and Bjorn Billhardt.
Other titles: Twelve week MBA
Description: First edition. | New York: Hachette Go, [2024] | Includes bibliographical references.
Identifiers: LCCN 2023022282 | ISBN 9780306832369 (hardcover) | ISBN 9780306832376 (trade paperback) | ISBN 9780306832383 (ebook)
Subjects: LCSH: Management. | Leadership. | Executive ability. | Master of business administration degree.
Classification: LCC HD31.2 .K727 2024 | DDC 658—dc23/eng/20230519
LC record available at https://lccn.loc.gov/2023022282
ISBNs: 978-0-306-83236-9 (hardcover); 978-0-306-83513-1 (international edition); 978-0-306-83238-3 (ebook)

Printed in the United States of America
LSC-C
Printing 1, 2023

To Emily J. Kracklauer and Jost Billhardt

In memory of Aloysius F. Kracklauer and Jutta Billhardt

# CONTENTS

*Acknowledgments*                                                    *ix*

*Preface*                                                            *xi*

*Introduction*                                                      *xix*

*Book Overview*                                                     *xxv*


## PART I THE NUMBERS

CHAPTER 1      Value                                                  3

CHAPTER 2      Profitability                                         13

CHAPTER 3      Growth                                                27

CHAPTER 4      Risk                                                  41

CHAPTER 5      The Balance Sheet                                     51

CHAPTER 6      Cash Flow Basics                                      69

CHAPTER 7      Cash Flow and Working Capital                         77

CHAPTER 8      Cost Structures                                       93

CHAPTER 9      Valuation Foundations                               109

CHAPTER 10     Creating Value                                      129


## PART II THE PEOPLE

CHAPTER 11     Joy and Frustration                                 143

CHAPTER 12     Trust and Expectations                              149

CHAPTER 13     Adventures in Feedback                              159

CHAPTER 14     Engagement and Motivation                           173

CHAPTER 15     Leadership                                          189

CHAPTER 16     Collective Action and Decision-Making               203

CHAPTER 17     Defining the Decision                               215

# CONTENTS

CHAPTER 18    Deliberating and Executing    227

CHAPTER 19    The Power of Dissent    239

## CONCLUSION

CHAPTER 20    Embracing Responsibility    251

*Next Steps*    *257*

*Appendix*    *259*

*Glossary*    *263*

*Notes*    *283*

*Bibliography*    *293*

*Index*    *305*

# ACKNOWLEDGMENTS

This book is the result of what we have learned teaching leadership and business acumen classes to rising and senior leaders at Fortune 500 companies for twenty years. We have to thank many, many people who have shaped our professional journey: our students, our clients, our business partners, and the hundreds of people we've had the honor of collaborating with at Enspire Learning and at Abilitie. Special thanks go to our fellow leadership team members, who not only left their mark on the content but also kept the ship afloat whenever this project took us from our day jobs.

Many people taught us valuable leadership lessons as colleagues, and others devoted their time and their critical thinking as they reviewed our work: Deaton Bednar, Julia Bojko, Seth Caplan, Matt Confer, Mike Daross, Andreas Dittrich, Karen Dube, Megan Fanale, Ben Glazer, Sean Hennessey-Hsieh, Joel Hock, Marianne Inman, Pelle John, Sebastian Jülich, Rebecca Kaloo, Paulash Mohsen, Joana O'Neil, Luke Owings, Trey Reynolds, Adrian Taylor, Jörg Uhde, Michael Watkins, Nick White, Paul Woodruff, and many others.

Our collaboration would never have started without the intervention of Professor Jan Hammond of Harvard Business School, who believed in both of us when we had little in the way of track records. Our collaboration would not have been as creatively fruitful over many years without the advice, assistance, and friendship of Professor Steven Tomlinson, who currently teaches at Seminary of the Southwest. Many teachers and mentors opened our eyes to the ideas whose surface we've merely scratched in this book. Among them are Larry Carver, Elva Gladney, Robert Kane, Tatjana Schönwälder-Kuntze, and Lloyd Walker, as well as all our fellow students and faculty at the University of Texas Plan II Liberal Arts Program, the Harvard Business School MBA Program, and the Philosophy, Politics, and Economics Executive Masters Program at the Ludwig-Maximilians-Universität München.

We owe Lisa Shannon, Leah Spiro, and Dan Ambrosio and all the other good people at Hachette Go a debt of gratitude for believing in this project and bringing it from our minds to the page.

Finally, we are deeply indebted to our families—Billhardt's Kirsten, Aaron, Carter, and Evan; Kracklauer's Emily, Anna, and Emma; and Loraine Roy—for their support and forbearance as they kept our *other* ships afloat whenever this project took us away from our true calling.

# PREFACE

On day one of Harvard Business School's entrepreneurship class, Professor Bill Sahlman began by displaying charts of industry valuations. The graphs told stories of rising and falling fortunes: plastics peaking and crashing in the 1970s, investment banks in the 1980s, dot-coms in the 1990s.

Then Sahlman showed the number of Harvard Business School students entering those industries in the years before the crashes. Each time, the influx of MBAs seems to predict the demise. The more Harvard graduates flocking to an industry, the deeper its plunge.

It was a tongue-in-cheek performance, meant to put aspiring Harvard MBAs, not known for their modesty, in their places. Still, the data is real, and it raises important questions: Does the traditional MBA do as advertised and give you skills and knowledge that help you "administer a business"? And aren't there a million successful business leaders who never bothered to get the MBA stamp of approval?

Jokes about the value of MBAs are a dime a dozen. (How many MBAs *do* you need to screw in a lightbulb?)* Yet hundreds of thousands of smart, ambitious people enroll in MBA programs annually. They do so not only for the promise of new expertise, knowledge, and skills that will vault

---

* "One. She holds it firmly and the universe revolves around her." And that's just one of several of the lightbulb type alone.

them to advancement, higher salaries, or perhaps the confidence to start their own companies. They also hope to build valuable personal contacts and professional networks. They hope to signal their leadership potential to employers. Like a peacock's feathers, the ostentatious expense of two years and tens of thousands of dollars displays their fitness for the corporate ladder.

Networking and signaling value also play roles in the decision to attend law school and medical school. But no one questions the need for doctors and lawyers to complete several years of study before they are allowed to practice their profession. The question remains: Outside of specialized fields like investment banking or accounting, is there a body of management expertise that you can (a) learn in school and (b) apply in any business organization and functional area?

Our answer is an emphatic but qualified yes! For those who can afford the time and the expense, a traditional two-year MBA might be a perfect fit to acquire that knowledge along with the network and pedigree. But make no mistake: You'd be paying for the latter. And because spending lots of time and money is actually the point—the more you spend, the more exclusive the network and the higher the value you're signaling—you may as well go for the elite institutions only. Meanwhile, what options do you have if you'd rather dedicate your time and money elsewhere but want to learn how to manage your own business or someone else's?

This book's premise is that you can acquire the essential skills and knowledge to "administer a business" at lower cost and in less time. The teachings of a traditional MBA program aren't fluff. But in an age where disruption is the only constant, it is difficult for the MBA to keep up. In the early 1900s, when the degree was invented, most businesses made money in similar ways, and you could rely on the fact that most skills you were taught would be relevant twenty years later. Today, many skills you learn in an MBA program will be outdated soon after you accept your first job.

There are two reasons for this. One is that today's business skills evolve quickly. By the time the latest best practices on how to use social media marketing make it into an MBA curriculum, they are already outdated. The second reason is that the world of business has grown more complex. Much of what you learn in an MBA program will not be relevant in the industry, company, and function you enter. Today's business schools teach fascinating supply chain topics that are misleading when a pandemic disrupts the global supply chain or if the job you aspire to is in enterprise software sales. The case studies about marketing you'll work through in the traditional MBA? They're based on marketing channels as passé as Friendster.*

As the functional and industry expertise you need in management has become more diverse and complex, much of the knowledge that you gain in an MBA can be acquired in a more timely fashion and at lower cost *on the job.* In fact, much of what you learn in your MBA you'll have to unlearn or relearn on the job.

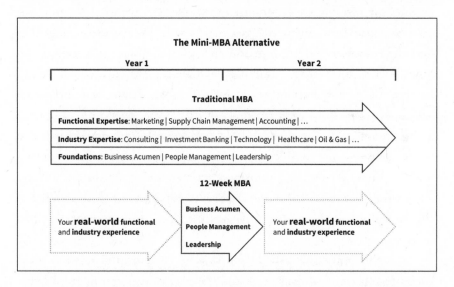

When you strip away the two-year MBA's function-focused and industry-specific content, we believe that you are left with two timeless and universal topic areas. Part I of this book is about numbers: using the

---

* Wondering what Friendster is? Exactly.

tools of accounting and finance to measure the value a business is creating. Part II is about people: how to work *with* and *through* others.

On what basis have we performed this distillation? For the past two decades, we've created leadership development and business acumen programs for some of the world's largest and most admired companies— companies like Coca-Cola, Marriott, and Dell—as well as hundreds of start-up companies on all continents except Antarctica. Our mini-MBAs and leadership programs have helped over a hundred thousand professionals. We've seen firsthand the truly universal gaps when it comes to the skills required to administer real-world businesses. To promote employees to management positions from within, organizations consistently struggle to identify people with business acumen and leadership skills. Companies spend fortunes trying to fill those gaps, even though many of their employees are credentialed MBAs!

Not surprisingly, we experienced the same pain points as we grew our own two businesses during the past twenty years. We've also struggled to find and empower leadership teams, and yes, we've made just about every possible business acumen and people management mistake ourselves. Even in the narrow human resources field in which our two companies have operated, lessons we learned about marketing, operations, and even human resource management did not transfer well from one company to the other. We've had to unlearn and relearn these lessons as the world has evolved. But some hard-won business acumen and leadership skills have stood the test of time. This book is a product of both our clinical observation of real-world companies and our time in the entrepreneurial school of hard knocks.

When Harvard established the first MBA class in 1908, it was called a "delicate experiment." This book and the twelve-week online mini-MBA program on which it's based reflect our own commitment to advance that experiment, delicately, and with a laser focus on what matters in a world that has evolved significantly.

The world offers no shortage of challenges that can only be addressed by organizations, whether single-digit teams or giant corporations. There are far more management positions than there are people with elite MBA credentials to fill them. And these positions ought to be filled by people with a greater diversity of backgrounds than those with the time and means to go through a graduate-school curriculum. Good business acumen and management practices are simply too important to our flourishing: individually—as consumers, citizens, colleagues, employees, or shareholders—and collectively, as organizations, communities, nations, and a precariously interconnected world.

# THE
# 12-WEEK
# MBA

# INTRODUCTION

**W**hat do aircraft engines, medical devices, and wind turbines have in common? Not enough, decided the board of directors of General Electric (GE) in November 2021, and they split the iconic US conglomerate into three companies.

Few corporations had epitomized American enterprise as GE had. Launched in 1892, GE was one of the original constituents of the Dow Jones Industrial Average stock index, where, unlike any of its initial peers, it stayed for over a hundred years. In 2000, it was the world's most valuable company, with a stock market valuation of over $600 billion.

Jack Welch, CEO of GE at its zenith, was held in awe by a generation of aspiring managers. Under Welch, GE was considered a marvel of good management. The company's leadership development curriculum was admired as the gold standard of executive training. In 2008, standing in a wood-paneled conference room, we pitched one of our training solutions to GE's corporate leadership development team. We felt like knock-kneed teenage musicians auditioning at Juilliard.*

However, by that time—2008—the bloom was off GE's rose. The company's stock price had never regained its high-water mark after the dot-com

---

* Nothing came of that meeting, but GE eventually became a client. In fact, its big November 2021 breakup was communicated to company managers during one of our training workshops for its high-potential leaders.

crash of 2000, and the global financial crisis took it deeper still. From 2000 to 2020, GE's stock market valuation dropped from $600 billion to $100 billion. It was against this backdrop of value destruction that CEO Larry Culp and the board of directors split the company into three parts.

Was the breakup a good business decision?

You could argue either way. No doubt GE's board did. We don't think the answer is truly knowable. Suppose all three successor companies wind up doing spectacularly well afterward. Could they not have done even better together? If they eventually fail individually, maybe their demise would have been quicker if they had stayed joined at the hip. And what do we mean by "doing better"? Is there a score that we can use to measure the three successor companies' performance—individually or as a unit—to determine whether the breakup was the right call? Is it the stock market valuation? If the market valuation is the score, how long does the game last?

There are no simple answers to these questions. But the questions themselves—and the decision GE faced—illustrate the essence of what it means to administer a business. Business decisions like GE's involve the following:

**Coordinating to create value:** The fundamental task of management is to coordinate the actions of many—possibly hundreds of thousands of people—so that they accomplish more together than they could individually. GE's history as a conglomerate shows that you cannot take for granted that the whole will always be greater than the sum of the parts. Sometimes it is, but sometimes it isn't. GE's board decided in 2021 that it wasn't.

**Executing through others:** The board's decision was just the first step. Implementing it was a massive, multiyear undertaking. Many thousands of people were involved in disentangling the divisions, whether they agreed with the decision or not. They had to perform the disentangling well or face all sorts of problems, including lost customers and lawsuits. Along the way, they encountered new problems that demanded creative new solutions. And all that work had to happen while their day jobs—little things like, you know, making jet engines, medical devices, and power turbines—continued without letup.

**Making decisions under uncertainty:** GE's board could not predict the outcome before the decision was made, and even afterward, there would be no way to know for certain if the alternative might not have been better after all.

**Designating winners and losers:** The people making the decision didn't face its worst consequences. In the frictions of the transition, some people may have had to find new jobs, not all of which were better than the old ones. Others may have had to postpone retirement. Still, if the board had opted to keep the company whole, someone would have had to bear similar hardships. Either way, though, Culp and the other members of the board wouldn't be surviving on ramen noodles and cat food.

GE's breakup was a decision of epic proportions, affecting hundreds of thousands of people and hundreds of billions of dollars of assets. Few of us make decisions of similar import. Yet managers wrestle with fundamentally similar challenges in industries from high-tech manufacturing to building maintenance; in functions from human resources to research and development; at scales from single-digit start-ups to multinational corporations.

This book focuses on the timeless and universal knowledge and skills that apply in any management position.

## POETS AND QUANTS

We've divided this book into two parts, reflecting two different but complementary perspectives on business. You might look at a company and see a collection of *resources*, including human resources, with properties that you can arrange and rearrange in ways that create new resources. All of these resources can be quantified in terms of something we call monetary value. Alternatively, you might see an intricate web of *relationships* between people, with new relationships forming while others change or rupture. Not only does this web resist quantification, but within it, quantification is just another strategy to influence which bonds develop or strengthen, which weaken or break.

At business school, students sometimes get boxed into the categories of poets and quants, depending on a perceived tendency to look at a business from one perspective or the other.* People may naturally prefer one perspective. When you picked up this book, you might have scanned the table of contents with trepidation about one half and excitement about the other. Still, it's possible to look at the world of business through both lenses. What's more, knowing when to use one lens and being able to quickly switch perspectives are among the most important but underrated skills you'll need as you take on ever-greater responsibilities in an organization.

Our own facility with the two perspectives is the result of happy accident, a kind of advantageous occupational hazard. Our company delivers mini-MBA and corporate leadership programs using team-based business simulations. The simulations are computer-based multiplayer games that provide a hands-on platform for learning the concepts in this book. Designing those simulations and using them as teaching tools† forced us to switch between the two perspectives. So does playing them in our twelve-week MBA program.

We've tried to replicate as much of that magic as possible in book format. Although we've explored the perspectives in two separate parts, you'll find many places where we make explicit connections between

---

* There's even a popular MBA program comparison and information website called poetsandquants.com.
† Not to mention playing them more often than we care to admit.

them. Many more connections are implicit, and we're sure you'll find connections and echoes we didn't introduce consciously. Although the chapters in each part of the book build on each other, feel free to switch back and forth between parts as inspiration guides you.

The mini-MBA curriculum on which this book is based lasts twelve weeks, a pace that gives our students ample time to absorb the ideas and deepen them in discussions, exercises, and our simulations. If you organize your own book club as you read this book, a similar twelve-week journey might prove helpful. Alone or in a group, you can supplement your reading with some of the interactive exercises and resources at www.12weekmba.com.

# BOOK OVERVIEW

**R**eading this book over twelve weeks gives you time to digest some of the ideas and explore them in a book club or with friends and colleagues. But it also provides plenty of time for work and life to whisk you away on other adventures. The following outline serves primarily as a summary you can refer to when you return to *The 12-Week MBA* after a "leave of absence." It's also a helpful guide to which chapters you can safely skim or skip, depending on your prior experience.

**Part I** is about a company's scorecard. What is value, how do we create it, and how can we measure whether we're doing so successfully? **Chapter 1** provides an overview of Part I and examines the source of what's called shareholder value—sustainable flows of cash to the owners of a company—and its three fundamental drivers: profitability, growth, and risk.

In Chapters 2 through 4, we scrutinize those drivers one by one. **Chapter 2** defines profitability in terms of the value created for *customers* and the resources consumed in delivering customer value. We look at how the profit and loss statement reports profitability and then investigate what levers we can use to increase it.

Driving a wedge between price (what the customer is willing to pay) and cost (what it takes to deliver customer value) is one thing. Growing the volume of (profitable) business is another, and it's what we investigate in **Chapter 3**. We distinguish between market growth, market *share* growth, and expansion into new markets, and we consider how companies can take advantage of these options.

Future growth can't be reported. It has to be forecast. Forecasts are stories about how the world will evolve. Investors value more highly the stories in which they have greater faith. Investor confidence is the subject of **Chapter 4**, where we define risk in terms of investors' faith in the company's ability to make good on its promises, promises that ultimately have to be kept in terms of cash payments. The *predictability* of cash flows is just as important an input to value as are profitability and growth.

Investor confidence in cash flows is the lens through which we look at the two other important financial reports—the balance sheet and the cash flow statement—in Chapters 5 through 7. In **Chapter 5**, we look at the balance sheet both as a record of past transactions and as a record of future commitments to different stakeholders. **Chapter 6** provides an overview of the cash flow statement and spotlights the all-important distinction between *accounting profit* and the cold, hard reality of *cash flow*. **Chapter 7** deepens that insight by showing what drives a company's profit and cash flow apart, so that, paradoxically, an apparently growing, profitable company may actually be self-destructing.

Having examined the value drivers profitability, growth, and risk, we look at their interactions in Chapters 8 through 10. **Chapter 8** shows that cost structure—the relative importance of fixed and variable costs in a business model—affects how a company's growth profile translates into higher (or lower) profitability while increasing (or reducing) risk.

Chapters 9 and 10 unveil the mysteries behind company valuation. **Chapter 9** gets fairly technical. We describe the framework behind company valuation—discounted cash flow analysis—and how it is used to calculate the intrinsic value of a company. Our approach provides just enough rigor to convey the high-level concepts, not to turn you into a mergers and acquisitions specialist!

**Chapter 10** is about how you, as a manager at any level and in any function, connect to value through the three drivers: profitability, growth, and risk. We end Chapter 10 and Part I with a reflection on how shareholder value might also tell us something about value creation for a broader range of company stakeholders: investors, yes, but also customers, employees, communities, and the environment.

The concepts introduced in Part I permeate profit-oriented organizations to such a degree that organizational activity and decision-making are largely incomprehensible without them.* Still, they might not call attention to themselves every minute of your workday. The opposite is true for topics in **Part II**, where **Chapter 11** sets the stage: working *through* others to achieve organizational goals (Chapters 12 through 15) and working *alongside* others to make decisions and coordinate activities in a complex division of labor (Chapters 16 through 19).

Trust is the foundation of business, and setting proper expectations is the bread and butter of building trusting relationships. These are themes that underpin the discussion of investor confidence in Part I. **Chapter 12** picks them up and firmly places them at the heart of Part II, diving down to the manager-employee relationship as the building block of trust, on which coordinated organizational activity rests. In addition to giving practical tips for setting mutual expectations, Chapter 12 introduces another recurring theme for Part II: the manager's version of the Hippocratic oath: First, do no harm.

Day to day, some of the biggest opportunities to "do harm" to the trusting relationship come from giving feedback, the subject of **Chapter 13**. Giving feedback is essential as managers pursue the twin goals of achieving results in the present and building capabilities for the future.

**Chapter 14** looks at employee engagement and motivation, another area in which "first, do no harm" is the best guide. We'll look at different intrinsic motivators, how not to undermine them, and—occasionally,

---

* We'd argue that these concepts hold for not-for-profit organizations, too, but it's an argument that goes well beyond this book's scope.

with great care and respect—how to leverage them to help employees deliver their best performance.

Leadership is a huge and ambiguous topic. In **Chapter 15**, after running through some common interpretations of leadership—as opposed to management—we introduce an overlooked account of what leadership is all about: overcoming so-called social dilemmas, problems of collective action.

**Chapter 16** identifies aligned decision-making across all functions and levels of an organization as one of the central challenges of administering a business. We identify the team as the basic decision-making unit of the organization. We show how, under uncertainty, the quality of decision-making cannot hinge on the quality of the outcome. Instead, good collective decision-making is about having a good process. We introduce a basic model for decision-making—define, deliberate, execute—to structure decision-making, and we base the remaining chapters on these three elements.

Our general approach is to identify what goes wrong at each decision-making stage. **Chapter 17** covers the define stage. At this stage, teams tend to miss key decisions or spend too much time on unimportant ones. They may also overlook attractive options, get trapped in false choices, fail to use available data, or get caught in analysis paralysis. We look at techniques teams use to overcome these errors.

One common team decision-making pitfall is the failure to clarify how a decision is made and by whom. In **Chapter 18**, we look at three deliberation methods—consensus, majority rule, and sole decider—and weigh their pros and cons. When it comes to the execution stage, we discuss how consistently applying a well-defined process helps ensure that teams remain aligned in their downstream decisions and activities, even when agreement is not universal.

Agreement often isn't universal and, arguably, shouldn't be. **Chapter 19** looks at how dissent—rather than a hindrance to collective decision-making—is a powerful tool that often should be nurtured rather than avoided. For this, too, we suggest some simple techniques and highlight the importance of diversity in teams.

Our concluding **Chapter 20** weaves together our two strands—numbers and people—and allows us to share our views on what makes management, with its joys and frustrations, a worthy and rewarding calling.

# PART I

# THE NUMBERS

# CHAPTER 1

# Value

**"W**hat is the purpose of a company?"

We open many of our leadership training programs with that question. "Making money" is the immediate answer we hear most often. The more senior participants may offer the more sophisticated response "Creating value for shareholders." But after the easy answers are blurted out, we let an uncomfortable silence unfold.

Slowly, other responses emerge. "Creating great products for customers," someone will usually venture. More rarely, "Creating something that has value for society" or "Providing meaningful and gainful employment."

Our own answer is "All of the above." The purpose of a business is to create value for a wide range of stakeholders. Stakeholders include the company's owners, referred to as **shareholders** when ownership rights are partitioned into shares. But customers, suppliers, employees, and society at large also have a stake in a company's survival and flourishing. The view that creating **shareholder value** reigns supreme—an idea that has been called both the "biggest" and the "dumbest"* idea in business—is too narrow.

---

* Jack Welch's word, not ours. We'll hear more about the late former CEO of GE in Chapter 15.

But suppose creating broader *stake*holder—not just *share*holder—value is the true objective of a business? How do we know how much stakeholder value we're creating, if any?

There is no easy answer to this question. In this book, we focus on shareholder value—the value created for the owners of a business—and how to measure it. Partly, we want to keep things simple. Measuring shareholder value is tricky enough. However, by the end of Part I, you may be convinced that the ideas behind shareholder value, when properly understood, show us something about broader stakeholder value as well, even if seen through a glass, darkly. We certainly believe so. If ever we have the chance to meet, we'd be delighted to explore this question more deeply, over drinks.

Whether shareholder value is our indicator metric or a goal in itself, shouldn't we understand what it is? Quite surprisingly, we've seen that many managers have hazy notions of what shareholder value means and how their activities create—or destroy—it. In preparation for an executive education program, we had the opportunity to interview the chief financial officer (CFO) of a global car manufacturer. We asked him what knowledge gaps he saw among the high-potential senior managers being groomed for executive board positions. Even at that level of seniority, the CFO complained about widespread misconceptions about value and financial management!

In a traditional MBA, you learn several methods for valuing companies and assets, wrapping your head around concepts like company beta, the Black-Scholes model of option value, and how to use multiples to calculate the value of a company on the back of a napkin. All of this may be useful if you work on Wall Street. Or if you want to engineer the next global financial crisis.*

We believe a lot of this knowledge is, at best, overkill for most managerial positions. At worst, it's a dangerous distraction. But managers ought

---

* No joke. Two of the originators of the Black-Scholes model, Myron Scholes and Robert Merton, who earned the Nobel Memorial Prize in Economic Sciences for their efforts, went on to found a hedge fund based on their insights. In 1998, their fund—Long-Term Capital Management—famously went belly-up and nearly dragged the whole financial system with it.

to understand the drivers of shareholder value, how their decisions connect to those drivers, and how they interact with the decisions made by other managers in other functions. To achieve that, managers must become fluent in the language of finance: the lingua franca that allows different functions like sales, marketing, logistics, HR, customer service—each with their own quirky success metrics—to communicate and coordinate, and to measure progress on value creation.

So what is shareholder value? Let's get straight to the point:

*Shareholder value originates in a company's discounted future net cash flows.*

Part I is all about unpacking this clunky eleven-word sentence. The remainder of this introduction is a preview.

In early 2007, the shareholders of Finnish technology company Nokia had good reasons to be optimistic. Nokia's brand was strong. Its feature phones, famed for their sturdiness and battery longevity, dominated the market. Global standards of living were rising, and Nokia had a good foothold in countries with emerging middle classes. Waves of innovation in portable devices were imminent, and Nokia looked like the company best positioned to ride them. After all, one of Nokia's subsidiaries produced the network infrastructure that made the phones useful.

Shareholder value originates in a company's discounted future net cash flows.

Investors could tell themselves an attractive story about Nokia's future. That said, history abounds with sudden reversals of fortunes, particularly in industries characterized by quickly evolving technology, like consumer electronics. There was, for example, the case of Apple, whose early success in personal computing had never translated to market dominance and whose operating system was an also-ran next to Microsoft's. In fact, Apple had only escaped bankruptcy thanks to a timely infusion of cash from its rival. As rosy as Nokia's outlook may have seemed in early 2007, there were also reasons to be anxious. You never know what threats might be lurking around the corner.

Still, the optimistic view seemed more persuasive, and Nokia's stock price rose steadily during 2007. Starting the year at around $21 per share, the upward trend continued into November, when it reached a decade high above $40.

Twenty-one dollars. Forty dollars. What's behind those numbers? *Shareholder value originates in a company's discounted future net cash flows.*

Let's start unpacking. As we said earlier, a shareholder is someone who owns a business in whole or in part.* So much for shareholders. Meanwhile, *value*, like beauty, is in the eye of the beholder. If a shareholder sells a stake in the company, the price at which it sells says something about how much they valued the company. If someone had valued it more highly, they would not have sold their shares at that price. Likewise, the buyer agreed to the same price, so the price also reflects the value this person sees in it. If the buyer believed it had less value, they wouldn't have bought it. In early July 2007, Nokia shares traded at around $29. Buyers must have thought they were getting at least that much in value. Sellers may have had misgivings about Nokia's value and decided that $29 was as good as it gets. Each party may see different value. The price is just a point where their perceptions of value overlap, making a transaction possible.

The first important point is that value is always subjective. It's the perspective of a particular person. Although the *price* is established objectively in the contract between buyer and seller, it derives from their subjective perspectives. Second, current owners and potential buyers value the

---

* Whether stockholders of a publicly traded company are truly its owners in the same sense that you might own your house or your phone is a matter of some controversy. We could go off on a fascinating tangent about the nature of property ownership and the history of the joint stock company. But not in this book! Also, for convenience, we'll speak of shareholders as people. In fact, publicly traded companies like those we've mentioned so far (GE and Nokia) are owned by both people and institutional investors such as pension funds. Institutional investors employ highly sophisticated investment professionals who invest on behalf of the institutions' stakeholders.

company, whether or not the transaction takes place. The value is there even when we can't observe it through a price.

Where does this leave us? Are we saying that creating value for share-holders means giving them warm, fuzzy feelings about the company? Yes, in a sense, that's exactly what we are saying. However, a company is different from a piece of jewelry, a fitness machine, or a home with a yard. The benefit of owning a company is to generate cash that you can use to buy the things your heart desires. Most people don't have warm, fuzzy feelings about cold, hard cash itself. However, owning a company offers the *promise* of cash in the future: next year, two years from now, and a long time—an indefinitely long time—thereafter.

The thing about promises is that they can be broken.

When you own a company, you look forward to those promised future cash flows. But you can also imagine any number of scenarios in which those cash flows do not materialize. A global crisis might eliminate demand for your service, as the Covid-19 pandemic did for countless restaurants. A change in customer preferences may permanently reduce demand for your product, as often happens to toy makers, whose customers' tastes are notoriously…shall we say "volatile"? Or a new technology might make your product obsolete. And yes, we will get back to Nokia.

Hindsight benefits us when we look at these examples. Restaurant owners and toy makers don't have crystal balls to warn them of looming threats. But neither are they caught entirely unawares. And here is where investor feelings come into play. You can envision a flow of future cash flows, but you may partly disbelieve in that story. And you may do so to greater and lesser degrees. Some investment stories inspire more confidence. Some cause stomach ulcers. Likewise, as an investor, you probably feel more confident in nearer-term cash flows than in longer-term ones. As you count up your company's forecasted cash flows, you probably feel that later ones count less. You **discount** them, in other words.

How does an investor forecast the future cash flows? A company enjoys a sustainable source of cash *inflows* when customers buy what it is selling.

So, the investor needs a forecast of the company's future sales. But cash will also flow *out of* the company to its suppliers and employees and, in taxes, to governments. The cash theoretically available for the shareholder can only be the **net cash flow**, the difference between what flows in and what flows out. It's all about buying low and selling high: If the company buys stuff (including labor) from its suppliers at a lower price than it can sell its product to a customer, then it makes money.

We all know this, and we generally use the term *profit* when we talk about buying low and selling high. But it turns out that cash flow and profit are not the same thing. Why they are not, and what makes them diverge from each other, is a big part of what we'll explore in the next chapters. Diverging profits and cash flows are one of the major reasons that investors get queasy about a company's prospects.

The following picture emerges: A company's owner values the company because it can deliver a stream of future cash flows that this shareholder can use to buy the things they need and want. The owner can forecast those cash flows with explicit numbers that are based on a story about the company's future performance. Next year may deliver a $1,000 cash flow, the year after that $5,000, and then $10,000 every year after that, indefinitely. But the shareholder recognizes that there is always a risk that the cash won't flow as projected. They will discount each flow in proportion to their confidence in the company—or lack thereof.

So, what does that mean for us as managers? What can we do to create value in these terms? We can increase the company's net cash flows, which means growing the inflows faster than the outflows. And we can raise shareholders' confidence in the company's ability to deliver net cash flows. In this chapter and the rest of Part I, we'll look at three drivers of value that we as managers influence with our actions every day:

**Profitability:** Driving a wedge between what our customers are willing to pay and the costs required to create what they pay for

**Growth:** Getting more and more customers to buy more and more of what we offer

**Risk:** Increasing shareholder confidence in our ability to keep our promises

In its 2007 annual report, Nokia summarized what looked like a spectacular year. Sales were 24 percent higher than they were in 2006, and pretax profits had increased even faster, by 44 percent. In the same report, Nokia forecast further growth of 10 percent in the mobile device market, and the company targeted an even higher share of that market. It sure looked like Nokia's engine was firing on at least two of our three value pistons. Interestingly, however, the annual report for 2007 was released on March 31, 2008, when shares were trading at around $32, around 20 percent lower than the high reached the previous fall. Had anything happened that might have made investors feel queasy about Nokia's future?

If you've been paying attention—surely you are!—then you may be wondering if there was a problem with cash flow. Sorry, no. Net cash flow had increased over sevenfold.

But something *had* happened. During the previous summer, Nokia investors had seemingly shrugged off a little event: the release of a new gadget by Apple on June 29, 2007. But by March 2008, it was clear that the iPhone posed a serious threat to the story Nokia's investors had believed as late as November.

With the benefit of hindsight—knowing that the iPhone effectively drove Nokia out of the mobile device business*—we might wonder why anyone was willing to buy shares even at $29 in March 2008. But again, Nokia's decline and Apple's success were not certain at that point. It remained unclear whether Nokia would be able to keep the promises of

---

* Nokia eventually sold what had previously been its core, the mobile device business, to Microsoft in 2014, choosing to focus on network infrastructure instead. In 2016, another Finnish company, HMD Global, began producing smartphones and feature phones under the Nokia brand, with decidedly modest success.

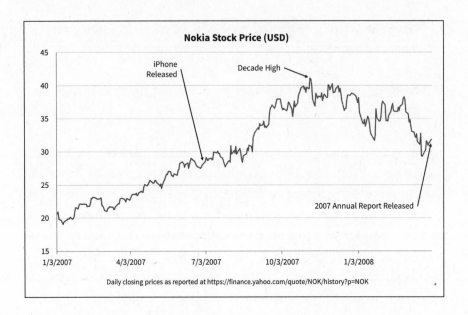

**Nokia Stock Price (USD)**

Daily closing prices as reported at https://finance.yahoo.com/quote/NOK/history?p=NOK

future cash flows, the promises investors had once valued as highly as $40 per share.

You may be wondering why we keep using the word *promise.* There are two parts to keeping promises: You keep the ones you make, and you don't make ones you can't keep. A central theme of this book is *trust,* which is fundamentally about keeping promises. A company's value may show up in a valuation or a stock price, but it is founded on the trust between the shareholder and the company's managers. They are the ones who make and keep promises about cash flows, making only those they can keep and keeping those they make.

In business, numbers and people are inextricably intertwined.

# CHAPTER 1 KEY TAKEAWAYS

The purpose of a company is to create value for a range of stake-holders: investors, customers, employees, suppliers, the community, and the environment.

The value of a company is in the eye of the beholder; the price at which a company is bought and sold is where two people's perception of value overlap, making an exchange possible.

Shareholder value originates in a company's discounted future net cash flows.

The main drivers of shareholder value are profitability, growth, and risk.

## CHAPTER 2

# Profitability

People born before 1984 remember a world divided into two camps, each pointing nuclear weapons at the other. Arguably, the Cold War was a conflict between ideologies that disagreed about whether the profit motive should be the organizing principle of our economic relations. One would hope the concept of profit is well defined and important enough to be worth setting the world aflame over. You decide at the end of this chapter!

Business begins with needs and desires. We all have them, and we're all forever trying to get what we want using our scarce resources like money, time, and skills. Suppose you wanted to share an exquisite dining experience with that special someone. The prices at a Michelin-starred restaurant might spoil your appetite. But imagine the money and time it would cost you to single-handedly replicate the exact same experience: Consider not just the finest (and priciest) ingredients and top-notch equipment but also the years of training to reproduce the meal. Compared to all that, the restaurant bill is a steal!

That's where the opportunity for profit comes from: the difference between the resources a customer would have to devote to satisfying a need and the resources a business has to devote to create the same thing for that customer. Somewhere in that gap lies a price at which the customer will say, "OK, I'm getting enough value here to shell out my money. After all, it's considerably less than I would have to spend if I tried to create that value myself." Profitability is about driving a wedge between what a customer is willing to pay and the cost of the resources a business consumes in delivering that value.

> Profitability is about driving a wedge between what a customer is willing to pay and the cost of the resources a business consumes in delivering that value.

A business can pull two levers to make more profit. It can try to consume fewer resources even as it creates the same amount of customer value. Or it can increase the customers' willingness to pay more by helping them perceive greater value. The two levers may work at cross-purposes. Skimp on fresh ingredients, and the customer won't pay $50 for a salad. Spend half a day sculpting the Eiffel Tower out of mashed potatoes, and your costs explode. Managing profit is a balancing act between these two levers, an act performed with customers, competitors, employees, and suppliers all shaking your tightrope.

## CONSTRUCTING THE PROFIT AND LOSS STATEMENT

Imagine we're planning to launch a simpler eatery: a food truck specializing in grilled cheese sandwiches. We'll need to determine what kinds of resources we'll consume as we create value for our customers, who value things like flavor, nutritiousness, and convenience. The resources we consume are called **expenses**. If we can convince customers to buy at our chosen price, we'll realize **sales**.* The difference in the dollar value of sales and expenses is that thing we call **profit**.

---

* *Sales* is a common word for the number of things we sell multiplied by the price at which we sell them. Another term for the same thing is *revenue*. In the United Kingdom, you may see *turnover* as well. Unless you're a poet, having many words for the same concept is not terribly helpful. But there you have it. We don't make the rules; we just report 'em.

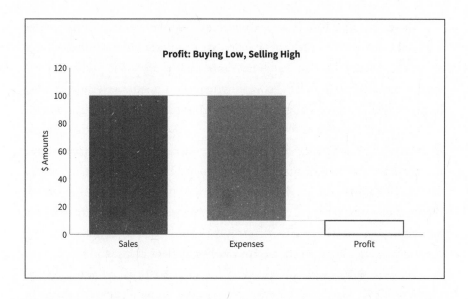

Customers are prepared to pay for the value we create, to a point. They could also prepare and pack a sandwich each morning. The food truck is a viable business because it can deliver a fresher, tastier meal faster and cheaper than the customer could produce, including (importantly) preparation time.

We can look at profit from different scales: at the level of the individual sandwich or on a daily, weekly, monthly, quarterly, or even annual basis. When it comes to sales, the monetary impact of scale is pretty straightforward. The more sandwiches we sell, the more sales we record. But when we look at the resources we consume, things get complicated quickly for two main reasons. Some resources are hard to value monetarily. Additionally, we may not always be able to attribute one resource's consumption to a specific meal or even to a specific period. Eventually, for example, our cutting board will wear out. But to which individual sandwich, day's tally, or weekly, monthly, quarterly, or annual tally should we attribute its monetary value as an expense? Questions like these make the definition of profit ambiguous and keep accountants busy.

The **profit and loss (P&L) statement**\* records sales and expenses—
what we delivered to consumers and what resources we consumed—over
a specific time. Companies whose shares trade on stock exchanges are
legally required to publish P&L statements on a quarterly and annual
basis, and you can typically access them from the company's website.

Our first category of expenses is the resources consumed creating the
sandwich, the thing the customer values. In the case of our food truck, these
resources are the ingredients, labor, and energy inputs. If we ran a delivery
service with a bike courier, the biker's labor would also count as what we call
the **cost of sales**. That's a confusing term, because it specifically does *not*
refer to the cost of selling activities. It is the cost of producing and delivering
the things we sell†: grilled cheese sandwiches, bags of chips, and sodas.

The difference between sales and cost of sales is called **gross profit**.
Gross profit is a particularly revealing measure of the business's health. In
principle, customers could have assembled the inputs themselves. Their
willingness to pay a price higher than our input costs reveals that we must
have special capabilities: a particularly tasty recipe, an extremely efficient
production process, or cheaper access to suppliers. Or we might be able
to offer intangible benefits. If a celebrity raves about our grilled cheese
on social media, then by dining at our truck, our customers also buy a
moment's respite from the fear of missing out.

Besides producing what our customers buy, we also have to persuade
them to buy in the first place. They need to hear about our food truck,
and not because we've been associated with a salmonella outbreak. We
may pay for our location to appear on Google Maps or print and distribute flyers. Gross profit is such an important measure because it determines
how much money we have left over to spend either on persuading more
customers to buy or on persuading customers to buy more: our selling and
marketing expenses.

---

\* Frequently also called the income statement.
† You may also see *cost of revenue*, *cost of goods sold (COGS)* for companies selling goods, and *cost of services* for companies selling services.

Running a food truck involves other unavoidable expenses. At the very least, we have to do the accounting, and because we're better at cooking beans than counting them, we pay someone to run the numbers. That expense has nothing to do with creating customer value or with persuading customers to buy, but it is part of our business model. More complex businesses than food trucks may have many other **general and administrative expenses** beyond accounting, for example a human resource function, an IT function, or a group of executives who make sure the corporate jet gets a workout. Most corporate financial reports lump together **selling, general, and administrative expenses** into a single line item (**SG&A**).

The simplicity of our menu is part of our charm, but we're turning away vegan customers. That's why we're experimenting with different all-vegetable cheese substitutes. We haven't quite got the recipe right yet, but if we keep spending time and money on **research and development (R&D)**, we'll get there eventually, right?

What about the cutting boards that are wearing out? And for that matter, what about all the other kitchen equipment, not to mention the truck itself? Those resources cost money to buy in the first place and to replace once they've broken down for good. The consumption of long-lived resources is impossible to associate with any one sandwich, day, week, month, or year. Our accountant Margaret calls these long-term resources **assets**, each of which has its characteristic expected useful life. The only way Margaret can account for the consumption of **tangible assets** like cutting boards is to assume they get used up over their useful life, in what we call **depreciation**. Meanwhile, we don't use up our accounting software in any meaningful sense. But it does become obsolete over time and will also have to be replaced. Margaret refers to this kind of resource consumption—consumption of **intangible assets**—as **amortization**.

Together, cost of sales, SG&A, R&D, and depreciation and amortization make up what we call **operating expenses**. They are intrinsic to our business, and after we take them out, we are left with **operating profit**. A business that can generate an operating profit can continue indefinitely, at

17

least in principle. Or perhaps it's better to put it the other way: A business that consistently generates an operating loss is doomed. It consumes more resources than it can replenish using the money its customers are willing to part with.

Have we truly accounted for all the business's expenses, though? The answer is no. Businesses also have expenses that are hard to characterize as operating expenses—in other words, nonoperating expenses. For one, our food truck uses many resources that we do not explicitly pay for. We drive it on roads and bridges, we park it in a public square, we rely on police and a legal system to make sure people don't take the grilled cheese and run. **Public goods** are paid for by the government, which raises the funds to do so via **taxes**. Taxes and the relationship between government and commerce raise many questions and much disagreement, none of which fall within the scope of this book. Suffice to say that businesses use and consume public goods that have to be paid for somehow.

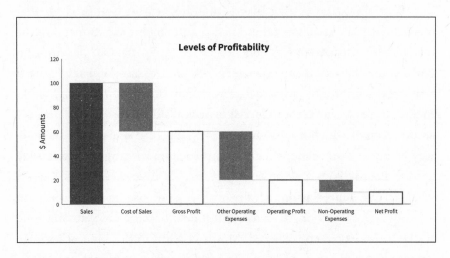

We still have not considered all the expenses that a business consumes as it creates value for customers. The missing factor hinges on time. The P&L's structure is misleading in one sense: It *begins* with sales, then subtracts out all the expenses. In reality, customers buy our grilled cheese menu *after* most of the resources have been paid for and after many have been consumed. Before our cash register first rings, we have to buy or lease the truck, the equipment, and our raw materials; we have to advertise; we have to develop a tasty recipe. Sales don't occur until after resources have been committed—some irrevocably. We call resources we commit up front our **investments**. To be able to commit resources up front, somebody has to have an available stockpile. In practice that means a stockpile of cash that can be transformed into grilled cheese production resources. The person who contributes that cash is called an **investor**. The stockpile is called **capital**.

A business that only generates operating losses will eventually deplete the initial investment. Not only does that mean the investor loses capital, but it also means the business can no longer create value for our customers, employees, and suppliers. A sustained operating loss is bad news all around, except maybe for our rival grilled cheese truckers.

Finally and crucially, because the capital has to be committed before sales can take place, investment is always an uncertain enterprise. Our food truck may never

> Investors do not know if they will ever get their capital back. They expect to be compensated for accepting this anxiety.

generate an operating profit. It might not even generate a gross profit. In fact, when the initial investment takes place, neither we nor the investor can be certain that it will even generate sales.

These observations take us straight back to our introductory discussion and the uncertainty that investors face. A business endeavor typically involves an up-front commitment of resources before customers pay for the value we created for them. Investors do not know if they will ever get their capital back. They expect to be compensated for accepting this anxiety.

Different investors may choose different structures of compensation. In the investment agreement called **debt**, the business agrees to pay back the amount initially contributed by the investor by a specific time and pays a fee called **interest** along the way.

Interest is another expense of the business, but it is not considered an operating expense, because it is not intrinsic to the business itself. A business could avoid paying interest entirely with no change to its operating model by resorting to a different structure of agreement with its investors. In the **equity** agreement, the company does not commit to returning the investor's capital on a specific date. And it does not commit to any specific rental fee. In return, the equity investor has an indefinitely valid claim on anything that remains after all other expenses—the entire list we've gone through so far: cost of sales, SG&A, R&D, depreciation, interest, and taxes—have been paid for. Those leftovers are called **net profit.*** And net profit is ultimately what we're talking about when we buy low and sell high.†

| Simple P&L Statement | |
|---|---|
| | in US Dollars |
| **Sales** | **10,000** |
| Cost of sales | 6,000 |
| **Gross Profit** | **4,000** |
| SG&A | 1,500 |
| R&D | 1,500 |
| Depreciation/amortization | 200 |
| Operating profit | 800 |
| Interest | 300 |
| Taxes | 100 |
| **Net Profit** | **400** |

* You may also see the word *earnings*.
† If you already have a background in finance, you'll probably quibble with a dozen things in the last two paragraphs. We know. There are many ways to structure debt and equity agreements, including exotic mélanges to titillate all manner of investment tastes. And the interplay between interest, taxes, and profits combined with thousands of regulations in hundreds of jurisdictions is like a candy store for lawyers and accountants. But for most of us, the bread-and-butter description here should suffice.

In a sense, the P&L statement tells us something about how value is created and shared among all the stakeholders. Customer value is reflected in sales, particularly in the price. The value employees and suppliers gain from the business is reflected in several of the individual line items: Those expenses are their income. By way of taxes, companies contribute to the public goods from which they benefit along with everyone else. And investor value is reflected in interest (creditors) and net profit (shareholders). It's a far-from-perfect lens through which to look at stakeholder value. But it's a start.

## PROFITS, MARGINS, AND COMMON-SIZING

So far, we've been speaking about profit in absolute terms: a specific amount of dollars, euros, or any other currency. If we sell a grilled cheese sandwich menu at $10 and the ingredients and labor cost us $6, then we make a $4 gross profit. If we sell a thousand meals in a three-month quarter, we make $4,000 gross profit. But we can also speak about profit

| Simple P&L Statement | | | |
|---|---|---|---|
| | in US dollars | | as a % of sales |
| **Sales** | **10,000** | | 100% |
| Cost of sales | 6,000 | | 60% |
| **Gross Profit** | **4,000** | **Gross Margin** | **40%** |
| SG&A | 1,500 | | 15% |
| R&D | 1,500 | | 15% |
| Depreciation/amortization | 200 | | 2% |
| **Operating Profit** | **800** | **Operating Margin** | **8%** |
| Interest | 300 | | 3% |
| Taxes | 100 | | 1% |
| **Net Profit** | **400** | **Net Margin** | **4%** |

in relative terms, as a percentage of sales. How much of our sales turns into gross profit? For every $1 in sales, we make $0.40 in profits, or 40 percent. The term *profit* is usually used for absolute amounts, and *profit margin* for relative amounts. So if we sell a thousand $10 meals and consume $6 worth of cheese, bread, labor, and so forth on each meal, we have a gross profit of $4,000 and a **gross margin** of 40 percent. Similarly, if we have $3,200 in other operating expenses, then we make an operating profit of $800 and an **operating margin** of 8 percent. And if we're left with $400 after paying interest and taxes, we'd have a **net margin** of 4 percent. Unfortunately, you can't rely on everyone using the same nomenclature, but it's handy to have two distinct words ("profit" and "margin," respectively) for the two distinct concepts, so that's what we'll use throughout this book.

Absolute dollar amounts and relative percentages are both important ways to look at quantities. If we cheese-preneurs want to know whether we'll have enough money to pay next month's rent, we definitely care about the absolute amount of profit. But if we want to understand how our food truck's performance evolves over time, day to day, month to month, year by year, the absolute amounts may tell a confusing tale because sales and expenses go up and down over time. When we are comparing across time, margins may tell a clearer story. As our operation increases its sales, it may grow its profits in absolute terms, too. But our margins may be decreasing, revealing that we need to work more efficiently.

We might also want to benchmark our performance against other food service businesses. We're obviously not going to achieve absolute amounts of profit comparable to those of Burger King. But it would be instructive to see if we are as good at turning a dollar of sales into profits as this larger company is. By **common-sizing** using margins—profit levels per sales—instead of absolute dollar amounts, we can better benchmark our performance against our own historical performance and that of other companies.

## COST AS A LEVER OF PROFITABILITY

Profitability is one of our three drivers of shareholder value, along with growth and risk. You might say it's the wellspring of value. Our other two drivers—growth and risk—further characterize future profits: Will profits increase or decrease? Do we feel more or less confident in them?

To increase profitability, we can decrease expenses or persuade customers to pay a higher price. But what can we do specifically to engage those two levers?

When we ask that question rhetorically in a management training program, most of the answers we get relate to reducing expenses. That's probably to be expected, because everyone can look for ways to do more with less. Just about everyone has been asked to do so at some point!

There are countless ways to reduce expenses. For example, we can *negotiate with our suppliers*, driving bargains to lower their prices. Labor is often the biggest cost, whether in production/delivery, sales, administration, or R&D. Salary and wage negotiations can be famously tense on both sides. Employees band together in unions and bargain collectively, sometimes shutting down operations. Companies may threaten to move their business activities to areas with lower labor costs and weaker unions and often make good on those threats. In the 1960s, one of our grandfathers ran a manufacturing business. He decided to seek out lower labor costs within the United States, moving the company and its many-ton machinery by river barge from Wisconsin to Texas. In recent years, East Asia has been a popular destination to move manufacturing.

We can also try to *use fewer inputs or cheaper ones.* In our food truck, we can slice the cheese thinner. Or we can try to *redesign our processes.* Reconfiguring our cooking station to reduce the time it takes to make each sandwich might allow us to serve more customers during the lunch rush.

Negotiations and process improvement methodologies are skills you can learn. But what works depends on what kind of a business you're in and what function you perform. What makes you a more effective manager—as opposed to a negotiator or a process engineer—is your ability to understand how different levers interact with each other, sometimes working together, sometimes working at cross-purposes.

In the late 1990s and first years of the twenty-first century, Nokia was famous for producing reliable mobile phones at affordable prices. One of Nokia's key strengths was design-to-cost. The company designed its phones to make the production process highly efficient in terms of raw materials and labor. This design-to-cost approach allowed the company to realize a substantial gross profit based on the low cost of sales. What were the trade-offs? On the one hand, Nokia consciously chose to trade up-front expenses in R&D for savings in cost of sales. As we'll see in Chapter 3, though, orienting R&D toward design-to-cost may have involved another trade-off.

Balancing acts like that happen everywhere. Skimping on cheese may lower our cost of sales, but a less tasty sandwich won't launch a free word-of-mouth advertising campaign. We'll have to spend more on flyers to get the word out. Buying a used truck may conserve money now but may cost more in maintenance in the long run.

## PRICE AND VALUE PERCEPTION AS LEVERS OF PROFITABILITY

So much for expenses. Pricing, however, is at least as important a factor in profitability. Arguably, it's more important. Because relatively few people in an organization contribute actively to pricing decisions, pricing often gets taken for granted by those working outside of sales and marketing departments. At the same time, activities and decisions in other areas of the business indirectly affect pricing in profound ways that might make the key difference to a customer's willingness to pay. Customers can, in fact, be convinced to pay a higher price. Or at least, in a highly competitive market, with rivals dropping prices, they may be persuaded to keep paying the same price. The secret is to offer more value.

Again, there are infinitely many industry, market, and customer-specific ways to increase customer value. We can **improve the quality** of our offering, with the trade-off being that we might have to spend more on better ingredients, on R&D to concoct a tastier recipe, or on marketing to figure out what customers look for in a superior sandwich. Or perhaps we can **bundle** different products together, as fast food restaurants do. McDonald's, Burger King, and others sell their burgers close to their production costs, enticing you to buy a whole meal with what looks like a discount. They make their profits on the fries and the soda, whose input costs are low.

Finally, we might focus on a small subset of customers and shape our offering to their highly specific needs so that they are willing to pay a higher price. We could skip the lunch rush entirely and instead cater to harried parents leaving the surrounding offices at day care pickup time. They might be happy to pay a 50 percent premium for a to-go box with a little toy. **Customer segmentation**, higher quality, and savvy bundling are all ways to keep prices high. But the trade-offs they involve may not necessarily drive that wedge between price and cost to produce higher profits.

Whether we're driving profitability through cost savings or by persuading customers to recognize the value in our offering and pay a higher price, management is about evaluating the total impact of a decision, factoring in the trade-offs.

# CHAPTER 2 KEY TAKEAWAYS

Profit compensates shareholders for contributing their capital to a business endeavor for an indefinite period. Profit is the difference between the monetary value of sales and the monetary value of the expenses within a given accounting period.

The P&L statement:

- Shows the sales achieved and the expenses incurred over a given period, usually a quarter or a year
- Categorizes expenses according to the purpose they serve

We define different profit levels by including or excluding some of the expenses to answer different questions about the health of a business. The most common levels include gross profit, operating profit, and net profit.

Common-sizing by calculating profits as a percentage of sales—gross, operating, and net margins—allows us to better compare performance across time and between different companies.

Profitability can be increased in two ways:

1. Reducing expenses, for example by negotiating aggressively with suppliers, consuming fewer inputs per unit sold, or improving processes in all the different areas of the business.

2. Creating more value for customers and asking them to acknowledge this value by paying a higher price.

Managerial choices almost always involve trade-offs. Understanding the trade-offs lies at the heart of managing for value.

## CHAPTER 3

# Growth

Is big beautiful? Is a large company necessarily more valuable than a small company? How should we measure size? Number of employees? Number of customers? Sales?

From the viewpoint of creating shareholder value, profits are what matters. All else being equal, more profit is better than less profit. A company that promises to steadily increase its profits is more valuable than one whose profits have plateaued—assuming the promise is credible. In principle, you could increase profits by steadily decreasing expenses or increasing prices, as we saw in the previous chapter. But there's a limit to how low expenses can drop for each product or service sold and a limit to how high prices can rise. That's why the most realistic way to grow profits is to increase the number of units sold while keeping profitability as high as possible. Growing profits is the goal. Growing sales is—usually—the means.

> Growing profits is the goal. Growing sales is—usually—the means.

For one type of investor—creditors, such as banks—growth is not very important. Creditors are happy as long as the company makes all its interest payments and repays the principal on time. In contrast, companies are not contractually bound to deliver regular payments in a set amount to the other type of investors: shareholders. Instead, shareholders may be able to take money out of the company in what are called **dividends**, if and when surplus cash is available.

That's a humongous if. If a company doesn't consistently earn more in sales than it pays in expenses, it won't have surplus funds sitting around when shareholders want them. Even when cash is momentarily available, extracting it may cut the company off at the knees, wrecking its ability to generate surplus cash in the future. If our food truck shares all its surplus cash with its owners, it will lack the cash to replace the cutting board or the truck itself when those assets wear out. As we'll explore in greater detail toward the end of Part I, shareholders' claims on cash are far weaker than creditors'. Shareholders accept greater risk than creditors do because they hope that the company will eventually pay out not just regular dividends but steadily growing dividends. Growing dividends can only come from growing profits.*

Increasing your sales is straightforward. You convince more customers to buy. Or you convince customers to buy more. That's what is called **organic growth**, like new branches from a healthy tree trunk. Alternatively, you can "buy more customers" by acquiring another company and its business. This **inorganic growth** is like transplanting a tree from someone else's orchard to your own.

## THE LEVERS OF GROWTH

If our food truck is selling sandwiches hand over fist, we might consider getting a second truck at another location and potentially double our

---

* Dividends are not the only way for shareholders to extract funds from a company. In recent years, many publicly traded companies have opted to return cash to shareholders by buying up the company's own shares on the stock market. The company's bid for its own shares keeps its stock scarce and, by reducing the number of shares available, increases the amount of company profit *per share*. Both factors may have a positive impact on the stock price. In addition, tax law may treat dividends differently from the gains investors earn by selling their shares at a higher price than when they bought them. Whether share buybacks or dividends are more advantageous, and for whom, is a matter of some controversy in the investment community.

profits. If our success continues, maybe we'll open a full-on restaurant and eventually more restaurants in the tristate area. Who knows where this concept will lead? Grilled cheese gondolas in the canals of Venice and Amsterdam? An eventual acquisition of McDonald's? At each stage of our expansion, we'll project our future sales and profits and then determine what steps we now have to take to put us on that trajectory.

It's helpful to break down the drivers of growth in terms of markets: sets of customers with desires and needs, and the ability to pay someone else to fulfill them with products or services. For our grilled cheese food truck, our market is hungry people who are within walking distance and have no aversion to the hardened, curdled secretions of a ruminant's mammary glands.* What makes a market like that grow or shrink?

Both of us moved to Austin, Texas, in the 1990s to attend the University of Texas. At that point, Austin was a town of around half a million souls. Since then, it has more than doubled in size. If a halfway decent food truck had launched when we were students, it should have realized growth, thanks to all the people moving to the area. Markets can grow purely demographically. But they might also grow because of changes in how customers behave. Grilled cheese may go out of style as unsophisticated, only to come roaring back as a hearty vegetarian treat spiced with childhood nostalgia. Finally, whether or not grilled cheese is in style, overall economic conditions may change. When economic conditions put people out of work, many tighten their family budgets. They pack lunches instead of heading to the food truck.

The preceding three factors—demographic growth, customer behavior change, and economic conditions—clearly influence market growth. But in what sense are they levers that we control as managers? We can contribute to demographic growth in our own small way, but that's seldom a business matter. No individual company, not even the largest, can control overall economic conditions. At best, *what* we offer, the *quality* of what we offer, and our *selling and advertising activities* may have an impact

---

* Aka cheese.

on customer behavior. Market growth, although an important factor in our sales growth, is not easily manageable. At best, companies can make wise choices about which markets to address.

But there's another way to grow our food truck business. We could take a larger share of the existing market. In the office parks where we stop our truck, there are other options for hungry worker bees. A convenience store offers prepacked sandwiches of questionable freshness but unmatched prices. There's a smoothie kiosk. There's a decent Tex-Mex restaurant that serves half-price margaritas at lunchtime. We could grow our business by enticing customers away from all these options. Competition, in other words.

There are many ways to compete for market share. Price is the obvious way, and we may be able to grow—increase our sales at the expense of our competitors—by dropping the price. Of course, that approach trades off against lower profitability on a per-sandwich basis. And it may provoke a price war: a race to the bottom in the local food service market. Customers will be delighted, but sellers' profits will shrink, and market shares might well end up right where they started.

We can also compete by offering greater value to customers on all the things that customers find attractive about our offerings: tastier recipes, friendlier service, quicker service. Even when successful, that approach, too, involves trade-offs. Offering greater value will probably raise our expenses, and we may improve our sales without increasing profits. Meanwhile, our competitors are no fools. They will also find ways to make their former customers fall back in love with them.

Competitors may run themselves ragged trying to improve their offering while lowering prices and may still have nothing to show for it in terms of growth. An achievable goal is often just preventing shrinking. That's better than actually shrinking, of course. But in spite of all the things we can do to compete, growing by gaining market share is not easy. Market share is a **zero-sum game**. For someone to win market share, someone else has to lose it.

The zero-sum nature of market share explains why its growth is often accomplished inorganically through the purchase of a competitor and its customers. **Mergers and acquisitions (M&A)** also involve trade-offs. The financial resources dedicated to the acquisition could have gone to other value-creating investments. And M&A is still a zero-sum game. Competitors can also merge and acquire, leaving us out in the cold. Or maybe *they* will be the ones that make *us* an offer we can't refuse.

Market growth is great, but we have few tools to engineer it. In contrast, we can try many things to gain market share. But in a competitive context, the zero-sum game may limit the impact on growth. So where else can we turn to, to keep growing profits? Growth-minded companies are always on the lookout for *new markets*. What do we mean by a new market? Sometimes, technological innovation may offer a radically new way to satisfy human needs and desires. Personal computing, the internet, and AI all come to mind as examples of such innovations. For many companies, R&D is dedicated partly to improving existing products and processes and partly to entirely new ones: new offerings that will open or even define completely new markets. And if you don't come up with a great idea yourself, maybe you can buy a business that has already done so. Many mergers and acquisitions are not about gaining market share but about gaining access to a new market.

Other new markets are communities that have been historically underserved. In the last half century or so, much global growth—and individual companies' sales growth—has come from geographic expansion into the developing world.

Occasionally, it seems like someone discovers (invents?) an entirely new need or desire. The Pet Rock phenomenon in 1975 is a particularly fun example. Gary Dahl got tired of hearing friends complain about the tribulations of pet care. He boxed up rocks from a Mexican beach, along with an instruction manual for how to take care of this low-maintenance "pet," and sold the rocks for $4 each. Over a million times.

Many other times, **sociological**—as opposed to technological—innovation created an entirely new market. Take the MBA degree.

Someone had to come up with the idea that managing an organization required a set of skills that could be learned in a school, that a school could certify that someone possessed those skills, and that people with such a certification merited higher entry-level salaries. And thus the multi-billion-dollar market for the MBA degree was born.

Whether a market is truly new is often a matter of how you define your terms. Electric vehicle manufacturer Tesla's growth prospects come from its presence in a "new" market for electric vehicles. But of course, the market for personal transportation is not new. Tesla's offering may simply be a better match for evolving customer desires than are combustion-powered vehicles. The company's growth could just as easily be characterized as a particularly effective market share grab. At the same time, Tesla's cars and marketing strategy both ride and shape the shift in consumer behavior. When a competitive action like Tesla's has such a profound impact on a market that it essentially remakes the market, the fashionable word to use is **disruption**. A disruptive innovation typically involves a three-pronged attack: recognizing an underserved market, changing customer behavior, and, ultimately, radically shifting market share away from incumbents.

In summary, to generate growth, a business focuses activities in markets that are growing, and if possible, it will try to influence customer behavior to supercharge that growth. It does battle in the zero-sum game of grabbing market share at least to hold its own against competitive pressures. But some of the most significant growth opportunities come from new markets, whether these opportunities are defined in terms of underserved markets or are created through technological or sociological innovations.

On the job, you may contribute to any or all of these growth-oriented activities. As a manager, however, you need to understand the trade-offs involved. Will discounting to gain new customers contribute to profit? Or will it merely provoke a retaliatory discount from your competitor? Will your innovation allow you to price higher, gain market share, or open up an entirely new market? Or will it just **cannibalize** your existing sales, driving customers from one of your products to another, possibly a less profitable one? And if your new product doesn't feast on your old product's sales, will someone else's do so instead?

In 2004, Nokia pondered these questions as it evaluated something its R&D labs had created: a touchscreen, internet-ready phone. Nokia already had a dominant market share in mobile phones. The market for touchscreen phones was still hard to imagine. Would enough people really choose to stare at a four-inch screen? Meanwhile, the revolutionary touchscreen phone was expensive to

> Some of the most significant growth opportunities come from new markets, whether these opportunities are defined in terms of underserved markets or are created through technological or sociological innovations.

produce and therefore anathema to Nokia's famed design-to-cost principles. It would have to be sold at a high price at a time when the idea of paying up to $1,000—the retail price for many of today's smartphones—for something easily misplaced, stolen, or dropped seemed laughable. Nokia concluded that such a product wasn't viable and scrapped it. And so the company was utterly unprepared for the disruption that hit it in 2007.

## ON FAIRY STORIES AND HISTORIES

As we run our food truck over the years, our accountant can report how our sales and profits have evolved. We'll have a record of our past growth. But the past is a less-than-perfect guide to the future. When investors perceive value in a company they own, the value comes from future cash flows, not past cash flows. Past performance is only relevant insofar as it establishes a track record of a well-run business with competent managers and a solid resource base from which to conquer the future.

Projecting the future and planning for it lies at the heart of what we do as managers, whether we are CEOs or CFOs of giant corporate conglomerates, entrepreneurs in a small business, or leaders of small teams in larger organizations. A business has to project its sales and its expenses. Ideally, we'd want to know answers to questions like the following:

- Which customers will buy? How much? When? At what price?
- What resources will we need? When? Where? How much will they cost?

No matter how data-driven our projections, we won't know if they'll turn out as fairy tales or histories until the future arrives.

As food truck managers, we might be able to answer these questions on our own. A large business has to aggregate a lot of different information from many sources to project its future sales, expenses, and profit, a task that may involve thousands of people. Just channeling that information is an enormous challenge, about which we'll have more to say in Part II of the book. But even assuming that we had all the relevant information at our fingertips, we will never be 100 percent certain that our projections will come true. Our most reliable customers might get tired of grilled cheese. A global tomato blight might make tomatoes unaffordable. The local wholesaler might shut down.

Still, we can't just throw our hands in the air. We have to make some kind of plan. We have to come up with a likely story of what the future will bring, and we have to tell that story to our investors.

We're using the word *story* here very consciously. Sure, we might use spreadsheets and financial reports to tell the tale. But no matter how data-driven our projections are, they are always stories. Whether they turn out to be fairy tales or histories won't become apparent until the future arrives.

To see how a company's managers tell a story about growth, let's look at Swiss-based cement giant Holcim. Cement has been produced for over two thousand years; there's nothing more concrete than cement.* So at first blush, if there were predictability in business, you might expect to find it in this industry. Cement, however, is used in big, physical infrastructure: buildings, bridges, railways, roads. The construction industry is highly sensitive to the economic environment. Projects are often frozen or even abandoned during economic downturns. Demand for cement can be quite volatile in the medium term, as recessions remain notoriously unpredictable.† Cement is also a highly fragmented market with global behemoths, many midsize players, and even thousands of small, local, single-plant companies. Competition is fierce.

All annual reports display financial statements with backward-looking data about how a company performed. Investors look at the recent results and equally closely at what executives say about the future. Holcim's 2020 annual report has a helpful discussion by the CEO Jan Jenisch, framed as an interview. Asked how Holcim‡ was positioned for 2021, he answered, "I am very confident about the growth momentum we are taking into 2021, with positive demand trends in all regions. With infrastructure and climate action on top of governments' priorities—and an unprecedented wave of stimulus packages being deployed around the world to drive the recovery—we are ready to play our part."

Terms like *growth* and *positive demand trends* explicitly communicate the expectation of growth. But Jenisch qualified this growth, as well he should. He was "very confident" about it, but he was not crossing his

---

* Sorry.

† As the joke goes, economists have successfully predicted nine out of the last five recessions (a joke attributed to economist Paul Samuelson).

‡ The company name at the time was LafargeHolcim, a postmerger moniker that was dropped a few months later. Incidentally, company reports always contain a blanket disclaimer about the nature of forward-looking statements like the ones cited here. It's a disclaimer written by lawyers for lawyers and is sometimes longer than anything the CEO says about growth.

heart, hoping to die. At the same time, he told a story about what would drive that growth. The Covid pandemic had hurt the construction business along with most of the rest of the global economy. In response, governments around the world were spending to stimulate their economies. And when governments spend, it's often on big-ticket infrastructure that consumes a lot of cement.

When asked about where growth would come from in the medium turn, Jenisch had a longer, more nuanced response in which he cited "urbanization, population growth," "an unprecedented worldwide investment in infrastructure," and the "unique opportunity to accelerate the transition to sustainable building at scale."

There are three main themes to this growth story. The infrastructure investments by governments should continue to unfold over the medium term. Building infrastructure takes time, and government spending is much less sensitive to the vagaries of the economy. That pours a solid foundation for growth.* The two larger, longer-term themes are about market growth and new markets. Population growth is obvious. More people means more houses. But market growth will also come from a change in customer behavior: urbanization. Denser settlement patterns require more infrastructure: roads, rails, ports, airports, and train stations. Finally, there's a hint of a new market as well: sustainable building. Cement manufacturing is a notoriously carbon-intensive process, by itself accounting for 8 percent of global greenhouse gas emissions. A cement company that can get ahead of the sustainability trend stands to benefit.

But will Holcim benefit? This growth story sounds good. Don't call your broker to buy Holcim stock just yet, though. As we write, we have no idea whether this story will turn out as projected. By the time you read this, all the world's cement manufacturers may have been put out of business, disrupted by a hot start-up called WÛD, whose revolutionary new building material grows straight out of the ground and captures carbon. On the flip side, maybe wearable cement will have become a

---

* Last cement pun. We promise.

thing. Or maybe everything will have gone exactly as Jenisch described, but in the zero-sum battleground, some other cement maker came out on top for a hundred individually insignificant but collectively decisive reasons.

We should take stories told by company executives with a grain of salt. Executives are biased—consciously or unconsciously, for personal financial and reputational advantage—toward telling happy stories, not tragedies. Even with the purest hearts, business leaders have to be careful about how they set expectations. A gloom-and-doom forecast could demotivate the entire workforce, thereby causing the predicted poor performance. Investors made skittish by dark prophecies will sell their stocks, driving the price down and thereby fulfilling the prophecy themselves. For these reasons, CEOs may err on the side of optimism in their public statements, for everyone's benefit.

At the same time, they have to beware of overpromising and under-delivering, because nothing will shake investor confidence more than broken promises. It's a fine line executives have to walk. But it's not that different from the balancing act you might have to perform as an employee when your manager asks you how long it will take to accomplish a task!

Investors look for independent confirmation of the executives' stories. They look at the stories competitors are telling. They'll read reports by industry analysts and put everything into context with the wider economic and political news.

> Nothing will shake investor confidence more than broken promises.

Investors can gain insight into growth through the company financial statements, too. Growth has to come from somewhere. It has to be set up in the here and now, just as you have to do shopping today for the recipe you plan to cook tomorrow. The financial statements reveal what recent spending by the company might set up a growth spurt. Where would we find these clues?

We'd expect to see elevated spending on things like sales and market-ing, R&D, or new productive assets—for example, a second truck for our grilled cheese business. Spending does not guarantee growth but may be a precondition for it. If the CEO promises rainbows and unicorns, but at the same time we see reductions in spending, then at the very least, our BS* detectors should start blinking. What the company is actively doing now should be consistent with the story. The CEO should be putting their money[†] where their mouth is.

But regardless of whether company leaders believe their own stories, whatever will be will be. How we come to grips with that uncertainty is the subject of the next chapter.

---

* "Business subterfuge." This is a family book.
† It's the investors' money, of course. But that's precisely why executive compensation often includes stock and stock options so that they align their interests better with investors. In theory, at least. Whether that works in practice...let's just say that opinions diverge.

---

## CHAPTER 3 KEY TAKEAWAYS

Growing sales is the most sustainable way to achieve profit growth.

Companies can try to capture the underlying growth in the markets they currently serve; they can grow by gaining market share or by addressing new markets.

Growth has to be projected, not reported. Projections may or may not come true.

Managers instill confidence in investors by setting appropriate expectations for future performance.

---

# CHAPTER 4

# Risk

**W**e all know that risk lies at the heart of business and investment. There are many definitions and interpretations of risk.* They all wrestle with a basic challenge: We do not know what the future holds for us, but we have to base our present actions on what we think might happen.

For our part, we like to talk about risk in the simple terms of promises. A company can be described in many ways. It's a collection of resources. It's also a collection of people. More than that, it's a web of relationships between people. We find it useful to look at a company as a bundle of promises—promises made to many stakeholders. Customers are promised goods and services on time and at an expected quality level. A company promises employees that it will make payroll. It promises suppliers that bills will be paid. It promises to make interest and principal payments to creditors on a precisely defined schedule. And a company promises that after it keeps all its other promises, there will be something left over for shareholders: the thing we call profit.

We make promises all the time, sometimes without meaning to. Sometimes we hear a promise when none was intended. By some strange

---

* The area of mathematics called probability theory represents one way to get a handle on our uncertain future. But interpreting what probability *means* is a remarkably controversial subject.

alchemy, "You're going to like the Avengers movies" translates into "We're going to watch one right now" in the ears of a nine-year-old some five minutes before bedtime.* The things we say (and the things we don't say) create expectations. On the one hand, we try to avoid making promises we cannot keep, and on the other, we try to convince others that we intend to keep those we do make (like a child's "cross my heart and hope to die"). Companies don't cross their hearts, but they use things like contracts to really, really, really commit to a promise.

> We set expectations, and in turn, we form our own, whether they are based on others' promises or fabricated by our own imaginations.

We set expectations, and in turn, we form our own, whether they are based on others' explicit or implicit promises or fabricated by our own imaginations. Some of our expectations go unmet. Maybe we mistakenly interpreted something as a promise. Maybe we were intentionally misled. Maybe a contract left wiggle room. Or maybe the world left our promise-partner no choice but to break the most solemnly sworn oath. Every year, many thousands of businesses have to break promises to creditors and declare **bankruptcy**, often because of circumstances beyond their control.

We cannot take *any* promise made to us at 100 percent face value. We have to *dis*count that promise. An investor looks at a company as the promise of future cash flows, a promise in which lesser or greater confidence is warranted. As we saw in Chapter 3, much of what executive management does is shape investors' expectations and therefore their level of confidence.

## THE INVESTOR PERSPECTIVE

Let's look at the world through the eyes of an investor, Ingrid. For Ingrid, funding a new food truck to the tune of $10,000 is the opportunity to

---

* "But you promised!" No. We. Did. Not.

achieve a payoff. But of course, the future is uncertain; she does not know what will happen exactly. It might turn out that Ingrid is funding the next McDonald's. She can imagine, she can yearn, but she also knows that pigs will fly before the wildest dreams come true. She imagines some truly amazing outcomes that are, however, unlikely. There are also some satisfying outcomes that have decent odds. Some disappointing outcomes might also be likely. A catastrophic outcome for Ingrid would be her losing every cent she put into the venture, but she thinks that's unlikely to happen.

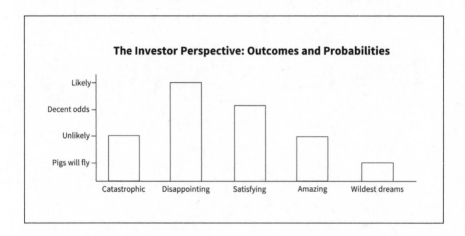

The outcomes are monetary. That doesn't mean we can know exactly what they might be. For Ingrid, the worst possible outcome is a catastrophic loss of capital—she loses everything she put in.* Beyond this worst-case scenario, Ingrid has to choose some representative outcomes:

- She just about breaks even (disappointing results) ($0).

---

\* That there is a worst possible outcome and that it has a specific monetary value is not a fact in the way that "the earth revolves around the sun" is a fact. If our food truck caused a mass salmonella outbreak, with millions of dollars of medical bills and punitive damages in lawsuits, should Ingrid be on the hook for all of them? Under the legal concept of *limited liability*, Ingrid's responsibility for the damages as owner would be limited to her investment and no further. But it was a sociopolitical choice to allow organizations to incorporate as companies with limited liability for their owners. The choice could have gone otherwise, and indeed, throughout much of history, owners were fully responsible for damages caused by their companies.

- She makes a satisfying amount ($1,000).
- She gets a windfall (amazing results) ($5,000).
- She lives her wildest dreams ($50,000).

Is that enough information to help Ingrid decide whether to go for it? Clearly, an investor's level of confidence in the different outcomes needs to feed into a decision: Ingrid will calculate the **expected value** of this investment.

First, she will translate her level of confidence for each possible outcome into a probability: a number between 0 and 1 usually expressed as a percentage, for example, 50 percent.

| Outcome | | Probability | |
| --- | --- | --- | --- |
| | in US dollars | | as a percentage |
| Catastrophic | −10,000 | Unlikely | 10% |
| Disappointing | 0 | Likely | 50% |
| Satisfying | 1,000 | Decent odds | 25% |
| Truly amazing | 5,000 | Unlikely | 10% |
| Beyond my wildest dreams | 50,000 | Pigs will fly | 5% |

The expected value is what she calculates by weighting each of the possible outcomes by her level of confidence in it and adding up the result. In this case, the expected value is $2,250:*

Two thousand two hundred and fifty dollars: Ingrid's investment decision condensed into one pristine number.

So...what does it mean?

That's the tricky part. Let's first clarify what it does not mean. This expected value of $2,250 is not the likeliest outcome. In fact, it's not even among the options that Ingrid chose to calculate her payoff. Could it be something like "If you invested $10,000 in each of a thousand food

---

* *Expected Value = -10,000 × 10% + 0 × 50% + 1,000 × 25% + 5,000 × 10% + 50,000 × 5% = 2,250*

trucks, then your average payoff per truck would be $2,250"? If that's your hunch, then you know a thing or two about statistics. But then you probably also know that this interpretation is valid only if investing in a food truck is an experiment that you could hypothetically run over and over, with each experiment having no influence on the others. Those aren't realistic assumptions for a business.

The best interpretation of the expected value is this: Expected value says little by itself but does help us compare different investment options offered at this moment, right now. Ingrid could also just sit on her cash, in which case she has one outcome, $0, and this outcome is certain.* "Aha!" you say. "An outcome of $2,250 is greater than $0. The expected value clearly tells Ingrid she should choose the food truck investment over sitting on her money."

Well…it depends, doesn't it? How much would losing the $10,000 hurt her if the worst case occurred? How life-changing would an extra $2,250 or $5,000 or even $50,000 be for her? Far be it from us to judge Ingrid foolish or wise for forgoing this opportunity. The expected values help us compare investments, but they aren't the whole story.

What else might Ingrid consider? Suppose she had another investment option with these payouts, side by side with the food truck for reference. The expected values are the same. But the new opportunity differs in two important ways:

1. It takes less to play the alternative game: only $5,000 to enter, limiting the total loss of capital to $5,000.
2. The results are much more tightly clustered around two of the more attractive options.

We would say those are two compelling reasons for Ingrid to choose the new opportunity over the food truck. Now what if we told you that the new opportunity is the *same* food truck?

---

* Ignoring things like inflation, interest on bank accounts, and government bonds. For now.

| Initial Food Truck Case | |
|---|---|
| Outcome (US dollars) | Probability (as a percentage) |
| −10,000 | 10% |
| 0 | 50% |
| 1,000 | 25% |
| 5,000 | 10% |
| 50,000 | 5% |

**Expected Value: $2,250**

Let us explain. Suppose we, the grilled-cheese-preneurs, realized that Ingrid felt queasy about our proposal. We did some research and came back to her with the following new information:

- We found a food truck we could rent instead of buy, reducing the need for up-front capital.
- We did more market research and discovered many more watering mouths than we had expected.
- We found a bunch of ways to reduce costs without compromising on quality.

| Revised Food Truck Case | |
|---|---|
| Outcome | Probability |
| (US dollars) | (as a percentage) |
| −5,000 | 10% |
| 0 | 24% |
| 1,000 | 25% |
| 5,000 | 40% |
| 50,000 | 1% |

**Expected Value: $2,250**

We showed Ingrid charts and graphs. We made her a sample sandwich (she loved it!). We impressed her with our get-up-and-go. Where before she felt queasy, she now feels excited. She decides to invest.

## CREATING VALUE BY INCREASING CONFIDENCE

What happened here? We reshaped Ingrid's expectations in two ways. We limited the worst-case scenario, and we raised her confidence in a narrower range of outcomes. Ingrid came to prefer the new scenario to the first offer. And what could preference mean other than that she *values* the offer more highly? In a very real sense, we created value. Of course, we will just as quickly destroy it if we do not deliver and we lose Ingrid's confidence.

A business promises an investor flows of future cash. The value the investor sees depends both on the size of those flows—as measured, for instance, by the expected outcome—and on the investor's confidence in them. Part of what a business does is shape the investor's confidence, both through what the business's managers say and through what they do. As managers, our words and actions create and destroy value by raising and undermining investor confidence.

In the next chapters, we'll explore how company performance and, equally importantly, how a company *communicates its performance* together shape investor confidence. For a brief preview here, let's consider the shareholder's perspective one more time. To a shareholder, the company promises that there will be something left over for them after all the company's other promises have been kept. Consequently, shareholders will want to understand what promises the company has made and to whom. They'll also want to know about the receiving end: what promises have been made to the company, and by whom. Finally, shareholders will want to know what resources the company can deploy to live up to its promises.

Along with the P&L statement that we discussed earlier, the **balance sheet** and the **cash flow statement** help answer these questions. All three financial statements working in concert report on a company's most recent performance. In doing so, they help shape investors' confidence in the company's future.

The toolkits of probability theory and statistical analysis can help investors and managers quantify the monetary values of business outcomes and their degree of confidence in them. Nevertheless, the future remains irreducibly uncertain, and many of the risks that might prevent a company from keeping its promises remain unquantifiable. As famed economist John Maynard Keynes said about uncertainty, "The sense in which I am using the term is that in which the prospect of a European war is uncertain…or the obsolescence of a new invention….About these matters there is no scientific basis on which to form any

> As managers, our words and actions create and destroy value by raising and undermining investor confidence.

calculable probability whatever….Nevertheless, the necessity for action and for decision compels us…to do our best to overlook this awkward fact."

Or in other words, business will never be truly boring.

# CHAPTER 4 KEY TAKEAWAYS

Companies make future promises to stakeholders—promises usually made in terms of cash flows. Future cash flows are always subject to uncertainty.

Investors feel more anxious the higher the stakes they are playing, and they will feel more anxious when the range of possible outcomes is wide. They value more highly the business opportunities that instill less anxiety.

As managers, our words and actions create and destroy value by raising and undermining investor confidence. Managing for value includes improving the predictability of cash flows, not just their size.

# CHAPTER 5

# The Balance Sheet

The more confident shareholders are in their company's future cash flows, the more valuable those cash flows become. Now imagine two companies, Company T and Company P, both with multiple billions of dollars of annual sales. Company T is loaded down with around $175 billion of debt, on which it pays roughly $7 billion in interest every year. Company P has no debt to speak of and pays no interest whatsoever. Which company gives you the heebie-jeebies?*

If you're like us, your anxiety level spiked when you read the word *debt*. Most of us have been exposed to debt, whether through home mortgages, car loans, student loans, or credit card debt. Debt is a contract obliging us to make cash payments, usually on an inflexible schedule. We may have to keep this promise using cash we haven't yet earned—otherwise, why would we have needed to borrow in the first place? Even with our best intentions, the money we hope to earn in the future may not materialize at the exact time we need it to keep our promise.

---

* Some of our reviewers with accounting backgrounds felt that we overemphasized the subjective experience of uncertainty. After all, the movement of stock markets is overwhelmingly driven by investment professionals doing securities trading and asset allocation based on cold-blooded risk assessments, right? Although we understand this perspective, economic history has painfully demonstrated that the pros are humans, too. For a fascinating look at the neuroscience of professional investing, see investment banker turned Cambridge neuroscientist John Coates's book *The Hour Between Dog and Wolf.*

A company may borrow money to fund its ambitions for growth and profitability. It then agrees to return that money to its creditor along with a fee: interest. The company pays for interest with future profits. From the shareholders' perspective, interest lessens the profit to which they have a claim. Decreasing profits sounds bad by itself. But even more importantly, some circumstances may prevent the company from sticking to the debt contract. When a company does not make its promised payments—what is called **default**—the creditor can have the courts force the company to make its payments, if necessary, by transferring ownership of the company from the shareholders to the creditors. In that case—in what is called **bankruptcy**—the shareholders may experience the worst case, the total loss of capital.

Creditors' claims on a company rank higher than shareholders' claims. Consequently, a company's shareholders are rightly more anxious about their prospects of future cash flows than the company's creditors are about the loan payments. Therefore, it's tempting to assume that an investor will feel more anxious about a debt-ridden company like T than about a debt-free one like P, all other things being equal. But all other things aren't equal. In fact, it may be precisely because Company T is low risk that creditors were willing to lend it money and that shareholders are happy that its managers borrowed. Its debt may be a symptom of financial strength rather than a cause of financial weakness. Conversely, the debt-free P may have no debt because no creditor would dare touch it.

These aren't hypothetical cases. *T* is the stock ticker symbol for AT&T, the US telecommunications giant. Company P is Palantir Technologies, a US data analytics company that sports over $1 billion in annual sales but has never made a profit in its roughly two-decade existence. The lack of profit is just one factor that explains why Palantir might have a hard time attracting debt capital. AT&T faces no such reluctance. In this chapter, we'll investigate why investors might have such high confidence in AT&T's promise-keeping abilities that its shareholders are willing—perhaps even happy—to allow creditors to stake higher-ranking claims.

As entrepreneurs, we're keenly aware that a company's foundation is the value it creates for a customer. No customers, no business. End of story. The company assembles resources and transforms them into goods and services valued by customers. Customers honor that value by forking over cash to the company, cash that the company can use to produce more goods and services, and so on, in what can become a never-ending cycle of win, win, win...But what sets that cycle in motion?

> A company's foundation is the value it creates for a customer. No customers, no business. End of story.

Rarely do customers trust a company enough to provide the impetus, paying their cash up front so the producer can acquire resources and transform them into what the customer wants. It's far more common for a company to first make something customers want and then convince them to pay for it. To get started, though, the company needs resources: raw material, tools, labor, intellectual property, you name it. Those resources can be bought, but with whose money? Investors' money.

## CONSTRUCTING THE BALANCE SHEET

When we launch our food truck, suppose we contribute our own $25,000 in savings as owners—**equity** capital—and get another $25,000 in a business loan from a bank. In its initial state, the company has $50,000 in its bank account. Two parties have a claim on the company: The bank has a claim for $25,000 (plus future interest). And we have a claim on anything left over after all other obligations have been met. Initially, that is the "other" $25,000 that we invested in the first place. To keep track of all this, we could jot things down in a table, placing the company's resources—the $50,000 in cash—side by side with the outstanding claims on the company. We'd have created the

| Assets | | Liabilities and Equity | |
|--------|--------|------------------------|--------|
| Cash | 50,000 | Liabilities (debt) | 25,000 |
| | | Equity | 25,000 |
| **Total** | **50,000** | **Total** | **50,000** |

company's first **balance sheet**, a snapshot of what the company owns and what it owes at birth.*

The balance sheet is, by definition, always in balance. It is the output of the accounting method called double-entry bookkeeping. Double-entry bookkeeping was introduced to record a business's transactions in a way that reduced clerical errors and the opportunity for fraud.† The company's assets—in our example, its $50,000 cash balance—must always equal the sum of its **liabilities** and equity. The balance sheet shows that whatever the company may own, someone has a claim to these assets. Contractual claims against the company are its liabilities. In our example so far, the liabilities include only the $25,000 loan from the bank. Equity is what shareholders have a claim to if all liabilities are settled: $25,000.‡

Let's suppose the terms of our food truck's loan stated that at the end of each year for the next ten years, we had to pay $2,500 in interest and repay $2,500 in principal. That is not how most real-world loans would be structured, but let's keep the math simple. If we only ever serviced the debt, our banker should feel OK. Every year, we would make a $5,000 payment, and there would be enough money in the bank to do so, up

---

* All the figures in the tables in this chapter are in US dollars unless otherwise specified.

† Error and fraud are, of course, just some of the risks a company's investors expose themselves to.

‡ Is this "equity"—what shareholders put into the company—the thing we've been questing for, namely, shareholder value? Usually, the answer is no. As we described earlier, shareholder value originates in the *future* cash flows the company may yet pay out to the shareholder. But with nothing but our say-so at this stage—with no customers and nothing to sell to them yet—our company can offer no reason for a shareholder to believe in any future cash flows whatsoever. If we tried to sell the company to someone else right now, before having taken any meaningful steps, the only thing of value would be the cash left after paying back our creditor: $25,000.

If at some point *after* we start operating, we no longer see a way to make a profit in the future, then we will probably shut down the business and sell off its assets. Then, if there's anything left over after satisfying the creditors' claims, balance-sheet equity is again all that the shareholders have claim to; it represents the remaining value of their investment.

But in between the company's birth and (potential) demise, shareholder value lies in the company's ability to generate future cash flows for its owners and not in the accounting figure called *equity* on the balance sheet.

until the debt was repaid. But as equity investors, we'd feel terrible. After ten years, there would be nothing left for us to claim; we'd have experienced a total loss of capital.

Of course, the whole reason we set up and funded our company was to do something with that cash: buy cheese, bread, tomatoes; rent or buy the truck; make sandwiches; and delight some customers enough for them to hand over new cash, enough to cover all our expenses, including the interest payments. In fact, our loan contract exercises an enormous amount of pressure on us to get to work.

As a first step, we buy the resources we need: **inventory** and equipment. If we took a snapshot after our accountant Margaret diligently logged these transactions into the company's books, here's what our company would look like.

| Assets | | Liabilities and Equity | |
|---|---|---|---|
| Cash | 5,000 | Liabilities (debt) | 25,000 |
| Inventory | 5,000 | Equity | 25,000 |
| Equipment | 40,000 | | |
| **Total** | **50,000** | **Total** | **50,000** |

We have partly transformed one type of asset—cash—into two other kinds of assets: inventory and equipment.* The total value of the assets hasn't changed, nor has anything changed on the liabilities and equity side. Creditors and shareholders have the same claims as before. But how do they feel about this state of affairs? A creditor might feel a little more worried looking at this snapshot. After all, only one year's worth of loan payments—principal and interest—remains in the bank. To stay current on payments beyond then, the company will have to be successful. Of course, if things go south, the bank might be able to take possession of the equipment. But at that

---

* Other physical assets used over the long term include buildings and property in addition to equipment. Real-world balance sheets summarize these long-term assets under the heading **plants, property, and equipment (PP&E)**.

point, would the equipment still be worth enough to cover the outstanding debt? Possibly not. The bank might experience at least a partial loss of capital.

On the eve of our launch, as shareholders, we might feel just as anxious as when we first set up the company. But in the meantime, we face a different set of risks. We might not make any sales, and if that happens, then our inventory—mostly food—would spoil. It would be just as gone as if we had made it into a sandwich we sold, but no customer value would have been created and no customer payment received in return.

Suppose things go right in our first month. We sell all our inventory, collecting $20,000 in cash from our customers. In addition, we pay ourselves a small salary as food truck executives, we pay accountant Margaret, and we do some advertising, for a total of $5,000 in SG&A expenses. A simplified P&L statement for the month would look something like this:

| Month 1 Operating Profit | |
|---|---:|
| Sales | 20,000 |
| Cost of sales | 5,000 |
| SG&A | 5,000 |
| **Operating profit** | **10,000** |

The result would be a $10,000 profit.* Yes, *that* profit—the one we have a claim to as shareholders. As long as we don't pay any of it out to ourselves, this profit stays inside the company. So at this stage, it makes sense to distinguish between the equity capital we paid in initially (the **paid-in capital**) and the profit on which we have a claim but which we have decided to keep in the company: **retained earnings**. Retained earnings are all the profits that the company has ever made *and* that the shareholders have chosen not to extract *yet*. As long as the company has further

---

* Ignoring for now the interest and depreciation expenses, and ignoring taxation entirely, for simplicity's sake.

opportunities to grow profits, the shareholders may continue to make that choice, and retained earnings can fund new productive assets. We take another snapshot:

| Assets | | Liabilities and Equity | |
|---|---|---|---|
| Cash | 20,000 | Liabilities (debt) | 25,000 |
| Inventory | 0 | Equity | |
| Equipment | 40,000 | Paid-in capital | 25,000 |
| | | Retained earnings | 10,000 |
| Total | 60,000 | Total | 60,000 |

How did we get to $20,000 in cash? We had started with $5,000 after having bought our truck (–$40,000) and our inventory (–$5,000). Our customers paid us $20,000, and we paid for $5,000 in SG&A expenses.

If we, as shareholders, decided to realize some of our claim on the profits, we could pay out some of the company cash, say, $5,000, as a **dividend** to ourselves. Doing so would reduce the money in the company account on the assets side, and our outstanding claim on the liabilities and equity side.

| Assets | | Liabilities and Equity | |
|---|---|---|---|
| Cash | 15,000 | Liabilities (debt) | 25,000 |
| Inventory | 0 | Equity | |
| Equipment | 40,000 | Paid-in capital | 25,000 |
| | | Retained earnings | 5,000 |
| Total | 55,000 | Total | 55,000 |

How do our stakeholders feel now? There are both good and bad things to report. On the one hand, our bank account contains three years' worth of loan payments. We also have a one-month track record of making a profit and distributing it to shareholders. On the other hand, will we be able to repeat our performance next month? Will competitive pressures erode our ability to drive the wedge between the customer value we create and the expenses required to create it?

In any case, our inventories are depleted. We need to do something about that if we want to keep going. For the upcoming month, given that we were good customers, our wholesaler agrees to let us buy our ingredients now and pay for them a month later. The next snapshot shows that our inventories are back up to $5,000, without reducing our cash, taking into account the delayed payment. Although we conserved cash, now a new stakeholder, the wholesale supplier, has a claim on our company. This bill will come due eventually. We call it an **account payable**. It is also a liability, but it differs from the loan we got from the bank in that it is not interest-bearing.* We distinguish accounts payable with its own line item.

| Assets | | Liabilities and Equity | |
|---|---|---|---|
| Cash | 15,000 | Liabilities | |
| Inventory | 5,000 | Accounts payable | 5,000 |
| Equipment | 40,000 | Debt | 25,000 |
| | | Equity | |
| | | Paid-in capital | 25,000 |
| | | Retained earnings | 5,000 |
| **Total** | **60,000** | **Total** | **60,000** |

* There are other important ways that accounts payable differ from many loans. A business such as our food truck will usually only get a loan approved by offering up something as collateral. When we used the loan to buy the truck, our contract specifically stated that the bank could repossess the truck. The bank's secured claim on the truck takes priority over all other claims, including our supplier's claim. The priority of claims, which ones are secured, and which aren't all matter to stakeholders who individually have to consider how likely it is that the company will break its promises to them.

We're back in business. Over the remaining eleven months of the year, the following take place:

- Each month, we sell $20,000 worth of sandwiches.
- Each month, we use up $5,000 worth of inventory. We replenish it every month with the same payment terms with our wholesaler: Each month, we settle last month's bill for $5,000 and buy next month's ingredients on thirty-day credit. The wholesaler's claim on the company—accounts payable—stays stable month to month.
- Each month, we record $5,000 in SG&A expenses.
- Each month, we distribute $5,000 of dividends to ourselves.
- We make the first interest payment ($2,500) and first repayment of principal ($2,500).
- Our accountant deems that the useful life of our equipment is twenty years, so its value has been reduced by $2,000.*

| Assets | | Liabilities and Equity | |
|---|---|---|---|
| Cash | 65,000 | Liabilities | |
| Inventory | 5,000 | Accounts payable | 5,000 |
| Equipment | 38,000 | Debt | 22,500 |
| | | Equity | |
| | | Paid-in capital | 25,000 |
| | | Retained earnings | 55,500 |
| **Total** | **108,000** | **Total** | **108,000** |

---

* Feeling financially frisky? Try to reverse-engineer exactly how we got to the result from the list of transactions given. But don't worry about the details just now. We want to get to a big-picture impression of what the balance sheet tells us about risk, not turn you into an accountant! The Year 1 and Year 2 financial statements for our hypothetical food truck appear in the Appendix.

Now how do we feel? Pretty good, whether we are creditors or shareholders. We have a significant cash balance that will cover the outstanding debt and accounts payable. We have a year-long track record of making profits and distributing money to shareholders. If we wanted to expand, we'd also have the funds available to do so. Cash is available because we left it in the company instead of taking it out as dividends.

An expansion opportunity presents itself. Local cloud computing start-up Newage finds that many of its employees are driving a ridiculous distance to get to our truck during lunch break. The company offers to let us set up a kiosk on its premises as a kind of cafeteria. Newage intends to pay for its employees' meals and do so at higher prices, but there's a catch. It wants a single bill for all the sales at the end of the month, and it wants to pay thirty days after that bill. Taking advantage of this opportunity involves the following actions:

- Setting up the kiosk costs us $40,000 in cash.
- We have to double the amount of inventory we carry. Our wholesaler agrees to supply ingredients up front in return for later payment, as before.

Right before the kiosk's first day of operations, the next snapshot looks like this:

| Assets | | Liabilities and Equity | |
|---|---|---|---|
| Cash | 25,000 | Liabilities | |
| Inventory | 10,000 | Accounts payable | 10,000 |
| Equipment | 78,000 | Debt | 22,500 |
| | | Equity | |
| | | Paid-in capital | 25,000 |
| | | Retained earnings | 55,500 |
| Total | 113,000 | Total | 113,000 |

Our cash supplies are somewhat depleted now, and there is uncertainty about whether the new kiosk operation will thrive as much as the food truck did. In fact, the truck's business might suffer a little because of competition from our own kiosk! If business bombs, there is a lot more inventory that could spoil. Meanwhile, our total obligations have increased in the form of accounts payable. Again, our stakeholders' confidence is shaped by a mix of worries and hopes, weighted differently depending on their respective vantage points as suppliers, creditors, and shareholders.

We operate our two locations for a month, and things go as well as we had hoped. Our truck sells $20,000 of sandwiches, and customers pay in cash. Our kiosk even achieves $25,000 in sales, for a total of $45,000 in sales. To achieve those figures, we had to double our SG&A expenses to $10,000, and of course, we consumed $10,000 of supplies. Our profit for the month is $25,000, and based on that performance, we decide to double our dividend payment to $10,000.

For the sales at the kiosk, we send Newage, our corporate client, a $25,000 bill. But that does not result in a flow of cash yet. How should we characterize the promise of payment by that single corporate customer? Just as a liability is a claim someone else can make on our company, a claim we can make on someone else is an asset for the company. We call it one of our **accounts receivable** and take another snapshot:

| Assets | | Liabilities and Equity | |
|---|---|---|---|
| Cash | 15,000 | Liabilities | |
| Accounts receivable | 25,000 | Accounts payable | 10,000 |
| Inventory | 10,000 | Debt | 22,500 |
| Equipment | 78,000 | Equity | |
| | | Paid-in capital | 25,000 |
| | | Retained earnings | 70,500 |
| Total | 128,000 | Total | 128,000 |

Our grilled cheese business may now look as solid as a nicely aged block of Gruyère. But a lot now rides on whether Newage pays its bill. Suppose the overall economy were to tank? Our individual customers would stop coming to the truck, and our corporate customer would have trouble keeping its promises to its creditors, never mind to us. The value of our accounts receivable and our inventory might go to zero, leaving us with just $15,000 in cash to cover $32,500 of liabilities to our suppliers and to the bank. All our stakeholders would start hitting the antacids.

There's no reason to panic yet, though. Sure, we do not have enough cash to cover all our liabilities. But there's a schedule to those promises. We promised to pay our supplier in thirty days, so that liability is coming up fast. We'll also have to make another $2,500 principal payment on our loan this year. But the remaining $20,000 of our loan isn't due until a year or more later. By then, the economy may have turned around. We may only need to weather the immediate storm. Wouldn't it be helpful if our balance sheet communicated to stakeholders whether promises were due in the near term or further down the road?

Balance sheets do exactly that. In them, we distinguish between **current** and **noncurrent liabilities**. By convention, current liabilities are the promises we have to keep in the next twelve months. Noncurrent liabilities are all other liabilities. Generally speaking, **current assets** are, correspondingly, those we expect to convert into cash in the next twelve months.* Usually, inventory will either sell (and turn into cash) or spoil soon. We also expect our customers to make good on their promises—recorded as accounts receivable—in the next twelve months. Cash is already a current asset. And because we don't expect to turn our equipment into cash in the next twelve months (or ever), equipment figures among our **noncurrent assets**.

---

* Accountants define current assets more broadly to also include any asset that the company expects to use to generate sales, even if it intends to keep the asset around longer than twelve months. For example, distilleries may hold inventory of whiskey for many years as it matures.

| Assets | | Liabilities and Equity | |
|---|---|---|---|
| **Current Assets** | | **Current Liabilities** | |
| Cash | 15,000 | Accounts payable | 10,000 |
| Accounts receivable | 25,000 | Short-term debt | 2,500 |
| Inventory | 10,000 | | |
| | | | |
| **Noncurrent Assets** | | **Noncurrent Liabilities** | |
| Equipment | 78,000 | Long-term debt | 20,000 |
| | | | |
| | | **Equity** | |
| | | Paid-in capital | 25,000 |
| | | Retained earnings | 70,500 |
| **Total** | **128,000** | **Total** | **128,000** |

We split our bank loan into two parts. The long-term part is due more than a year from now, so it figures among the noncurrent liabilities. We characterized the amount due at the end of this calendar year among the current liabilities as **short-term debt**. In real-world balance sheets, it may be explicitly called the **current portion of long-term debt**.

With this display of our financial position—the balance sheet is often called *the statement of financial position*—we can easily see how our short-term promises to our stakeholders match up with the short-term promises made to us. In the short term—within twelve months—we have enough cash to keep our promises even if our corporate customer defaults and our inventory spoils. Displaying our financial position in this way informs stakeholders about some of the primary risks to which the company is exposed, as well their urgency.

The balance sheets of publicly traded companies are usually much more complex than our example. They are weighted down with all sorts of promises given and promises received, including pension commitments, long-term lease agreements, customer prepayments, financial securities, and many more elements. But our simplified example covers the main features that managers need to understand. Managers don't need to know the exact accounting calculations. But they should understand how their actions may make those line items increase, decrease, and trade off against each other and how those movements may affect the confidence of all stakeholders.

## A REAL-LIFE EXAMPLE: AT&T'S BALANCE SHEET

Let's look at AT&T's 2021 balance sheet as an example. In this sheet, the amounts are in millions of dollars, and several line items have been condensed.

Given the line items "short-term debt" and "long-term debt," it looks like AT&T has about $175 billion in interest-paying debt, and a roughly equal amount in other promises, current and noncurrent. Equity makes up only one-third of the company's financing: For every $1 of equity there is $2 in liabilities.* Rather than thinking of AT&T as burdened with debt, let's ask, Why were creditors willing to lend so much? Why are its shareholders willing to allow such a heavy load of claims to outrank theirs? We're not going to give an exhaustive account, but consider the following questions:

**From how many customers does AT&T receive incoming cash?**
Telecom operators will typically have many millions of customers, of all shapes and sizes. Some of these customers might

---

* We're really simplifying a complex picture. The "other long-term liabilities" shown on the balance sheet are valued at $130 billion, which is hardly chump change but consists of pretty esoteric stuff. About half of those other long-term liabilities are "deferred income taxes," for example. This liability constitutes an important promise that has yet to be kept—a promise to the government. But few AT&T managers will have any impact on that number.

| AT&T 2021 Balance Sheet (Simplified) | | | |
|---|---:|---|---:|
| **Assets** | | **Liabilities and Equity** | |
| **Current Assets** | | **Current Liabilities** | |
| Cash | 21,169 | Accounts payable | 50,661 |
| Accounts receivable | 17,571 | Short-term debt | 24,630 |
| Inventory | 3,464 | Other short-term liabilities | 10,297 |
| Other current assets | 17,793 | | |
| | | | |
| **Noncurrent Assets** | | **Noncurrent Liabilities** | |
| Plants, property, and equipment | 125,904 | Long-term debt | 152,724 |
| Intangible assets | 311,699 | Other long-term liabilities | 129,455 |
| Other noncurrent assets | 54,022 | | |
| | | | |
| | | **Equity** | 183,855 |
| **Total** | **551,622** | **Total** | **551,622** |

switch providers or fail to pay their bill in any period. But it's very unlikely that a substantial portion would do so all at once. Also, telecommunication is a basic and essential service. Unlike, say, cruise vacations, it's not something people choose to do without when the economy hits a rough patch.

**On what terms do customers pay?** Telecommunications operators often collect from customers monthly, from subscription contracts that are not easy to break, that lock in customers for as much as two years, and that auto-renew. Some customers do not lock themselves into contracts, but they prepay for the most part. Therefore AT&T has very strong visibility into regular and frequent flows of incoming cash. That's quite different from, say, a car company whose product customers may buy at unpredictable and long intervals, with the possibility of the customer opting for a competitor each time.

Similarly, companies like Amazon offer rich enticements—free shipping, access to unlimited content—to get you to sign up to their subscription offerings, because regular, predictable cash flows are so attractive. In IT, many companies offer software as a service (SaaS) based on subscription contracts. For example, Microsoft strongly encourages its business and individual customers to buy the subscription-based Office 365 rather than purchase single licenses, making incoming cash flows more regular and predictable. Subscriptions to software can be advantageous for its customers, too, because expenses become more predictable. As we'll discuss in more depth in a later chapter, businesses often base decisions not only on price, expenses, and profits but also on smoothness and predictability.

**How is the debt secured?** This item is a bit harder to discern from our simplified balance sheet. About a quarter of AT&T's assets are tangible, which for AT&T means all the infrastructure of a telecommunications network, including real estate and cables stretched across North America. Some of these assets are high-tech gear that may become obsolete with innovation or may degrade on their own. But much of this gear can be used for a long time. Meanwhile, a lot of the intangible assets consist of licenses to use segments of the radio spectrum for cellular wireless networks. If for any reason AT&T were unable to meet its financial obligations, its creditor could seize a set of highly useful assets that other companies covet.

In short, creditors look at AT&T and see steady, frequent, and predictable flows of cash that comes from a huge and diversified customer base and is secured by highly marketable assets.

Creditors are willing to offer AT&T debt capital at attractive interest rates because of the strength of the company and its business model. The debt is a symptom of the company's financial solidity more than it is a cause of financial vulnerability. AT&T's apparent strength doesn't mean there is no reason to worry—even companies with the best business models may bite off more debt than they can chew. But a company with predictable cash flows is an attractive investment for creditors and shareholders alike.

The term *statement of financial position* is instructive. The word *position* comes from a spatial concept: where something is situated in the physical world relative to other things. And our position in the world tells us a good deal about what might happen to us next. If we're on a mountain summit, we know where we can and can't go next; what effort it will cost us to move; what kinds of external circumstances— lightning, wind, and so forth—are likely to threaten us.

> The balance sheet helps inform investors about what threats we might face, what new promises we can make, and how credible they will be.

Similarly, the balance sheet tells us something about what might happen to our company next. What promises have been made, to whom, and with what urgency? What resources do we have at our disposal to make good on those claims? The balance sheet doesn't just tell us about the threats we might face. Our financial position also informs us about what new promises we can make and how credible they will be.

By itself, the balance sheet does not reveal everything we need to know about our vulnerabilities and opportunities. But it does outline the shape of things to come.

## CHAPTER 5 KEY TAKEAWAYS

The balance sheet is a record of past transactions. It displays what the company owns or controls (its assets) and what it owes (its liabilities and equity).

The accounting identity (*assets = liabilities + equity*) is true by definition. Whatever the company controls, someone ultimately has a claim to it. If the balance sheet is unbalanced, then there must be an accounting error.

The balance sheet embeds a time structure by distinguishing between current and noncurrent liabilities and assets.

The equity value reported in the balance sheet should not be confused with shareholder value.

As a statement of financial position, the balance sheet provides insight into what opportunities and threats loom in the company's future.

## CHAPTER 6

# Cash Flow Basics

**P**rofitability occurs when a company drives a wedge between the price a customer is willing to pay and all the expenses required to create that value. Bankruptcy occurs when a company runs out of cash and can no longer keep its promises to its creditors. Notice how we defined profitability and bankruptcy in completely different terms. That points us toward the central message of this chapter:

> Cash flow and profits are not the same thing.

*Cash flow and profits are not the same thing.*

What makes them diverge? There's no great mystery: Cash payments for goods and services are not necessarily made exactly when the goods or services are delivered. That's it. If you buy this book with a credit card and pay your credit card bill around six weeks later, you've pushed cash flow and profit apart for somebody somewhere in the value chain. As simple as that concept is, it's one that companies lose sight of often enough to lead to dramatic failures. Let's look at what disconnects cash flow from profits.

# CONSTRUCTING A SIMPLIFIED CASH FLOW STATEMENT

When we first set up our food truck, we put $25,000 of our own cash into the company account, and we persuaded a bank to pony up $25,000 as well. Those were two flows of cash into the company. But they were neither sales to a customer nor profits. Conversely, when we pay back principal on the loan or pay ourselves a dividend, those are outflows that have nothing to do with customer value or the expenses required to create it. These movements of cash between the company and its investors are invisible in the P&L statement.*

When we bought our cooking equipment, we transferred cash from our bank account to the suppliers of the truck, the cutting boards, and so on. Those transactions occurred all at once at the beginning of our history, untied to any particular sandwich. Cash outlays for assets are also not reported in the P&L.†

Cash flows associated with financing and investment don't correspond to the sales and expenses recorded on the P&L. For that reason alone, we

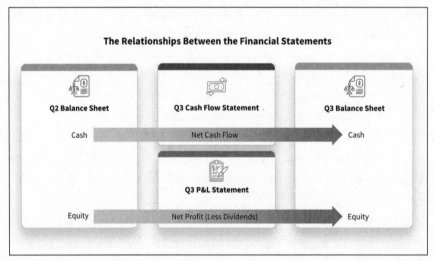

The Relationships Between the Financial Statements

Q2 Balance Sheet — Q3 Cash Flow Statement — Q3 Balance Sheet

Cash — Net Cash Flow — Cash

Q3 P&L Statement

Equity — Net Profit (Less Dividends) — Equity

---

\* By convention, the interest we pay to our creditors is considered an expense, and it appears on our P&L statement.
† The cost of the equipment is expensed in the form of depreciation over time, and the P&L does report depreciation. But at the point in time we recognize depreciation as an expense, it is not a cash flow. More on that later!

need to keep track of cash flows in a separate report called the **cash flow statement**. This statement records the movements of cash into and out of the company over a reporting period, between two snapshots of a balance sheet. Along with the P&L statement, the cash flow statement helps tell the story of how a company got from one snapshot of its financial position to the next.

To make the story easier to read, the cash flow statement groups flows into three areas, two of which we just outlined. *Cash flow from financing* tells us what cash flowed in from investors and back out to them. When a company takes out a loan or sells shares, those are inflows. When it repays loan principal or pays out a dividend, those are outflows.* *Cash flow from investments* speaks for itself, too. Purchases of new equipment are outflows. When we sell a piece of equipment—for example, if we sold our truck to generate cash for an upgrade to a restaurant—we realize an inflow.

It's not hard to see why financing and investment activities can make a company's overall cash flows diverge from profits, especially at key moments such as when the company first gets set up, when loans become due, or when new assets are needed. But what about the third area, *cash flow from operating activities*: cash coming in from customers and going out to suppliers?

For simple businesses, net profit and operating cash flow may be the same thing. In fact, many small businesses opt to do **cash-based accounting**. A real-world food truck might choose to do so. Its customers pay by cash or credit card right when they get their sandwiches. Its suppliers will usually demand payment immediately. The food truck isn't going to sit on large volumes of inventory, because things like bread, cheese, and tomatoes will spoil rapidly. Therefore, sales, expenses, and their related cash flows occur fairly close together.

The following table summarizes the cash flows, including the initial investments from us and from the bank, during our food truck's first year of operations.†

---

* When a company buys back its shares, the cash outflow is also recorded under cash flow from financing.
† For those initial investments, see previous chapter. All figures in this table are in US dollars.

| Food Truck Cash Flow Statement (Simplified) | |
|---|---:|
| **From Financing Activities** | **−12,500** |
| New loans | 25,000 |
| Loans repaid | −2,500 |
| Equity issued | 25,000 |
| Dividends paid | −60,000 |
| | |
| **From Investing Activities** | **−40,000** |
| New equipment purchased | −40,000 |
| Equipment sold | 0 |
| | |
| **From Operating Activities** | **117,500** |
| Customer payments | 240,000 |
| Supplier/salary payments | −120,000 |
| Interest payments | −2,500 |
| | |
| **Net Cash Flow** | **65,000** |
| Cash balance at beginning of period | 0 |
| **Cash Balance at End of Period** | **65,000** |

A company with a more complex product than grilled cheese faces very different challenges. Boeing makes jet aircraft and sells them to airlines. The company typically negotiates an up-front payment from its customers, followed by a second payment on delivery. The payments are separated by a process that could last years! During that time, Boeing has to pay its employees and buy inputs that may be stockpiled quite a while before use. If Boeing did cash-based accounting, it might have some quarters—even years—that looked really good, but only because a bunch of customer payments happened to coincide. Other quarters might look terrible, because no customer payments happened to flow in. Wide and unpredictable swings in cash flow can make it hard for a company like Boeing to plan for the future or even tell what's going on in the present. Did last quarter's cash outflows exceed inflows because Boeing is pricing too low or because that's just how the cash flow cookie crumbled? Did a record cash inflow mean the company can invest more in R&D, or is that an illusion caused by a spike in customer prepayments?

For companies like Boeing, cash flows from operations—never mind cash flows related to financing and investment—can be quite lumpy and volatile. The lumpiness obscures important information about whether the company is, fundamentally, buying low and selling high. If this uncertainty makes it hard for its managers to plan, it also makes it hard for its investors to predict long-term future cash flows. And it's hard to be confident in cash flows you can't predict. As we've been hammering home for several chapters now, confidence in future cash flows is one of the key drivers of shareholder value. To gain the insights needed for planning and to invest more confidently, wouldn't it be helpful if there were a way to average out the operating cash flows over time?

## ACCRUAL ACCOUNTING

Something like averaging out cash flows is precisely what all but the simplest businesses do; it's called **accrual accounting**. This method is not built on a statistical average, though. Instead, accrual accounting adopts some conventions about when something qualifies as a sale to a customer and when something qualifies as an expense. Accrual accounting matches sales to expenses in time and independently of when customer and supplier payments take place. The accounting rules are highly regulated and can be quite specific to an industry and a jurisdiction. Broadly, though, companies are allowed to recognize a sale during the period in which something was delivered to a customer. Expenses related to creating and delivering the thing the customer buys—the cost of sales—are recognized when they are related directly to a sale as just defined.

Boeing recognizes a sale when it delivers a jet to an airline. It recognizes all the expenses associated with that particular jet—the costs of all the parts and labor and so forth—at the same time.* The cash flows coming from the airline will happen in entirely different periods. For example, a prepayment might already have occurred years before. Cash payments made to suppliers might have been made throughout the preceding year, and others might not be due until the next period.

> Individually, the three financial statements—P&L, cash flow, and balance sheet—can be dangerously misleading; they have to be viewed in concert.

When we introduced the P&L statement a few chapters back, we defined profit as the difference between sales and expenses. For companies using accrual accounting, profit is defined in terms of sales and expenses recognized according to these rules. Because the rules are based on the timing of delivery, not on the timing of cash flows, profits and cash flow can diverge over and above the divergence caused by financing and investment activities. The P&L statement then helps managers and investors understand how well the company creates customer value while keeping expenses low.

But just as the P&L reveals one thing, it obscures another. The company still has to keep its promises using cold, hard cash. If cash does not flow in at the right time, the company can go under, even if the P&L looks just fine. Individually, the three financial statements—P&L, cash flow, and balance sheet—can be dangerously misleading; they have to be viewed in concert.

Sometimes, companies face a perfect storm: a coincidence of heavy outflows to suppliers, low inflows from customers, a new investment need,

---

* For a product like a grilled cheese sandwich or a 777 jet, delivery to a customer is easy to define. For a service like consulting or access to a telecommunications network, pinpointing the timing of delivery and the timing of expenses can be somewhat arbitrary and ambiguous. Many famous accounting scandals boil down to company accountants stretching the rules around sales and expense recognition to the breaking point and beyond.

and maybe a major principal repayment on a loan all due at around the same time. Because these payments are defined ahead of time in contracts with schedules, the company should be able to anticipate them. If the underlying business is sound—as demonstrated by the P&L—then a bank should be willing to provide a bridge loan. A bridge loan allows the company to make good on its commitments in return for a fee, until the cash flow situation turns around for the better. Much of the time, the partnership between the worlds of industry and finance works smoothly.

However, during a financial crisis, banks may become reluctant to lend to anyone, even to solid businesses. In the global financial crisis of 2008, banks lost confidence in each other's investments (specifically, mortgage-backed financial assets) and refused to lend to one another. Banks need to borrow cash from each other to finance short-term loans to nonfinancial businesses. Consequently, cash-crunched companies—even those completely unrelated to mortgage banking and real estate—couldn't find banks that would help them, no matter how strong their business models. People spoke of Wall Street's problems spilling over onto Main Street. Many companies failed, having done nothing wrong other than to be in an industry characterized by lumpy cash flows.

That's why investors will—all else being equal—prefer companies with regular, frequent, and predictable cash flows over companies with lumpy flows. These companies are less exposed to risks that they could not possibly manage, such as global financial crises.

# CHAPTER 6 KEY TAKEAWAYS

Cash flow and profits are not the same thing.

Cash flow and profits diverge because of timing issues:

- Investment activities may require more cash than operating activities generate in a given period.
- Financing activities may not align perfectly with the cash needs for investment and for shortfalls in cash flow from operations.
- Cash flows from customers may not align well with cash payments to suppliers.

The cash flow statement tracks the cash flows that occurred in a specific period and thereby helps reconcile the balance sheet and the income statement.

Only when used in concert do the cash flow and P&L statements tell the full story about how the company evolved between balance sheet snapshots and reveal many of the company's strengths and vulnerabilities.

## CHAPTER 7

# Cash Flow and Working Capital

Timing issues can drive profits and cash flows apart, especially when payments are lumpy and irregular. Now let's look at another circumstance in which a profitable company can run into cash flow problems. In doing so, we'll tie together the drivers of value: growth, profitability, and risk. Let's suppose we started up a new company—not the food truck—and are now reviewing its first business quarter (three months) of operations. Let's take a look at the P&L statement.*

With just a few bits of additional information about the company's

| Profit and Loss | |
|---|---:|
| Sales | 10,000 |
| Cost of sales | 6,000 |
| SG&A | 1,500 |
| R&D | 1,500 |
| Depreciation | 200 |
| Interest | 0 |
| **Net Profit** | **800** |

---

* We'll ignore taxation for the purposes of this discussion. All figures in this table and the other tables in this chapter are in US dollars.

contracts with customers and suppliers, we can reverse-engineer operating cash flow from this P&L statement. Let's use these assumptions:

- Customers pay on *net 90* terms; they are allowed to pay ninety days after delivery (these agreements are called **customer payment terms**).
- Suppliers accept payment on *net 30* terms; the company pays them thirty days after delivery of their services and goods. For simplicity's sake, we'll assume that these terms apply only to the cost of sales, not to SG&A and R&D expenses, which are paid immediately.
- In the first quarter (Q1), the company bought $1,000 worth of inventory that was not incorporated into any products sold and remained available for use in the next quarter.

How much operating cash flow did the company generate in Q1?

In the long run, we would hope that net profit and operating cash flow are equivalent. Sales should correspond to customer payments, and expenses should correspond to supplier payments, even if the lumpiness of cash flows might make them diverge from one another at any given time. So as a first approximation, let's assume that net profit and operating cash flow are the same: $800.

| Profit and Loss | | Operating Cash Flow | |
|---|---:|---|---:|
| Sales | 10,000 | Net profit | 800 |
| Cost of sales | 6,000 | | |
| SG&A | 1,500 | | |
| R&D | 1,500 | | |
| Depreciation | 200 | | |
| Interest | 0 | | |
| **Net Profit** | **800** | **Operating Cash Flow** | **800** |

This assumption—that net profit equals operating cash flow—is unwarranted. There are several reasons we know this assumption to be wrong. We will now systematically walk through each error and correct it.

The first error concerns **depreciation**. Depreciation lessened our profit by $200. But depreciation is an expense introduced to account for the fact that our equipment gets consumed over its useful life. We did not cut a check for $200 to someone named "depreciation." Therefore, net profit *understates* cash flow by $200. With respect to depreciation, cash flow must be $200 higher than the $800 profit shown in the P&L statement because the $200 depreciation expense did not involve an outflow of cash. To get from net profit to cash flow, we would have to adjust it upward by adding the depreciation back in.

| Profit and Loss | | Operating Cash Flow | |
|---|---|---|---|
| Sales | 10,000 | Net profit | 800 |
| Cost of sales | 6,000 | Adjustments | |
| SG&A | 1,500 | Depreciation | 200 |
| R&D | 1,500 | | |
| Depreciation | 200 | | |
| Interest | 0 | | |
| **Net Profit** | **800** | **Operating Cash Flow** | **1,000** |

So, even though "depreciation" appears in the "operating cash flow" column, it is not a true cash flow. It is an adjustment that compensates for the error we introduced by assuming that net profit and operating cash flow were equivalent.*

---

* Feeling nonplussed about a phantom cash flow in an official company report on the movements of cash? Join the club! We—along with 95 percent of anyone else we know who's been confronted with this—struggled to wrap our heads around it. You may have to ponder this again (and again). Even if you shout out "Eureka!" right now, you might feel your forehead creasing when you try to recall the idea in the shower tomorrow morning. Assuming you also use shower time to meditate on life's great questions and counterintuitive accounting concepts.

Depreciation is just the first of a string of these strange adjustments we'll make to contend with our incorrect assumption that net profit and operating cash flow were equivalent. What other errors did we introduce?

Our customers pay us ninety days after delivery. By the rules of accrual accounting, we recorded $10,000 worth of deliveries to customers during Q1 in the P&L statement. But with payment terms of net 90, every customer payment from this quarter's sales will fall into the next quarter. While we can recognize $10,000 of sales in Q1 in our P&L statement, we received no cash at all from customers in Q1! Therefore, by assuming that net profit and operating cash flow were the same, we overstated cash flow. By a huge amount.

| Profit and Loss | | Operating Cash Flow | |
|---|---|---|---|
| Sales | 10,000 | Net profit | 800 |
| Cost of sales | 6,000 | Adjustments | |
| SG&A | 1,500 | Depreciation | 200 |
| R&D | 1,500 | Customer payments outstanding | −10,000 |
| Depreciation | 200 | | |
| Interest | 0 | | |
| **Net Profit** | **800** | **Operating Cash Flow** | **−9,000** |

Like the "depreciation" we recorded under the "operating cash flow" heading, the "customer payments outstanding" is not a real cash flow. It's another phantom: an adjustment to correct our unwarranted assumption.

Just as customers deferred their payments to us, our contracts with suppliers allow us to defer payments to them. Here's where the math gets a tiny bit more complicated. The quarter consists of three months. Let's assume suppliers have been delivering goods and services to us at a steady rate across the entire quarter. In the first month of the quarter, we received and used one-third of the total supplies, that is, $2,000 worth (one-third of the total cost of sales, $6,000). But our net 30 payment terms allowed us to defer paying the supplier until the second month. In Month 2, we took delivery of and used another third of the total (another $2,000 worth). We deferred payment for those supplies to Month 3, but we also paid out cash for the first month's supply. In Month 3, we received another $2,000 worth of supplies and paid up for Month 2. However, we won't pay for Month 3 until the first month of the next quarter, outside of our current reporting period. So overall, although we received and consumed $6,000 worth of supplies, we only paid $4,000 in cash this quarter.

| Example: Accrued Expenses Versus Cash Flow | | | | |
|---|---|---|---|---|
| | Month 1 | Month 2 | Month 3 | Total for Quarter |
| *Value* of supplies received and used in units sold | 2,000 | 2,000 | 2,000 | **6,000** |
| *Cash* payments to suppliers on net 30 payment terms | 0 | 2,000 | 2,000 | **4,000** |

Consequently, our net profit understated operating cash flow by $2,000, and we have to add a corresponding adjustment.

| Profit and Loss | | Operating Cash Flow | |
|---|---|---|---|
| Sales | 10,000 | Net profit | 800 |
| Cost of sales | 6,000 | Adjustments | |
| SG&A | 1,500 | Depreciation | 200 |
| R&D | 1,500 | Customer payments outstanding | −10,000 |
| Depreciation | 200 | Supplier payments outstanding | 2,000 |
| Interest | 0 | | |
| **Net Profit** | **800** | **Operating Cash Flow** | **−7,000** |

We listed one more transaction among our assumptions earlier: Over and above the goods and services we bought from suppliers and recorded as cost of sales, we bought $1,000 of inventory that we did not turn into something we sold this quarter. Remember, the $6,000 of cost of sales only includes expenses tied to the sales achieved. According to the rules of accrual accounting, unsold inventory does not appear in our cost of sales on the P&L. The P&L statement is oblivious to it. Assuming we paid cash for this extra inventory in this quarter, though, our bank account balance diminished by that amount. We need to add another adjustment to get from net profit to true operating cash flow.

| Profit and Loss | | Operating Cash Flow | |
|---|---|---|---|
| Sales | 10,000 | Net profit | 800 |
| Cost of sales | 6,000 | Adjustments | |
| SG&A | 1,500 | Depreciation | 200 |
| R&D | 1,500 | Customer payments outstanding | −10,000 |
| Depreciation | 200 | Supplier payments outstanding | 2,000 |
| Interest | 0 | Inventory stockpiled | −1,000 |
| **Net Profit** | **800** | **Operating Cash Flow** | **−8,000** |

Our company earned $800 in profit, on $10,000 in sales, a net margin of 8 percent. We are clearly able to attract enough customers willing to pay prices so that the value of our sales exceeds the costs of our business. At the same time, our operating cash flow was painfully negative: −$8,000. Profit and cash flow diverged dramatically, even without considering cash flows connected to financing and investment. Suppose we had started with $10,000 in the bank. We would now be down to $2,000, dangerously close to running out of cash.

Outstanding customer payments are what we called accounts receivable in Chapter 5, so that's the nomenclature we'll use going forward. In every reporting period, some cash comes in from previously deferred payments, and some cash is deferred to a later period. The difference between the two tells us how accounts receivable has changed between balance sheet snapshots. If deferred customer payments exceed incoming payments, then accounts receivable increases. If deferred customer payments are lower than incoming payments, then accounts receivable decreases. Likewise, the difference between the supplier payments we catch up on and the supplier payments we can defer is the change in accounts payable. The same goes for inventory. If we buy more new inventory than the stockpiled inventory we consume, then the inventory asset in the balance sheet increases.

| Profit and Loss | | Operating Cash Flow | |
|---|---|---|---|
| Sales | 10,000 | Net profit | 800 |
| Cost of sales | 6,000 | Adjustments | |
| SG&A | 1,500 | Depreciation | 200 |
| R&D | 1,500 | Change in accounts receivable | −10,000 |
| Depreciation | 200 | Change in accounts payable | 2,000 |
| Interest | 0 | Change in inventories | −1,000 |
| **Net Profit** | **800** | **Operating Cash Flow** | **−8,000** |

What would happen if our business grew in the following quarters? Is the cash flow problem purely a matter of scale? The main cause of the problem is the difference between the customer and supplier payments deferred into the next quarter. Suppose that in Q2, we grew our sales by 50 percent, or by $5,000. In Q2, we could collect on $10,000 of customer payments from Q1, but we would be deferring $15,000 in payments until Q3.

| Profit and Loss | | | Operating Cash Flow | | |
|---|---|---|---|---|---|
| | Q1 | Q2 | | Q1 | Q2 |
| Sales | 10,000 | 15,000 | Net profit | 800 | 2,800 |
| Cost of sales | 6,000 | 9,000 | Adjustments | | |
| SG&A | 1,500 | 1,500 | Depreciation | 200 | 200 |
| R&D | 1,500 | 1,500 | Change in accounts receivable | −10,000 | −5,000 |
| Depreciation | 200 | 200 | Change in accounts payable | 2,000 | 1,000 |
| Interest | 0 | 0 | Change in inventory | −1,000 | 0 |
| **Net Profit** | **800** | **2,800** | **Operating Cash Flow** | **−8,000** | **−1,000** |

As long as we keep growing, customer payments from the previous quarter cannot catch up with the payments deferred to the next quarter. That problem is compounded by the fact that we pay our suppliers quicker than our customers pay us (net 30 terms versus net 90 terms). The more we grow—and the faster we grow—the worse the problem will get! Even as our business would be firing on two of our value pistons—growth and profitability—the cash flow dynamics would kill the company.

> When we pay our suppliers quicker than our customers pay us, the resulting cash flow dynamics could kill the company.

The cumbersome exercise we just went through—reverse-engineering operating cash flow from net profit—produces the standard form in which operating cash flow is displayed. We could do for a company what we do with our personal bank accounts: tally up inflows from customers and outflows to suppliers. Instead, a corporate cash flow statement like the one we just created does something more useful for analyzing why cash flows and profits may have diverged. It starts with the (unwarranted) assumption that net profit and operating cash flow are equal and then makes a series of adjustments. Although less intuitive than a tally of inflows and outflows, the cash flow statement and the P&L now tell us exactly what happened between two balance sheet snapshots.

Displayed in this way, the three financial statements reveal to investors not just what happened in the past but also the future risks the business model may harbor. Investors can discern how further growth, even if nominally profitable, could nevertheless lead to a cash crunch. At the very least, they can foresee that the company's cash needs will require future financing. As a current investor, you're generally not excited if your company needs to raise more cash. The more debt the company needs, the lower the profits will be, the greater the number of promises that have to be kept, and the greater the difficulty in keeping them. Or if the company raises more money by selling shares, then there may be less profit to distribute per share. Meanwhile, an upward trend in inventories may be a worrying sign that the company cannot find enough customers and that a future loss will come when inventory perishes or becomes obsolete.

## CHOKING ON GROWTH

Seeing your accounts receivable grow is especially ulcer inducing. Imagine you are thinking of lending money to a company with high and increasing accounts receivable. You not only need to worry about the borrower's business model and balance sheet but also have to worry about the borrower's customers. Can you count on them to pay for the goods and services they bought? Ninety days after their purchase, who knows what catastrophes will have befallen them? Are they businesses with their own sets of promises to keep and perhaps their own fears about collecting from *their* customers? When investing in a company with generous customer payment terms, you may have to worry about a domino game of contractually related companies. In such an arrangement, one falling block could set off a wave of defaults and bankruptcies.

A case in point is Lucent Technologies in the late 1990s. The company sold telecommunications equipment such as fiber-optic cables and switches just when global service providers like AT&T, Vodafone, and Singtel were building out the infrastructure on which our connected world now rests. Lucent grew rapidly and offered its customers generous payment terms. Some of its customers were companies like AT&T—firms with reliable cash flows, as discussed in the previous chapter. But some of Lucent's customers were start-up companies looking to build entirely new business models for the information age. When the economy sputtered in 2001—as it sometimes will—many of those start-ups went out of business, taking with them the suppliers to whom they owed money. The entire telecommunications technology industry was shaken. Companies that were more resilient bought out the more vulnerable ones. This fate eventually happened to Lucent when investors lost faith that it would keep its promises. The loss in faith sent Lucent's stock price from over $100 per share at its high to less than $1 at its low, wiping out more than $100 billion of stock market value.

Another company, a small, struggling start-up called Netflix, nearly went under a few years later for a different set of reasons related to cash flow. Today, the company is known for streaming entertainment, but when it was founded, the digital network infrastructure was not yet robust enough for streaming video. Instead, Netflix operated a website and a subscription service. As a customer, you signed up and selected a list of movies you wanted to see. Netflix then sent out—by snail mail—the next three items in your list as digital video disks (DVDs), with a postage-paid return envelope included. Whenever you were done with the disks—and there was no time limit—you sent them back to Netflix and received the next items on your list. To entice customers, Netflix allowed you to subscribe with a three-month free trial period. With this attractive offer, Netflix experienced explosive growth.

You've probably guessed, though: Netflix's business model engaged the dynamics we described above. Allowing customers to sign up for three months of free service is equivalent to granting ninety-day payment terms. Meanwhile, to support a sufficiently large library—including multiple copies of popular blockbusters—Netflix had to sink a lot of money into the DVDs themselves, up front. For each new customer, Netflix had to buy three additional DVDs. The cash flow that was required every month to satisfy new customers exceeded the payments coming in from the customers who had signed up three months earlier. Netflix nearly choked on its own growth. The company turned things around only by reducing the free phase to a single month and by negotiating with its suppliers, the film distributors. It reduced the up-front payment for DVDs in return for a share of Netflix's sales. Netflix survived and led the film industry into the streaming age.

## WORKING CAPITAL

Cash flow tragedies and near tragedies like Lucent and Netflix hinge substantially on the gap between when customers pay and when suppliers get paid. Let's take a close look at current assets and current liabilities in the example we worked through.*

| Q1 Current Assets | | Q1 Current Liabilities | |
|---|---|---|---|
| Cash | 2,000 | Accounts payable | 2,000 |
| Inventory | 1,000 | | |
| Accounts receivable | 10,000 | | |
| **Total** | **13,000** | **Total** | **2,000** |
| | | Imbalance | 11,000 |

In the Q1 statement, the current portion of the balance sheet is unbalanced, by $11,000. For the balance sheet to remain in balance overall,

---

* These figures report the balance sheet implications of the operating cash flows we described earlier in this chapter.

the company needs OPM, as they call it on Wall Street. Other people's money. Some form of capital has to weigh on the liabilities and equity side of the balance sheet to bring it into balance, over and above the financing required to fund the long-term assets, the equipment. The capital required to make up for the shortfall is called **working capital**. From an accounting point of view, working capital is the difference between current assets and current liabilities.

*Working Capital = Current Assets – Current Liabilities*

Leaving aside the cash balance itself, **trade working capital** is the difference between accounts receivable plus inventory on the one hand and accounts payable on the other.

*Trade Working Capital = Accounts Receivable*
*+ Inventory*
*– Accounts Payable*

> Working capital management is a crucial and often-overlooked leverage point for creating shareholder value.

Working capital management is a crucial leverage point for shareholder value, and it's one that managers sometimes overlook as they focus on keeping customers happy and costs low. What can we do to manage working capital efficiently?

If our payment terms with suppliers were calibrated to our customer payment terms, we would need less working capital. In our example from above, if we had supplier payment terms of net 90, we could defer all cost of sales entirely to the next quarter: $6,000 instead of just $2,000. That would reduce our trade working capital to $5,000.

| Q1 Noncash Current Assets | | Q1 Current Liabilities | |
|---|---|---|---|
| Inventory | 1,000 | Accounts payable (net 90) | 6,000 |
| Accounts receivable (net 90) | 10,000 | | |
| **Total** | **11,000** | **Total** | **6,000** |
| | | Imbalance (trade working capital) | 5,000 |

Managing working capital may have little to do with how great your product is or how skilled you are at producing it. Managing accounts receivable and accounts payable comes down to how you negotiate your contracts.

Reducing your inventory also reduces working capital. Over the past few decades, much business innovation has centered on supply chain management and so-called lean manufacturing: setting up just-in-time ordering and delivery processes that minimize the time raw materials and finished products sit in warehouses or in transit to customers. Meanwhile, accelerating *production* processes means that unfinished products—work in progress—will spend less time encumbering the balance sheet.

Have you been wondering what happens if you stand the working capital dynamic on its head? What if you really squeeze your supplier while collecting early from your customer? Some retailers like Amazon can benefit from **negative trade working capital**. With this practice, customers pay on delivery and suppliers get paid on extremely long payment terms. When you buy in bulk, you might even convince—perhaps *force* is the better word—suppliers to get paid 120 days later. In that setup, cash flows into the company from customers faster than it flows out to suppliers. Like when a dam across a river creates a lake behind it, cash pools inside the company, and that pool of cash can be used for many things, like growing the company through sales and marketing or R&D, maintaining a rainy-day fund, or rewarding shareholders for their confidence and patience.

Especially for a growing company, the negative working capital dynamic can launch a virtuous cycle in which positive operating cash flow funds new investments, which generate new operating cash flow, and so on. The computer company Dell got started when Michael Dell took orders and credit card payments over the phone and then got to work on assembling computers from parts he bought with long supplier payment terms. In this way, he and his team stamped a multi-billion-dollar company out of the ground in just a few years—with the help of customers' and suppliers' money.

The secret to business does not lie in managing working capital efficiently alone, of course. Have you reduced inventory to near zero? Congratulations. But what happens when an unexpected large customer order comes in and you can't fulfill it on time? Or perhaps you get your customers to pay on delivery (terms of net 0)? Your competitor may eat your lunch by offering net 30 payment terms. If you string out your supplier on long payment terms, don't be surprised if the supplier charges higher prices, puts your orders on the back burner, or goes out of business because of its own cash crunch.

As we write, the world is experiencing the highest rates of **inflation** in decades. Inflation—when this year's dollar buys you fewer goods than last year's—has many causes. A major contributing factor in the early 2020s has been the supply chain disruptions caused by the Covid-19 lockdowns. A global economy in which every link in the supply chain manages inventory to the bone is one in which capital is available for growth-oriented investment, instead of sitting on balance sheets in working capital. It's also one in which there is very little slack in the system. Even modest disruptions in one link can be amplified up the chain, for example, when car manufacturers ran out of computer chips in 2021: They had not kept an inventory of chips on hand, and when chip producers in Taiwan temporarily shut down fabrication facilities during the pandemic, car production slowed to a crawl and car prices rose, even for used cars.

The immediate cause of the disruptions might have been the pandemic. Their severity may be due to working capital management practices. We cannot predict where inflation will go from here or what its consequences will be. Historically, inflation has been a catalyst for social upheaval, as it was in Germany in the 1920s, when inflation sowed the seeds of World War II. Our relentless focus on just-in-time working capital management may yet have wider-ranging consequences than just a decade or two of solid shareholder value creation!

## CHAPTER 7 KEY TAKEAWAYS

The "cash flow from operations" portion of the cash flow statement displays information about routine cash flows in a way that is counterintuitive but that helps reconcile the balance sheet and P&L statement.

*Trade Working Capital = Accounts Receivable*
*+ Inventory*
*– Accounts Payable*

Positive (and growing) trade working capital makes the company vulnerable to several risks, including

- The need for ever more capital when the company grows
- The threat of customer nonpayment
- The threat of losses due to perished or obsolescent inventory

Negative working capital results when companies collect from customers quicker than they pay suppliers while keeping inventories low. When cash flows in faster than it flows back out, the resulting pool of cash can be deployed to fund growth-oriented investments without the need for other people's money.

## CHAPTER 8

# Cost Structures

"**S**ure, we're losing money on every unit we sell. But we'll make it up in volume!" That's been the rallying cry of many ambitious start-ups. Sometimes, it's the punch line to a joke about Silicon Valley hubris. Sometimes, it's the foundation of a wildly successful business model. And for some companies, the jury is still out. Ride-sharing behemoth Uber Technologies had accumulated losses exceeding $26 billion according to its 2021 annual report, in spite of over $17 billion in sales that year. By early 2022, there was no clear end in sight to the losses. Uber itself acknowledged the financial challenges: "We expect our operating expenses to increase significantly in the foreseeable future." Can Uber eventually "make it up in volume?" We've looked at the three drivers of value—profitability, growth, and risk—individually, and we've started to see some of the interplay between them. This chapter is all about the interplay between growth and profitability, to which the idea of making it up in volume refers. And we'll see that risk lies at the heart of the interaction.

# ECONOMICS VERSUS ACCOUNTING

In Chapter 2, on profitability, we looked at expenses—what a company consumes—in terms of the accounting buckets used to describe what the expenses were used for: making the product, persuading the customer to buy it, improving products and inventing new ones, compensating debt holders. *What* we expend resources on is one question. *How* we consume them is another. Our food truck uses up the resource cheese in direct proportion to the number of sandwiches we sell. Other resources are consumed in ways that don't tie clearly to our sales. Renting the food truck, employing our accountant: We incur those costs whether we sell a thousand sandwiches or none at all. In our food truck's business model, cheese is a **variable cost**. Rent is a **fixed cost**. The more we sell, the more our variable costs increase. The fixed costs don't change according to how many sandwiches we sell...to a point, at least. But let's not get ahead of ourselves.

Most managers we meet in our training programs are familiar with the distinction between fixed and variable costs. Familiarity breeds contempt. Although the concepts are familiar, the implications are frequently misunderstood. There are at least three misconceptions we encounter all the time.

> **Economics is not accounting:** The first misconception is that the accounting categories and the economic categories overlap exactly, that costs of sales, like cheese, are strictly variable and that the other operating expenses—sales, marketing, R&D, and so on—are strictly fixed. Those distinctions are not necessarily true. Some expenses related to making or delivering a product are fixed—for example, the salary of a plant manager. Likewise, some expenses on the SG&A side may be variable—for example, sales commissions. The more you sell, the higher the commission payments.

**Timing and scale:** The second misconception is to overlook the fact that whether an expense is fixed or variable can depend on scale, in terms of both volume and time. What your team of four salaried employees costs may be fixed over the next quarter, regardless of how much business your company is doing. But the CEO of a 50,000-employee organization might look at head count as a variable cost over a multiyear time horizon, something that can be increased and decreased as the volume of business rises and falls. Even the smallest variable expense can be fixed at the smallest of scales. We have to buy cheese in twenty-slice packs, regardless of whether we sell one or twenty sandwiches. And the largest fixed expense looks variable at the largest of scales. In addition to the timing, scale also matters when we are deciding whether a cost is variable or fixed. A TV ad campaign is fixed for one media market, but it is variable when we decide how many media markets we want to cover.

**Applicability:** Finally, another misconception concerns the applicability of the fixed-versus-variable distinction. *Fixed* and *variable* are relative terms. Fixed relative to what? Varying along with what? Much of the time, we're interested in how expenses relate to *sales*. But we can also relate expenses to other target outputs in the organization. In our own business, we interact with large corporate learning and development departments. Their target output is human capital, and one of their units of measure for output is the number of people trained. When they organize a leadership development workshop, some costs vary according to how many people attend the workshop: things like materials, software licenses to our business simulations, or travel. Other costs may be fixed regardless of whether three people or thirty attend: our faculty's day rate, for example.

Different business models and industries will naturally have different **cost structures**, some with a preponderance of variable costs, others heavily weighted toward fixed costs. Still, in a given business, we can make many decisions that push the cost structure in one direction or the other. We're going to look at what criteria inform cost structure decisions in areas that directly relate to the volume of business: the number of units we sell. This insight will help us understand whether a company like Uber can—or cannot—make it up in volume.

> Pricing below the variable costs is like pressing a business's self-destruct button. That doesn't mean companies never do it.

Let's say the raw materials—bread, butter, cheese, tomatoes, spices—used in each grilled cheese sandwich cost us $4. From the get-go, we see that we cannot charge customers any less than $4. If we were to charge less, we'd lose money on every sandwich sold, and the more we sold, the more we'd lose. *There would be no way to make it up in volume.* Pricing below the variable costs is like pressing the business's self-destruct button. That doesn't mean companies never do it. In 2019, journalist and Uber user Josh Barro pointed out that the customer loyalty discounts Uber kept sending him must have driven the prices he was paying below the variable costs—in this case, the driver's time at the legally mandated minimum wage. But when companies like Uber price below variable costs—in a process sometimes called **dumping**—it's usually to pursue a strategic goal. They are playing a business version of the game of chicken, trying to drive competitors out of the market. Prices can be raised to profitable levels later, when theirs is the last company standing.

Alternatively, in business models like the previously discussed Netflix and other network-based ones, selling a product initially below cost—even giving it away for free—can lead to a later lucrative stream of future profitable sales from enthusiastic customers. But free lunches are not sustainable. As long as your price sits below your variable costs, you cannot make it up in volume, even if you have no fixed costs at all.

# BREAKEVEN ANALYSIS

If your price exceeds the variable costs by even the smallest amount, making it up in volume is possible in principle. Whether you can do so in reality is another matter and depends on the fixed costs. Suppose we priced our sandwiches at $4.01. We'd make what is called a **contribution margin** of $0.01 on each sandwich sold. It's called a contribution margin because each unit sold contributes to covering the business's fixed costs. Suppose our fixed costs per month were $6,000 for rent, permits, and other things. With a contribution margin of $0.01 per sandwich, we'd have to sell six hundred thousand sandwiches every month to cover our fixed costs.

That number is, of course, absurd. Even if that many people wanted grilled cheese sandwiches, we'd have to deliver fourteen sandwiches per minute nonstop, twenty-four hours per day, every day of the entire month. Maybe with multiple locations, that goal might not be impossible. McDonald's serves thousands of burgers per minute. But the fixed costs for McDonald's are considerably higher than $6,000 per month. If we added trucks to serve the volume, we'd see very quickly how the distinction between fixed and variable costs is a matter of scale!

With a sandwich price of $10, we'd make a contribution margin of $6 per sandwich. At that price, we'd have to sell a thousand sandwiches every month, or fifty sandwiches a day for twenty days. This goal is much more reasonable. Of course, we'd make zero profit. The volume at which our contribution margin exactly covers the fixed costs is the *breakeven point*. If we sell less than the breakeven amount, we lose money. If we sell more, we are profitable.

Calculating the breakeven point is simple: Subtract the variable cost from the price, and divide the resulting contribution margin by the fixed costs.

$$Breakeven\ Point = \frac{(Unit\ Price - Unit\ Variable\ Cost)}{(Fixed\ Cost)}$$

$$= \frac{(Contribution\ Margin)}{(Fixed\ Cost)}$$

We can visualize the breakeven point by graphing sales, total costs (including variable and fixed), and fixed costs against the number of units sold.

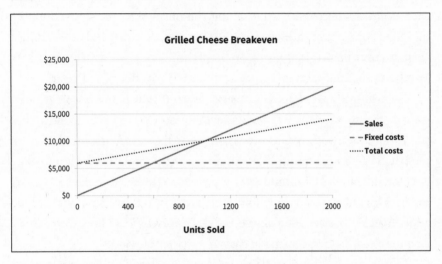

Looking at a business's fixed costs, variable costs, price, and potential volume and deciding whether the product is viable is called **breakeven analysis**. The fact that we can calculate the breakeven point with sixth-grade math and display it with a simple graph is deceptive. As always in business and in life, it's not about calculating a single number. Suppose we take our grilled cheese breakeven point at $10 per sandwich to be 1,000 sandwiches per month, or about 50 per day on twenty days in the month. That means we'd need to sell more than 1,000 to be profitable. Can we sell more than 50 a day? Or do we need to stay open for twenty-four days or even all thirty days? We could drop the breakeven point by increasing our price. At \$12.00, the breakeven drops to 750 sandwiches. But with this higher price, do we still feel confident we'll find enough customers to hit the lower breakeven point? Reducing our costs also lowers the breakeven point. If we found a way to squeeze \$1 in variable costs out of the system, the breakeven drops to 858 sandwiches. But what impact will less cheese or lower-quality cheese have on customer satisfaction and sales?

Breakeven analysis helps test our assumptions and discover what questions to ask, and ultimately, it suggests what real-world experiments to run. What winds up working is up to customers.

## THE TRADE-OFFS BETWEEN PROFITABILITY, GROWTH, AND RISK

Different business models naturally have different cost structures. Brick-and-mortar retailers may have high fixed costs to rent* desirable locations with high foot traffic. That's why they will often offer steep discounts to bring traffic in the door: They have to get those fixed costs covered. Whatever the natural tendency of a business model or industry, we can still make decisions about how to structure some of the costs, including decisions such as

- Hiring a full-time, salaried employee with benefits versus hiring a contractor on an hourly or piece-rate basis
- Maintaining an expensive downtown office or flexibly renting workspace and conference rooms at a coworking space
- Hiring in-house legal and tax teams or paying for external legal and tax advice on a billable hour basis

Companies may even go back and forth between different cost structures as their needs and market context evolve. In its earlier history, online

---

* Whether they recognize the fixed costs as rent on a leased space or as depreciation of real estate they have purchased does not ultimately matter from the perspective of the cost structure.

retailer Amazon paid logistics companies like UPS and the US Postal Service on a delivery basis. Later, Amazon built out its own logistics arm, with all the fixed costs that doing so entailed, including its own fleet of Boeing 737s. Nowadays, Amazon is going back in the opposite direction and is encouraging its drivers to become entrepreneurs and start their own business by driving packages for Amazon. Essentially, it is reconverting a fixed cost—a driver's salary—into a variable cost of paying former drivers only when a package is actually delivered. Because these new Amazon-sponsored businesses are much smaller than UPS, Amazon has substantial negotiation leverage over them, enjoying the benefits of variable costs at a much lower total delivery cost than when the company started.

When you do have a choice, why prefer fixed over variable costs, or variable over fixed? There are many possible reasons that are specific to a business's particular situation: It might make sense to bring on people with rare skills on a full-time basis to prevent their expertise from flowing to a competitor, for example. Generally speaking, however, what cost structure you choose may hinge on how you expect the volume of your business to evolve in the future. Imagine, for instance, that you believe your market is growing and that your company will capture that growth

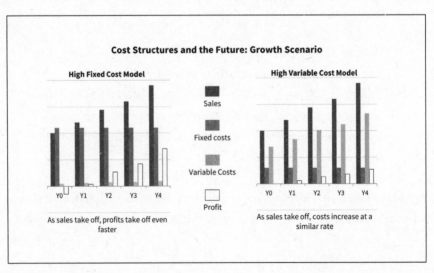

with steadily rising sales over the next few years. Given the choice, you might want to make as many costs independent of your sales volume as possible. As sales increase, profits will increase even faster. With fewer fixed costs and higher variable costs, although profits will increase with sales volume, they will increase much slower.

Conversely, if your outlook is pessimistic and you see declining sales in your future, you might favor variable costs over fixed costs. You can control variable costs and glide your overall expenses down along with your sales, maintaining profitability. High fixed costs could quickly lead to losses.

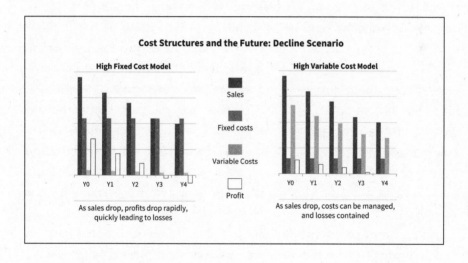

Many companies serve multiple markets with multiple products. At any given time, Product A may be early in its life cycle, with low current sales but a rosy outlook, just like the models in the growth scenario in the first pair of charts. Another product, Product B, may be aging, facing a long, slow decline, as depicted in the second pair of models. Correspondingly, Product A's manager may be looking for ways to make more costs fixed, whereas Product B's manager will try to maintain profitability by making costs variable.

Some of the company's expenses may be impossible to attribute to any specific product line; these expenses are often called **overhead**. The two product managers may have very different perspectives on how overhead expenses should be allocated to the two products and how those costs should be structured, especially when their own compensation is tied to their respective products' profitability. This is just one of many thorny problems posed by business administration, making collective decision-making so challenging that we've dedicated several chapters to it later in this book!

We founded our own first business in 2001, when online e-learning was still in its infancy. We believed we were boarding a rocket ship of growth. Corporate training, academia, and even much of K–12 education looked ready to shift from in-person, instructor-led training and paper textbooks to rich, interactive online media. And once we got past the near-death experiences all new companies seem to go through, our growth story started to unfold as envisioned. Our client list and our sales grew. We won awards for our highly interactive multimedia courses, and the awards attracted new clients and new sales. Our orders came in as individual service projects, but with more and more projects, we felt the need to increase our fixed-cost base to leverage growth into higher profitability. We made full-time job offers to people with amazing talent. We expanded the management team. We rented office space with room to grow.

> Our choices about cost structure dictate how growth, profitability, and risk interact to create value...or destroy it.

We were young and naive. We weren't entirely wrong, either. Online e-learning has grown massively. What we misunderstood was our particular market segment: custom-developed, high-end, interactive multimedia. Market demand grew steadily, but simple e-learning courses could be developed fairly cheaply in regions with much lower labor costs than those at our base in Austin. We were cost competitive when it came to solutions that were more complex. Demand for complex higher-end multimedia experiences grew, too. But there were far fewer such projects. Fewer learning and development departments had the budgets, business cases, and timelines to spend six figures on custom-developed projects. It became hard to predict when we might find one of those projects or when a project might find us. Unlike in the preceding graphs of cost structure scenarios, we could plan confidently neither for steady growth nor for decline.

It was the kind of feast-or-famine environment that many service businesses face, and our fixed costs became highly problematic. Sure, when our order books were full, our profits were quite high—high enough to fund the development of The 12-Week MBA programs on which our current business rests. But when times were lean—as they inevitably were once in a while—we experienced huge losses, losses that a small self-funded business could ill afford. We tried to make it work, but we eventually ran into roadblocks that made us sell the custom-development operation. The competitors we know who stayed in that market succeeded by relying more heavily on contractors—whose costs are variable—than on employees.

Our choices about cost structure connect directly to our value drivers and how they interact. Much of the time, growth and profitability seem to trade off against each other. Dropping prices may lead to more sales but at a lower level of profit. We might be able to attract more customers with a catchy radio jingle or a product with more bells and whistles. Jingles, bells, and whistles cost money and may reduce profits. However, we can use a high-fixed-cost structure to turn growth into higher profitability, *if we are confident* about growth. If our confidence is misplaced and we don't grow—if we shrink or if demand fluctuates unpredictably—then high fixed costs lead quickly to losses. We take on high fixed costs to drive value through growth and increased profitability, but we do so by exposing our business to greater risk, magnifying the consequences of sales shortfalls. Conversely, in weighting variable costs more heavily, we take less advantage of growth but mitigate the risks of low sales.

## SALES, PREDICTABILITY, AND BUSINESS MODELS

The *variability* in the volume of sales clearly affects profitability. The *predictability* of sales is an important input into the cost structure decision. Macroeconomic conditions, competitor action, technological disruption, and changes in consumer behavior are just a few of the risks that express themselves in unexpected—usually lower—demand. So it should come as no surprise that many business activities are focused on reducing variability and increasing the predictability of sales. Yes, we all know that businesses try to sell more while consuming less. But much of what happens in business is better understood as an attempt to tame sales rather than just to grow them. Here are a few business models whose target is predictability of sales—and of cash flows from customers.

> Much management effort goes into taming the sales rather than just growing them.

**Brand:** Although both of us know that it's perfectly irrational, our teeth don't *feel* clean unless brushed with the toothpaste that both of our sets of parents bought when we were toddlers. The great dream of a Colgate-Palmolive marketer is to have consumers think that only this company's brand of toothpaste gives them the feeling of freshness and that, when they beget children, their kids, too, will associate the clean-teeth feeling with the same brand, passing on the association to their children and to their children's children and so on through a biblical chain of begats, until our sun goes supernova.

Every time a consumer faces a buying decision, the person might choose something new, especially if enticed to do so with a discount. If consumers only based their decisions on price, not only would there be an unrelenting race to the bottom but each provider's sales would swing wildly and unpredictably from one period to the next as competitors found new ways to produce things more cheaply and to lower the price. Brands lock consumers into a buying pattern that secures not only a slightly higher price but also a long-term customer-provider relationship, reducing variability and enhancing predictability of sales. And of course, brands also create customer value by making the customer experience more predictable.

**Subscriptions:** Another approach to smoothing sales figures is to reduce the number of times customers have to make a choice.* For many years, Microsoft looked at each purchase of a new computer as an opportunity to sell another license to its suite of office software. By moving to the Office 365 *subscription model,* customers make a lower initial payment and might even sometimes pay less. But now, once they have agreed to the subscription, they have to make a conscious decision to leave. Many other software providers have switched to the *SaaS* (software as a service) *model* as well: It provides a steady and predictable flow of cash. And it's not just software. Amazon entices users into a Prime membership in part because of the steady flow of subscription cash, even though it could conceivably make more money on individual streaming rentals and purchases.

**The razor blade model:** Game console makers like Sony and Microsoft sell their consoles at low margins, sometimes even at prices below the production costs. They do so to entice gamers to commit to a platform for which these consumers buy high-margin games. Game consoles have a useful lifetime of a few years. GE Aviation sells jet engines to airlines at a modest margin because it is assured of service and parts contracts that can last *decades.*†

---

\* Or is it "get to" make a choice?

† And then it doesn't hurt that maintenance and regular parts replacement are required by regulation, thankfully for us all.

Both cases are instances of the so-called **razor blade model** used by makers of (cheap) razors and their (expensive and very profitable) replacement blades.

We haven't even begun to list the many ways **insurance** providers shift some of the risks to a company's sales from things like natural disasters, political crises, and health crises. For a fee, of course. There's even a financial service specializing in helping companies deal with the risks associated not with customer sales but with customer cash flows. Companies that provide what is called **factoring** buy up the accounts receivable of other businesses—at a discount—so that those businesses don't have to worry about collecting and can make their cash flows more predictable. These are just some of the business models deployed by companies to smooth sales and cash flow and to raise confidence in projections of future performance.

So what about Uber Technologies? Uber is clearly betting on the steady growth scenario, hoping that the slim—at times questionable—contribution margins above the drivers' variable costs will eventually make up for the considerable fixed costs. As CEO Dara Khosrowshahi put it in an internal email from May 2022, "We have to make sure the *unit economics* work before we go big." One wonders what "big" means if the $32 billion reported for 2022, another loss-making year, is not big enough yet. As of this writing, Uber certainly has its work cut out for it, even if the company was finally able to eke out a nominal profit midway through 2023.

# CHAPTER 8 KEY TAKEAWAYS

A company's cost structure is the relative weighting of expenses that increase with sales volume (variable costs) and those that do not (fixed costs).

The economic concepts of fixed and variable costs do not match up precisely with the accounting categories reported in the P&L statement.

Cost structure influences a company's profitability as it grows:

- In a high-fixed-cost structure, growth turns into rising profitability, but slow sales quickly lead to losses.
- For companies with high fixed costs, variability in sales tends to lead to even higher variability in profit margins.
- In contrast, a high-variable-cost structure allows companies facing declining or less predictable sales to control costs and maintain profitability but limits the upside.

The breakeven formula tells us how high the sales volume has to be to make up for fixed and variable costs.

Much of the cost structure of a business depends on its business model, but managers at all levels make decisions that affect the company's cost structure.

## CHAPTER 9

# Valuation Foundations

On April 19, 2022, the entertainment streaming service Netflix announced that for the first time ever, its subscriber base had declined. During the Covid-19 pandemic, millions of people had been stuck in their homes with little to do. Streaming was an attractive way to while away the hours. But once lockdowns ended, people who had been glued to their screens for business and pleasure were raring to rediscover the real world. Cutting back on monthly subscriptions freed up money to spend on restaurants, concerts, theme parks, and nonpajama clothes. Two hundred thousand fewer subscribers were reported. Not only that, but management also warned that it expected to lose another two *million* subscribers in the next quarter. Netflix's stock price dropped immediately by around a third, wiping out about $50 billion in shareholder value.

That's a pretty dramatic statement about value. On the surface, it looks as if Netflix's shareholders believed that 2.2 million customers were worth $50 billion.* Our journey started with the question "What is shareholder value, and how do I create it?" And we gave away the answer up front:

---

* That would imply a value of around $23,000 per customer. As we'll see in the following chapters, it's not quite as simple as that.

*Shareholder value originates in a company's discounted future net cash flows.*

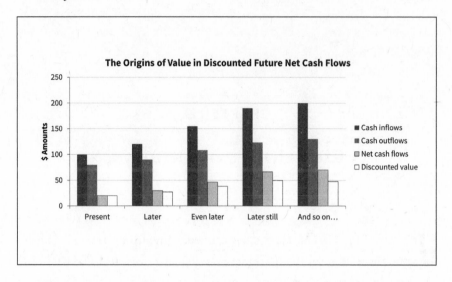

Since then, we've built the scaffolding to make sense of that sentence. Now you're hoping for some payoff! But here comes a big caveat: If you're hoping to learn the tools that allow you to value companies and become a day trader or launch a career in mergers and acquisitions, you're reading the wrong book.* There are such tools, in fact many of them. Some can be applied both to investments in entire companies and to investments in long-term assets like food trucks and subscription-paying customers.

You may have opportunities to apply that analytical toolkit in your career. And you might not. In our own twenty-year experience, we've used the toolkit a handful of times. But even if a full crash course in advanced finance is beyond the scope of this book, the core ideas behind these financial toolkits haunt every business decision. Understand those ideas, and you will understand what drives business decision-making and

---

* The right book is *Valuation: Measuring and Managing the Value of Companies* by Tim Koller, Marc Goedhart, and David Wessels.

what role you play in creating value, no matter what function or level of the organization you're in. In this chapter, you can follow the core argument in the main text. But there are so many interesting sidetracks that we've peppered this chapter with footnotes for those who want to stop and smell the financial roses.

## RISK, RETURN, AND THE TIME VALUE OF MONEY

Let's begin with an abstract but extremely simple scenario of an investment: An investor gives up $100 now, expecting to get something back a year later.*

|  | Now | Next Year |
|---|---|---|
| **Cash Outflow** | –100 | |
| **Cash Inflow** | | *X* |

We lend things like books and tools to friends, family, and neighbors all the time. Maybe not *all* items are returned. But we usually just expect the thing itself back, hopefully not too much the worse for wear. With money and business partners, our expectations are different. To forgo $100 today, we want to earn a **return on investment** and get back some amount higher than $100.

Do we want a return on investment because we're greedy? Perhaps. However, the central point in this chapter is that although we may want the highest return possible, we actually need a minimum return. If we keep investing without earning the minimum return, our capital will dwindle, eventually to zero.

Why do we need a minimum return? And what is it?

Let's start with the why. The main reason is one that we've repeated frequently. Cash we invest today is no longer at our disposal. End of story.

---

* All the figures in the tables in this chapter are in US dollars unless otherwise specified.

When investors
provide capital
without earning
the minimum
return, their capi-
tal will eventually
dwindle to zero.

Meanwhile, next year's cash flow is really just a promise. And promises can be broken. In short, by investing cash now to get cash back later, investors are putting their cash at risk.

Risk is by far the most important reason investors need a minimum return on their investment. But at least conventionally, there is a second reason. That reason is tied to the idea that cash can be used for a dizzying array of pleasures or projects. Heck, you can wallpaper your room with it or use it as kindling. And one thing you can do with your cash is deposit it in a savings account and earn interest on it, essentially risk-free. Because you could always earn risk-free interest, any even slightly risky investment has to earn at least as much as what the savings account would earn. If the prevailing interest rate is 2 percent, a risky $100 investment has to return strictly more than $102 a year later, to compensate the investor for the $2 in interest forgone. The fact that investors have a risk-free option means that cash in the present is always more valuable than future cash.* We call this phenomenon the **time value of money**.

---

* Or so the conventional story goes. We can't help but share the following rant, placed in a footnote for your convenience. First, to expand on the conventional view: The risk-free rate is usually taken to be the interest rate on government debt of a stable, creditworthy country. The United States and its treasury bonds have been recognized as the closest thing to a risk-free bet.

In addition to risk, another reason an investor needs a return on investment is the fact that money tends to lose value over time, the phenomenon called inflation. Through a combination of market forces and the management of interest rates by central banks such as the US Federal Reserve, the interest rate on government debt is usually slightly higher than the rate of inflation. Consequently, the interest paid on government debt—also called the nominal rate—makes up for the effects of inflation. The difference between the nominal rate and inflation is called the real interest rate. When inflation is around 2 or 3 percent, interest rates ought to be around 4 or 5 percent. A positive real interest rate implies that even if there is no risk at all, not even inflation risk, investors still demand a return. The mainstream explanation for the real interest rate is cash's **option value.** Holding cash grants us the opportunity to choose: as long as we hold the cash, we can still choose between all the ways to deploy it. The opportunity to choose—also called optionality—is itself valuable, and we have to be compensated for losing it when we invest.

The two of us first learned the conventional story in the 1990s, a time when the story matched recent history. However, since the great financial crisis of 2007–2008, interest rate policy and behavior have been...weird, to say the least. Not only have real interest rates—nominal rates minus the inflation rate—often been negative, but some central banks have even turned to negative nominal interest rates: you paid the government to lend it money! The study of interest rate policy and behavior is part of the branch of economics called macroeconomics. Tellingly, in 2017, macroeconomics was not part of the economics curriculum of an interdisciplinary masters program at a top German research university where one of us studied. As one economics professor teaching the program explained (paraphrasing), "We're not really sure what to teach anymore."

In addition, there is risk. We previously discussed risk in terms of a level of confidence that a promise will be kept. A typical way we express confidence is to say something like "I'm 95 percent certain that..." That's how meteorologists report confidence in their forecasts of rain. Now suppose our investment was to lend our acquaintance Connie $100, and she promised to pay us back $100 one year later:

|  | Now | Next Year |
|---|---|---|
| **Cash Outflow** | –100 | |
| **Cash Inflow** | | 100 |

What would it mean to say "We're 95 percent certain she'll pay us back"? The most intuitive way to interpret this statement is that out of a hundred people about whom we felt similarly confident as we felt about Connie, we'd expect ninety-five to have merited our confidence, paying back our $100 a year later. But we also expect five Connie clones to be con artists, never to be heard from again. If we invested in one hundred Connies, we'd have laid out $10,000 and recovered $9,500, or $95 per person.

|  | Now | Next Year |
|---|---|---|
| **Cash Outflow** | –100 | |
| **Cash Inflow** | | 95 |

In other words, we'd earn a negative return; value would have been destroyed, not created. At that level of confidence, how much would we have to ask the one hundred Connie-like people to pay back next year if

---

With respect to the "risk-free" rate, neither are we. Our uncertainty is shared by Koller, Goedhart, and Wessels, the aforementioned authors of *Valuation*. They "recommend using a synthetic risk-free rate" by adding 2 percent to the current inflation rate ("synthetic" meaning "let's just pull it out of a dark hole")."

we expect five to pay nothing at all? The answer is $105.27.* We'd invest $10,000 and recover 95 times $105.27, which is $10,000. And 65 cents, but let's not be persnickety.

|  | Now | Next Year |
|---|---|---|
| **Cash Outflow** | −100 | |
| **Cash Inflow** | | 105.27 |

In absolute terms, in addition to the return *of* our investment of $100, we need to ask Connie for a $5.27 return *on* our investment to compensate for the risk we perceive. Because we ultimately want to be able to compare different investment opportunities with each other, we usually speak of investment returns in relative terms, relative to the investment amount, in this case, 5.27 percent. Put differently, it takes a 5.27 percent return to compensate us for taking the risk of accepting a promise of future cash in which we feel 95 percent confident.† To keep things simpler and the numbers round, let's dispense with the confidence level, speak only of the minimum return, and work with an even 6 percent for the discussion that follows.

What does a 6 percent gain mean? Are we $6 richer a year later? If Connie pays up, yes, we will be. But note that if she pays up, then we just got lucky and happened to choose the right Connie. If we make a habit of investments like this one, we'll eventually hit some scam artists or unlucky entrepreneurs who won't return us the money they promised. If we make enough such investments, we're going to preserve our $100 capital, no more, no less.

There are two ways to frame investments, depending on what question you are asking. To answer the question "What's the least reward I need to get in the future to motivate me to forgo cash in the present?" you

---

* Technically, $105.263158. To avoid a loss, we have to demand $105.27.
† If you want to account for the risk-free interest you forgo when you lend cash to Connie instead of to the US government, simply slap on the prevailing interest rate to the return required to cover risk.

multiply the cash you forgo by 100 percent plus the minimum return. Alternatively, you can ask, "What's the greatest amount of cash I can bear forgoing now in return for a promise of a future cash flow?" The answer: Divide the future cash flow by 100 percent plus the minimum return.

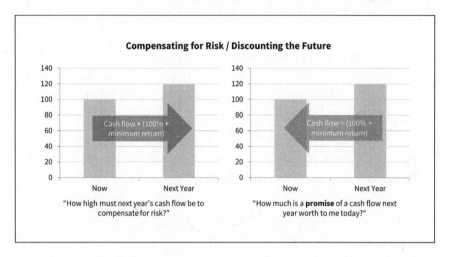

**Compensating for Risk / Discounting the Future**

"How high must next year's cash flow be to compensate for risk?"

"How much is a **promise** of a cash flow next year worth to me today?"

When we compare different investments, we usually do so in terms of their rate of return, which aligns more with the first framing. But when we evaluate an individual investment, we're usually asking the second question. We look at what cash flow is promised in the future. Then we use the minimum return to tell us how much of our current cash we should sacrifice—at most—in exchange for that promise. Because of risk, that future cash flow is always worth strictly less than its face value. In other words, we count its face value *less*: We are **discounting** the future value to what we call its **present value**. If the minimum return is 6 percent, then a promise of $100 next year has a present value of $94.34.

What if Connie agrees to our demand of a minimum return of 6 percent but tells us she can't pay back the $106 all at once? Instead, she proposes to pay it back in two installments of $53 each over two years. Does that still compensate us for the risk we're taking? Let's look at the **cash flow model** of this business proposition.

|  | Y0 | Y1 | Y2 |
|---|---|---|---|
| Investment | −100 | | |
| Cash Inflow | | 53 | 53 |

To answer that question, we discount those two future cash flows to their present values. Discounting the first year's flow is straightforward using our discounting formula, and it's an even $50.00. How do we discount the second year? Intuitively, the second year's $53 cash flow should be worth less than the first year's. Stuff happens, and the more time elapses, the more stuff will happen. A simple way to reflect that idea would be to discount the second year's cash flow twice by the same rate:

$$\frac{(\$53/1.06)}{1.06} = \frac{\$53}{1.06^2} = \$47.17$$

|  | Y0 | Y1 | Y2 |
|---|---|---|---|
| Investment | −100 | | |
| Cash Inflow | | 53 | 53 |
| Present Value | −100 | 50.00 | 47.17 |

The second year's cash flow is worth just $47.17 in present terms. In other words, once we factor in the risk of lending to Connie, we don't expect to recover the full amount of our initial investment: We recover only $97.17. Connie's two-year payment plan does not adequately compensate us for the risk we're taking.

The approach we just took to valuing promises of future cash flows is called **discounted cash flow (DCF) analysis**. Given a minimum return *r* and a time period *n,* the general formula for the present value of a future cash flow is:

$$Present\ Value = \frac{Future\ Value}{(1 + r)^{n}}$$

If formulas like this one aren't your cup of tea, just read it as:

*At the same level of risk, later cash flows are less valuable than earlier ones. And in the same time period, cash flows in which we are less confident are less valuable than ones in which we have greater confidence.*

## INTRINSIC VALUE

DCF analysis can be used to value any investment, including a company's individual investments in productive assets such as food trucks, intellectual property, and customer relationships. But we're going straight for the jugular: company valuation. So let's put on our investor hats and look at a company through the eyes of its owner. The owner looks at a company as a series of promises of cash flows. They won't be 100 percent confident in all the cash flows, and the farther in the future these flows are promised, the less confident the owner will be. And because of the **time value of money**, future cash flows are worth even less. The true minimum return has to compensate for both the risk-free return lost and the risk.

By projecting the future cash flows and discounting them with the minimum return, the owner can calculate a hypothetical price tag for the business: the sum of the present values of the future cash flows. At that price, the owner is indifferent between keeping a claim on the future cash flows or trading it for the sum of their discounted values now. That price is called the **intrinsic value**.

Let's bring back our food truck and walk through how we might value it as a business. First, we explicitly model the cash flows for the next few years. How many? That depends on the kind of visibility the company has, but let's say three years. Here are some of the basic elements in that projection:

**Sales:** Sales are the foundation. What are sales now? How much is the market growing? Will the company grow faster or slower than the market? What kind of pricing power does the company have? Will growth only be achieved by reducing prices, or can they be maintained or even raised?

**Expenses:** Calculating expenses comes next. What kinds of cost structures are in place? Will expenses rise at the same rate as sales, or will they increase slower because of high fixed costs? Will growth have to be fueled with initial high expenses in sales and marketing? Or by R&D?

**Working capital:** What kinds of contractual relationships does the company have with customers and suppliers? What level of inventory will it need to react to shifting customer demand? In short, will working capital consume more cash or provide it?

**Investment:** Will growth require further cash outlays to increase capacity?

With these factors in mind, we can calculate **free cash flows** for each of the first three years. Free cash flow is the incoming cash flow that doesn't get swallowed up by working capital and that isn't earmarked for investments in new long-term productive assets.* The company is free to distribute the

---

* Investments in other companies (through mergers and acquisitions) are generally not included in free cash flow.

cash to investors—both creditors and owners. Suppose our business plan entails free cash flows of $1,000 after the first year, $5,000 after the second year, and $10,000 after the third year and the following years.

|  | Y1 | Y2 | Y3 | Y4 |
|---|---|---|---|---|
| **Net Cash Flow** | 1,000 | 5,000 | 10,000 | 10,000 |

Two burning questions present themselves:

1. Exactly what number should we use to discount these future cash flows to today's values?
2. How far into the future can we reasonably project our food truck's cash flows?

## THE COST OF CAPITAL

How do you find the minimum rate of return that compensates investors for the risk-free interest forgone and for the risk taken? We're going to explore the answer at three depths. The first level is simple: Someone with specialized knowledge in corporate finance—someone like a CFO—will tell you what the minimum return is. The figure this expert will cite is called the **cost of capital**, so called because it represents the minimum compensation investors expect in return for having put their capital at the company's disposal.

Depending on a host of factors—some in a company's control and some definitely far out of it—the cost of capital will usually be anywhere from the mid-single digits (4 or 5 percent) to upward of 20 percent. Multinational companies operate in different countries through subsidiaries, and different countries may have very different risk profiles. One of the multinationals with which we work had, in early 2022, a cost of capital of 7.6 percent for its Canadian subsidiary and 23 percent for its Nigerian one.

Ask the CFO. What a copout! But in a moment, you'll thank us for providing it. Let's go one level deeper and see what considerations ought to guide a CFO's (and an investor's) risk evaluation, theoretically. Investors of all stripes invest to earn cash flow, and they face the risk that the cash flows promised will not materialize. Investors can invest in two structures: as lenders and as shareholders. Lenders set out a specific timetable of cash payments in a contract, which can be enforced by the power of the state. Equity investors—shareholders—simply hope that once the company makes good on its other promises, there will be cash left over to distribute to them, ideally without jeopardizing the company's ability to distribute still more cash in the future. If there's no surplus cash to distribute, tough…stuff.

Because the owner's claims have lower priority than the lender's, the owner is exposed to all the same risks and then some. Whatever the debt holder's minimum return is, the owner's minimum return ought to be strictly higher. So let's focus on how either sort of investor might look at risks to future cash flows.* It's really not all that different from how a bank considers financing your mortgage. Your mortgage holder quantifies the probability of a default on the basis of statistical facts about you and historical data for borrowers with a similar profile. That's not substantively different from what happens when an investor finances a company. The factors considered will be different, though, and they may include these:

- How predictable are sales in the company's markets? How sensitive are sales to underlying economic conditions?
- As sales volumes vary, does the company have the ability to vary expenses as well (i.e., what is its cost structure)?
- What is the company's track record for setting performance targets and then reliably hitting them?

---

* Readers with financial experience just spilled their coffee. They know that you have to treat the two sources of capital—debt and equity—differently, each with its own cost of capital, and combine them into what is known as the *weighted average cost of capital* (*WACC*) in proportion to the sources' importance in the company's financing model. Again, if you go into mergers and acquisitions, you will need to get WACC'd. For most managers, however, it suffices for them to understand that investors demand a cost of capital in proportion to the risk they experience.

- What is the company's track record for servicing debt? What other debt is outstanding? When is it due?
- Does the company expect to have the cash available to keep nearer-term promises?
- What's the company's business model, and in what structure does it generate cash flow from customers?
- Who are those customers, and how creditworthy are they?
- How many customers are there, and how significant are individual customers to the company's sales? Can one customer's departure destroy the company?
- Who manages the company, and what is their track record?
- If the company defaults, how easy will it be to convert assets into cash?

Questions like these help investors form a view of how likely it is that the promises of future cash flows won't be kept. They can compare the company with others having similar features and determine the frequency with which promises were broken by those similar companies in the past. For example, did these companies miss sales and profit forecasts, reduce or eliminate expected dividend payments, or default on loans and declare bankruptcy? Ultimately, all those considerations have to boil down to a single number: the cost of capital that compensates for both the risk-free interest forgone and the risks taken.

Are you feeling daunted by the sheer amount of data you'd have to sift, never mind the complexity of finding the cost of capital? No worries. Smart and efficient people know where to find shortcuts. Why should you do all the legwork yourself when you can crib from someone else's homework?

But whose work should you borrow from? The answer is, other investors'. Look at securities of publicly traded companies that are similar—in size, industry, markets served, and so forth—and see what returns investors have earned historically. Use those returns as a starting point for your own estimation of the cost of capital. Then make some adjustments upward or downward if you have good reason to believe your company might differ in risk from the benchmarks you're using. That's how the pros do it!

Now isn't it comforting to know that it will usually be someone else's job to figure out what the cost of capital is?*

## CONTINUING VALUE

We can easily calculate the present value of three future cash flows. But how many future cash flows should we project?

| | Y1 | Y2 | Y2 |
|---|---|---|---|
| **Net Cash Flow** | 1,000 | 5,000 | 10,000 |
| **Present Value at 10% Cost of Capital** | 909 | 4,132 | 7,513 |

We could set a point in time—say, three years—at which we shut down the business and sell its assets. Whatever the assets sell for at that point and whatever cash is left in the till would be a final cash flow to add to the model. That might be our best alternative if our food truck is unsuccessful after three years. But if grilled cheese is going strong, might there not be some go-getter looking for an opportunity to take over an established venture? Could we sell the business *as a business* instead of as a collection of assets? If so, at what price? How would we, the sellers, and the

---

* "But wait," you're thinking. "If investors crib from other investors' homework, and those investors crib from other investors' homework, who also just cribbed from somewhere else, isn't this all just one big hall of mirrors?" Well...you're not exactly wrong! The behavior of the stock market is not in this book's scope. Suffice to say that one effect of all this cribbing is that, indeed, individual stocks and the entire market may get systematically overvalued in the phenomenon we call a bubble. The bubble bursts when some of the more astute—and often ornery—cribbers realize that things have gotten out of hand and do some of their own homework. When the others start cribbing from these pioneering skeptics, stock values may even sink unreasonably low. Fun fact: This footnote doubles as a plot summary of *The Big Short*, the book (and its film adaptation) about the great financial crisis.

buyer value the business from the perspective of the end of Year 3? Well, we would start by projecting the cash flows for Years 4, 5, 6, 7, or longer; both we and the buyer would have to ask ourselves how far to project into the future. We'd be stuck with the same longevity question.

> In principle, companies can generate streams of cash flows indefinitely by inventing new products and addressing new markets.

Time to strike the *Thinker* pose and meditate on mortality. Is there a *necessary* reason why a company should expire? Unlike us mortals, a company could keep generating streams of future cash flows indefinitely, inventing new offerings as old ones become obsolete and addressing growing markets as old ones shrink.

Earlier in the book, we examined one company that has continuously reinvented itself. Nokia was launched as a humble Finnish wood pulp mill in 1865. Since then, it has steadily expanded into new areas of business while shuttering or selling off old ones, including the mobile phone business that made it a global brand. Today Nokia focuses on telecommunications infrastructure. Its pulp-milling founders would have a hard time understanding what telecoms infrastructure is, let alone the strange evolution their company would follow to become a major player in it.* Few companies manage such radical shifts. Discounting an infinite series of cash flows suggests that infinite survival is both possible and very unlikely.

That still leaves us with an infinite number of discounted cash flows to add up if we want to capture a company's value with a single number. If you were ever exposed to calculus, you know that even an infinite set of numbers can add up to a finite amount. If you're unfamiliar with that concept, you'll have to take our word for it! The present value of a **perpetuity**—a steady and perpetual cash flow *CF*—discounted by the cost of capital *r*—is simply:

---

* Along the way, Nokia was known as a maker of rubber boots.

$$\textit{Perpetuity Value} = \frac{CF}{r}$$

For example, we should be willing to invest, at most, $100,000 to acquire a perpetual $10,000 annual cash flow if we believe that its risk requires a 10 percent minimum return:

$$\textit{Perpetuity Value} = \frac{\$10,000}{10\%} = \frac{\$10,000}{0.1} = \$100,000$$

If we believe that the food truck will reach a steady state in Year 3 and deliver a regular $10,000 payout thereafter, with a cost of capital of 10 percent, then from the perspective of the end of Year 3, we and a potential buyer could reach an agreement at a value of $100,000. That hypothetical future value is called the **continuing value.**[*]

| | Y1 | Y2 | Y3 | Continuing Value at 10% Cost of Capital |
|---|---|---|---|---|
| Net Cash Flow | 1,000 | 5,000 | 10,000 | 100,000 |

The continuing value builds on educated guesses about the long-term size of the market, the degree of competition and pricing pressure, the supplier landscape, ongoing sales and marketing and R&D needs, reinvestments in assets just to make up for depreciation, financing costs, and

---

[*] You may also encounter the less uplifting expression *terminal value*. The continuing (or terminal) value formula can incorporate a growth rate. If you expect your cash flow *CF* to continue to grow at a rate of *g*, with a minimum return of *r*, then

$$\text{Perpetuity Value} = \frac{CF}{(r - g)}$$

Notice how the perpetuity value gets bigger the higher the growth rate is, because a higher *g* makes the denominator smaller. What happens, however, if the growth rate is greater than the minimum return? That would make the whole number negative and the calculation meaningless! The growth rate has to be lower than the minimum return. And that's not just a rule to make the numbers work out. Making the minimum return higher than the growth rate is like saying "A high long-term growth rate is implausible." Which it is. A company that keeps growing indefinitely would eventually swallow the world.

so forth. Educated guesses, yes, but still *guesses*. The inherent uncertainty in long-run estimations is part of why we need to discount.

## BRINGING IT ALL TOGETHER

We already discounted our three years' worth of explicit free cash flows, and now we can do the same to the continuing value. Remember, the continuing value is a catchall for all future flows beyond Y3, representing what we hope to get if we sold the company as a going concern at the end of Y3. The cash flow from that hypothetical sale also needs to be discounted to its present value.

|  | Y1 | Y2 | Y3 | Continuing Value at 10% Cost of Capital |
|---|---|---|---|---|
| **Net Cash Flow** | 1,000 | 5,000 | 10,000 | 100,000 |
| **Present Value** | 909 | 4,132 | 7,513 | 68,301 |

*Total Present Value* = $909 + $4,132 + $7,513 + $68,301 = $80,855

Add all the present values up, and we get a grand total of $80,855, one solitary number that expresses the value of our food truck business in consideration of its profitability, growth, and riskiness. Whew!

If this were a class, someone would now awkwardly ask, "Uh, is this going to be on the test?" This isn't a class, and the only test will be your application of these ideas to the real world. If your choices take you toward a career in which you determine the value of companies, hats off and good luck!

For everyone else: The point is not to produce such an analysis. Instead, you'll want to understand how you—through the tasks you perform, the decisions you make, and the information you share—are connected to the inputs that affect the intrinsic value of your company.

Whatever your role, responsibility, or area of expertise, you will have an impact on your organization's profitability and growth rate and, hence, on its projected future cash flows. Meanwhile the quality of the information you share and the reliability with which you deliver results will affect how consistently the company achieves its financial results. In turn, that consistency will affect investor confidence and perceived risk. Those inputs ultimately roll up into a single number, the intrinsic value of the company that you are a part of.

# CHAPTER 9 KEY TAKEAWAYS

The intrinsic value of a company is the sum of its expected future net cash flows, discounted by the cost of capital.

The cost of capital is the minimum return investors demand as compensation for forgoing the risk-free rate they could earn by investing in a safe asset and for the risk that the cash flows will not materialize as expected.

Estimating the cost of capital is an art and a science best left to true experts. The many considerations that flow into it include:

- The typical variability in the sales and profits of the company and its peers
- The extent and nature of the promises the company has made to all its stakeholders
- Its track record in setting and meeting expectations
- The extent and nature of the company's knowable risks
- Other investors' beliefs about the cost of capital, as revealed in the prices at which they are willing to trade shares

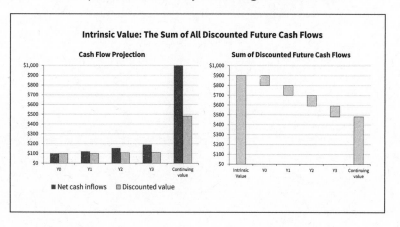

*Intrinsic Value: The Sum of All Discounted Future Cash Flows*

*(continues on next page)*

*(continued from previous page)*

To calculate the intrinsic value, we project future net cash flows and discount each one, with the more distant cash flows discounted more heavily.

For most managers, the mechanical details of the intrinsic value calculation are unimportant. It's far more important to understand how your decisions and activities contribute to profitability, growth, and risk and thus affect future cash flows and the confidence investors have in them.

## CHAPTER 10

# Creating Value

F ew managers are ever concerned with company valuation, but all managers are involved in creating value. To conclude Part I, we want to get a better sense of how we, individually and regardless of function or responsibility, connect to shareholder value.

Although you're unlikely to be involved in a company valuation, you may contribute to appraising the value of an investment project, which involves committing some financial resources immediately to generate benefits over the long term. The tools used to appraise a project are fundamentally similar to appraising a company. We'll look at project valuation briefly to deepen our understanding of value creation.

At the end of this chapter, we'll return to the question we raised at the outset: whether shareholder value tells us something useful about stakeholder value.

## VALUATION EXAMPLE: NETFLIX

As we try to answer "So what?" we'll use Netflix as a helpful example. Its stock price dropped from $348 to $226 in a single day, when the company reported the loss of two hundred thousand subscribers in the first quarter of 2022. How could the value of a company shift so radically in a matter of hours?

Let's look at how Netflix's report might have had an impact on the inputs into a valuation based on the discounted cash flow (DCF) analysis discussed earlier. We'll not do a full DCF analysis for Netflix. Instead, we'll imagine what hopes and anxieties would be going through the investors' minds as they projected a stream of future cash flows originating in subscriptions to an entertainment streaming service, making them willing to part with a share at $348 on one day and at $226 the next.

**Revised forecasts:** When Netflix announced the loss of two hundred thousand subscribers on April 19, 2022, it also warned about the potential future loss of two million more. But what investors were digesting—and factoring into their implicit or explicit valuation calculations—was that the previous forecast (issued on January 10 in the report for the last quarter of 2021) had been for the *growth* of 2.5 million subscribers for the first quarter, not a loss of two hundred thousand. Additionally, the January 10 report had been full of optimistic assessments, assessments that investors would have baked into their expectations and the $348 price. In other words, by April 20, investors were valuing not just the loss of 2.2 million current subscribers but also the loss of millions of previously expected new subscriptions.

**Surprise:** It's not only that the previously projected growth was stripped out of the projections of future cash flows; it's that Netflix executives did not see this coming. The forecasting miss, swinging from plus 2.5 million to minus two hundred thousand, and the radical change in tone eroded confidence in Netflix's ability to forecast demand. Warm and fuzzy feelings evaporated, and feelings matter.

**Reevaluation of the subscription model:** Part of the attractiveness of the subscription model is that it gives high visibility into regular future cash flows. But entertainment streaming subscriptions aren't locked in. You can drop the subscription at any point. Granting customers that degree of freedom probably makes sense for entertainment, a commodity that consumers will always want to keep flexible in their budgets. If streaming contracts forced too much of a commitment, many people wouldn't sign up in the first place. But as long as net new subscriptions were always positive, the evidence suggested to investors that subscriptions were sticky. A single quarter of net cancellations forced investors to reexamine that assumption. With consumers able to easily switch between different providers such as Disney+ and Amazon Prime, streaming subscriptions provide a lot less predictability than does a two-year phone service contract.

**The unpredictability of entertainment:** To attract subscribers and lock them in, Netflix and other streaming services have been producing more and more original content. If you can release a movie or a show that people tweet or talk about, millions of monthly cash flows are your reward. Or maybe not. Netflix had just scored such a hit with *Squid Game* in 2021. The success of this series partly explained why the company's numbers looked so rosy at the end of that year. But creating must-see content is not only expensive; it's also unpredictable. We doubt that anyone at Netflix expected that out of its entire lineup, a murderously violent Korean series would be the thing that attracted a global audience. What streaming providers—and their investors—are learning is that the creative industry is characterized by high-risk, high-reward bets, where one hit might just make up for dozens of misses. The loss of subscribers was not merely bad news. It showed that the previously reported good news from the earlier quarter may have been the sugar high of an inherently less predictable and more cost-intensive business model.

These are just some of the thoughts possibly swirling around a Netflix investor's head after April 2022. They are by no means the only reasons a given investor might have revalued Netflix and decided that $226 was a good price to sell on April 20, when just the day before, they were unwilling to sell at a price of over $300 per share. The Netflix story illustrates how breaking news might force a reassessment of the growth, profitability, and risks in a company's future.

## WHERE DO I FIT IN?

Most managers we work with have a good sense of how they contribute to sales and expenses, directly or indirectly. When it comes to generating cash flows, you can probably track how you affect them, even if your impact may be very, very small in a very large company. If nothing else, your salary is a fixed and known amount and sits right there in one of the P&L statement line items. But do you meaningfully contribute to the cost of capital? Think of the level of precision we used to describe the minimum returns. At best, we went to two decimal points, as in 5.27 percent. Precision beyond that would be absurd, given how much guesstimation is involved. Any individual action you take would have a tiny and *principally unmeasurable* influence that would get swamped by larger fluctuations due to investor sentiment, central bank policy, and whatever breaking news captured everyone's attention that day. So no, nobody comes home at the end of the day and says, "Honey, today was a win. We created a million dollars of value by nudging the cost of capital down by 0.005 percent!"*

---

* In their book *Valuation*, Koller, Goedhart, and Wessels do not treat the minimum return and the cost of capital as an operating lever a company manages, although the CFO does steer it by choosing the mix between debt and equity financing.

Still, we need to understand the trade-offs between the different drivers of value. Let's say you're in sales and you're about to close a deal that by itself will increase your territory's sales by a third. Great news, of course. But what consequences will the deal have on expenses? Will it entail stepping up the fixed costs in a way that raises the risk of higher losses later on? Or will it demand new long-term investments that consume cash? How dependent will your company become on that single contract?

Suppose you're on the production side. You have an idea for an investment that seems like a no-brainer and that will lead to sustained cost savings. But are your estimates of cost savings based on sales volumes of a product whose market is in decline? Could the cash your project would consume be deployed more fruitfully in attracting new customers or creating new products? Or say you're in HR and having trouble attracting the budgets you believe are necessary to build the organization's human capital.* Could you make the case better by illustrating how your ideas involve more than just more spending to build skill sets but also help mitigate key risks, such as the loss of employees who move to competitors?

> Executives know nothing that they haven't learned from the network of information collection and interpretation called *management.*

Think about some of the considerations involved in the cash flow projections and in weighing the risks. Among the key inputs was the company's track record of performance: making loan payments on time, forecasting sales and profits, and reliably hitting those targets. Whose actions constitute the performance? Yours do. And where do the forecasts—like Netflix's optimistic outlook on subscriber growth—come from? From you: from all the different reports flowing upward, downward, and across the organization about everything, from sales to

---

* You won't be surprised to learn that this is a song we hear in our corporate training business all the time.

customer satisfaction, inventory levels, supplier health, and cash sitting in a local account in the Singaporean subsidiary.

Investors rely on information shared by executives. But executives know nothing that they haven't learned from the network of information collection and interpretation called *management*. Investors may seem to sit in the catbird seat of the global economy, but the value they lay claim to is built substantially on the trust they have in the executives. These business leaders may seem to be all-powerful rulers of fiefs, but their power stems from their ability to make promises to investors and reliably keep these promises. Executives can neither keep the promises made nor, equally importantly, know what promises not to make on their own.

Day-to-day value creation boils down to the ability of managers at all levels to marshal the resources they control to grow the company and make it more profitable while channeling the information that executives use to shape shareholder expectations. Executives rely on a team—in fact, an entire organization—that they can trust and that produces both reliable results and reliable information. Trust lies at the heart of value: trusting relationships between people.

And the importance of these trusting relationships will be the focus of Part II.

## EVALUATING PROJECTS

As a manager, you're unlikely to have to perform a whole company valuation, but you may be involved in appraising the value of an investment project. Suppose you've got a great business idea for your area of the organization. You know the idea is great in spite of the upfront cash and people-time it will consume because, over the long haul, your idea will save money; generate new, profitable sales; or accomplish some other benefit for the company. You may feel intuitively that your idea will be worthwhile for the company, but what criteria should you use to determine whether it contributes to value?

Investors put cash at a company's disposal to gain future cash flows. Whenever a company invests, it deprives investors of cash that could otherwise be returned to them. Investors forgo cash only if they earn at least the cost of capital. Every investment project ultimately has to be considered in the same terms as the overall value of the company: It has to deliver positive net cash flows after taking risk into account.

The go/no-go decision for a given investment project involves applying the same valuation approach we learned about in the previous chapter:

- Map out all the project's expected cash flows, positive and negative.*
- Add up each year's inflows and outflows to a net cash flow.
- Discount each annual net cash flow to its present value using the cost of capital.
- Add up the result.

The result is called the **net present value** (**NPV**). An NPV of exactly zero means that the project returned the exact cost of capital. The standard interpretation of the NPV is that only projects with a positive NPV should be implemented; no negative-NPV projects should be greenlit. One way to look at a company is that it is nothing more than the sum of the projects it undertakes: If it undertakes only projects with positive NPV, it will generally compensate its investors adequately for forgone interest and for risk. That doesn't mean not a single one of those projects will fail. Some will, but that is precisely what we've factored in by discounting.

When you put together a cash flow model and pitch your idea to senior leaders, you may be able to impress them by calculating its NPV. Truthfully, though, they are going to be more impressed by the thoroughness

---

* Unlike companies, projects usually have a finite life span. The typical investment project will be something like the purchase of a major piece of equipment. It will have an expected useful life, which determines the number of years of cash flows to project, discount, and include in the analysis. Also, projects generally have an initial cash outlay—the investment—that figures into the valuation. Because it typically happens right at the beginning of the project, the initial outlay is not discounted.

with which you prepared your cash flow model and address their questions. They'll want to know things like

- How does your project align with company strategy?*
- What assumptions are built into it? How robust are they? What data informed your projections, and from what parts of the organization did you source them?
- Did you consider the impacts not only on sales and expenses but also on working capital?
- Did you consider a worst-case scenario? A best-case scenario?

If you've prepared answers to those questions, applying the company cost of capital to your cash flow model is practically an afterthought and takes a couple of keystrokes in a spreadsheet. Ultimately, your pitch will depend on the quality of your model, not on jargon-dropping terms like *DCF*, *NPV*, and *cost of capital*.

## SHAREHOLDER VALUE AND STAKEHOLDER VALUE

Years of skill-and-drill math education encourage us to accept the output of a calculation as some kind of cosmically correct fact. In the previous chapter, we showed how the value of a company can be boiled down to a single number, defined by a manageably complex formula. As we've pointed out, that number is not an objective fact about the universe. Not only are the inputs to the calculation a mix of questionably relevant historical data, blind hunches, and work cribbed from known cribbers, but the thing we're calculating is also itself fairly squishy. It's a shareholder's perceived value in their claim on an indefinite but uncertain stream of future cash flows. Ultimately, our valuation formula produces nothing more than a highly imprecise measurement of a highly subjective and fluid concept.

---

* Pro tip: If your pet project doesn't show a positive NPV, just say "it's strategic." Kidding! Mostly.

With an imprecise measuring tool, different people will get different readings at different times. The usefulness of the formula is not so much in the particular readings we get—$348 for a share of Netflix on one day, $226 the next—but in revealing directionally the likely impacts of business decisions and how those impacts might trade off against each other. Understanding the trade-offs of decisions on shareholder value is part of the essence of management.

> The valuation formula produces an imprecise measurement of a subjective and fluid concept.

Few of us get up in the morning just to create shareholder value, though. As we turn to the other timeless domain of managerial expertise—the art of getting people to cooperate with each other—we'd like to put shareholder value into a larger context.

It's not just shareholders who have a stake in a company's success. Customers gain goods and services that would have been out of reach if they had to produce them themselves. Employees find gainful and meaningful employment. Products, services, and employment opportunities can benefit a larger community but may also impose costs on it. And what counts as the community can be—and arguably should be—defined broadly, to include the natural environment.

When we use our valuation tools to get readings on shareholder value, do we also learn something indirectly about stakeholder value, in the same way that we measure temperature indirectly, via the height of a pillar of mercury in a glass tube?

First of all, as we discussed, the required minimum level of shareholder return simply preserves capital. If investors don't earn the minimum level, the world's risks will eventually whittle their stockpiles of capital down to nothing. Then there would be no capital left to fund all the wonderful assets that generate value for us all over the long haul: roads, bridges, power stations, combine harvesters, lithography machines, and, yes, masterpieces of arts and culture.

But especially compelling about the tools of valuation is their orientation toward the future. Creating value is not just about making a quick buck. It can't be. To create value, you need to instill confidence in an indefinitely long stream of future cash flows. You have to keep creating customer value year after year. Practices that don't create value for vendors and employees will lead to higher unpredictability as suppliers fold and employees go on strike or take their talents to competitors. And for there to be an indefinitely long stream of future cash flows, there has to be, you know, a future.

> For there to be an indefinitely long stream of future cash flows, there has to be a future.

It can't be a future characterized by the wildly erratic conditions of war, disease, and environmental degradation. Nor can it be a future in which people become too distrustful of each other to pool resources, knowledge, and skills to make the whole more than the sum of the parts.

Ours is not a perfect world. Managers can—and sometimes do—do things to goose company valuations by raising investors' hopes for the future in unsustainable ways, even in ways that permanently erode confidence in a company's future. Still, the long-term perspective deeply embedded in the valuation notions we've discussed may be a decent way to get a glimpse of stakeholder value. Let's talk about alternatives when we meet at the bar!

# CHAPTER 10 KEY TAKEAWAYS

As managers, we contribute to value creation in many ways simultaneously, and not always positively. Our actions and decisions involve trade-offs between profitability, growth, and risk.

The insights from company valuation and discounted cash flow analysis can be applied to individual company investment projects that require an up-front outlay of cash in the interest of generating net cash flow over a multiyear horizon.

The fact that much of the intrinsic value comes from the indefinitely projected future implies that the needs of all stakeholders have to be met sustainably and indefinitely as well.

# PART II

# THE PEOPLE

## CHAPTER 11

# Joy and Frustration

Adam Smith's *Wealth of Nations* famously opens with the example of a pin factory. Smith observes that a person could complete the pin production process from start to finish but might have a hard time even producing twenty pins on a good day. Ten people working in parallel could at best produce two hundred pins. But when ten craftspeople work in sequence, each person dedicated to a single step in the process, they become highly efficient at that step. Not only can they together produce tens of thousands of pins per day, but they also each need fewer skills. As a result, the laborers are more easily replaceable and are, therefore, cheaper. The cheaper labor drives down the unit cost to produce each pin. With cheaper pins, more people can make more and better clothes, shoes, and so on. The wealth of the nation increases, thanks to the division of labor. Though perhaps not the wealth of the average pin-maker!

It would be hard to overstate how foundational the division of labor is to, well, civilization itself, really. As a process, the subdivision of work into ever more specialized professions has been going on for thousands of years, to the point where few people, if anyone, can meet even basic individual needs in the sweat of their own faces. Not only are we unable to produce our own essentials, but also the very tools we use for our specialized live-lihoods are produced through complex production processes and supply chains that we couldn't re-create from scratch. We couldn't construct the laptops we're using to write this book, code the word-processing apps, or even make the paper you may be reading on, even if our lives depended on it. Which, in a sense, they do. As a species, we've thrown ourselves at each other's mercy. It's exhilarating and terrifying.

> As a species, we've thrown ourselves at each other's mercy. It's exhilarating and terrifying.

The division of labor is so woven into our lives that we easily take for granted that it just works, effortlessly. But try lending a hand during a holiday feast at your in-laws' and then tell us how effortless this coordination is! Look under the hood in a commercial kitchen, a pin factory, or any other area of coordinated human endeavor, and you'll see how much effort it takes to plan, to negotiate, to channel information from one person to another, and to make decisions in the face of uncertainty. To *manage*, in short. Through management, we ensure that the whole is more than the sum of the parts, that the individual pin-making steps add up to pins and not useless metal fragments.

Management is not the only way to coordinate individual activities. In fact, the premise of the way we have decided to arrange many of our economic relations—where prices of goods and services range freely according to supply and demand—is that the so-called market mechanism is often the best way to coordinate economic activity. At some scale, coordinating individual contributions through market competition does seem to be an efficient way to produce and distribute goods and services. But why do we need companies at all, then? Why aren't we all just independent contractors getting together in different configurations and selling our services to one another to make everything, from pins to jet engines?

It's a fascinating question that brings us back to one maker of jet engines: General Electric. In a sense, GE's board wrestled with this question in 2021 and concluded that far too many activities were sheltering under one umbrella—activities that were better done independently. By separating GE into three successors, the board members expressed their conviction that the new companies could better solve their business problems individually, through markets, rather than managing the allocation of capital within a larger firm.

As the GE story illustrates, there seems to be a tipping point where the effort to make the whole greater than the sum of its parts fails and where the parts are greater as separate pieces. Where is that tipping point? An entire branch of economics is dedicated to the *theory of the firm* to figure out when and why it makes sense to coordinate economic activity through management versus markets.* But that's another topic for our hypothetical future meeting at the bar. Clearly, we sometimes leave things to markets and sometimes try to manage resources—human and otherwise—through planning, within firms. And that's what we are concerned with in this part of the book: what it takes to get people to work together productively.

Coordination has many dimensions. Take process design at the pin factory. Defining the pin production steps, setting specifications of standards, arranging the specialists and their workstations in physical space—these are activities that can be planned, tested, evaluated, and improved. Whether planning activities are performed by yet another specialist, the manager, or the team collectively, they are part of the effort that goes into coordination. And there is a body of expertise about setting up and optimizing pin production processes, some of which might transfer to other manufacturing processes. But it's less clear that the

---

* The so-called gig economy—with people choosing to work as independent entrepreneurs rather than employees, for example, in delivery services—is a move to coordinate more human economic activity through markets rather than management.

same expertise helps you define optimal processes in film production, insurance, or software development. What all those settings do have in common, though, is that they involve the coordination of people and therefore what Canadian astrophysicist Hubert Reeves likes to call the "$%§! human factor," if you will pardon our French.*

This part of the book is about that delightful human factor, looking at it from two angles. The next four chapters deal with accomplishing work *through* other people. The remaining chapters deal with making decisions under uncertainty *along with* other people. We'll explore the challenges that people face as they interact with each other as human beings. These challenges are common to any organization, including families. Sadly, formal education, with its emphasis on individual achievement, rarely develops the competencies people need to coordinate with each other, and it often even hampers that development.

The impact of these insights goes far beyond any business. When we look back on our lives in their sunset years, few of us will say, "Gosh, I'm glad I helped create all that shareholder value." We're more likely to see the work we did as the vehicle for the relationships we built than the relationships as the vehicle for the work.

Thanks to the universal applicability of what we're sharing here, our examples can draw on a range of experiences, whether they occur in the family, nonprofit volunteer groups, sports teams, rock bands, housing co-ops, or business itself. We'll also be mining another rich source of examples: popular culture. Over the last two decades, we've seen an explosion of creative meditations on management and the workplace, such as the purely fictional show *The Office*, the nearly documentary approach of *WeCrashed*, the deep cynicism of *Veep*, and the feel-good *Ted Lasso*. It's no fluke that we're producing and consuming these workplace dramas with such passion. We're in the midst of profound social conversations about what it means to work, to manage, to lead, and to follow—conversations

---

* Reeves, who is Québécois, actually uses a French term, which we will also not print but which is abbreviated PFH.

provoked by technological change, demographic shifts, and crises like the Covid-19 pandemic.

Because of those fundamental changes, a commitment to the time and capital required by a traditional two-year MBA is so risky. We hope the following chapters provide you some solid ground amid the shifting sands we're all living with.

## CHAPTER 11 KEY TAKEAWAY

Markets and management are two ways we try to coordinate the work of specialists in the division of labor, allowing us to achieve much more than we could individually.

# CHAPTER 12

# Trust and Expectations

The early twenty-first-century mockumentary TV series *The Office* was enjoyed by millions, many of whom are now in positions of management. Of course, *enjoyment* doesn't describe what you feel watching Steve Carell* demonstrate all the ways a manager can make working life miserable and meaningless. The show aired just as both of us were cutting our teeth as young managers. Yes, *The Office* was hilarious, but it also made us feel more than a little uncomfortable, like looking into a fun-house mirror. The manager character, Michael Scott, is a gross exaggeration. But you could—as an extra-credit activity—binge-watch a season of *The Office* and then read these next chapters as a guide to not being "that boss."

Management is about getting people to coordinate their individual activities in such a way as to make the whole greater than the sum of the parts. What do we mean by *people* management, specifically? We'll define it in terms of what we ourselves found most jarring about the transition from individual contributor to manager. As kids and in our early careers, we did many tasks that were, in an important sense, up to us alone. Playing in a rock band? Of course it's a team effort. The bass player's sloppiness reflects on the band as a whole. But there's not much you can do about it.

---

* Or Ricky Gervais, in the UK version.

Meanwhile, you and only you can play that guitar riff perfectly. You may have neither chosen the song nor written the part, but nailing it is your individual contribution. Great power lies in that responsibility. The jarring thing about becoming a people manager is that you keep the responsibility and lose the power. Your success no longer comes from what you do but depends entirely on what others do.

As naive young individual contributors, we thought managers had all the power. Power to assign tasks. Power to set deadlines. Power to judge quality. In the end, power to decide whether we'd have an income next day. All these types of power were real. What caught us by surprise was the power we *lost* as managers. People management is a relationship of interdependence. It is inherently asymmetric. But the two parties—contributors and managers—wield different types of power over each other.

> You'll be a more effective manager if you come to terms with the power you *don't* wield.

If a direct report chooses to show up poorly or not at all, then sure, we may have the power to terminate this person's employment as a last resort. Firing people does not deliver results, though. The person is gone; the work still needs doing. Who holds more power is not always clear, and it's always irrelevant. You'll be a more effective manager if you come to terms with the power you *don't* wield.

As managers, all of us cede power over a task to the person we manage, but we stay responsible for the results. We can, of course, pitch in and get our hands dirty. We can help close the sale, write a few lines of code, or take over a shift to push a project across the finish line. Most managers do pitch in and have their own individual tasks to do. But as long as pitching in and taking care of our individual tasks is all we are doing, we are not managing. Management involves delegating tasks, hoping they'll be performed on time and at the required quality level. That's an act of trust.

Wiser heads than ours have written many books on delegation and trust. What we want to emphasize is that trust is a mutual affair. Trusting your employees may sometimes seem hard, but it's ultimately a simple choice that you'll just have to make. What you can work on—*must* work on—is building their trust in you. After all, can you truly have faith in someone who distrusts you? As Thomas Hobbes suggested, society is at risk of disintegrating into a war of all against all, because even people who are neither greedy nor aggressive will preemptively strike out against others they distrust. An employee who distrusts you will perform in counterproductive ways—withholding information, withholding effort, or spreading their distrust to others—and this employee may do so even if they are otherwise the kindest, most competent person you ever met.

The wonderful thing about trust is that pretty much anyone can gain it. It doesn't take formal training. It doesn't take charisma or likability. You can love a scoundrel you don't trust, and you might gladly put your life in the hands of someone you actually dislike. Yes, some people may unfairly get a leg up in the trust department: people with more symmetrical faces, or people who look and act like we do. We also place our trust in people who we believe—correctly or incorrectly—to have earned others' trust.

No matter what trust capital we begin a new relationship with, though, we can always build it up from there by consistently keeping the promises we make. On the flip side, we can instantly bankrupt our trust account by breaking a promise. As famed investor Warren Buffett supposedly put it, "it takes twenty years to build a reputation and five minutes to ruin it." That is why we strongly believe that the most important managerial mantra parallels that of the medical profession:

*First, do no harm to trust.*

People management is a true calling and something you can spend a lifetime mastering. We can't do it justice in four chapters, because we could not do it in four books. You might read a couple dozen books about management and psychology and then find that you learned twice as much reading the collected works of Shakespeare. There are dozens of theories and frameworks you can study and endless workshops you can attend. Like many others in our field, we are big fans of Paul Hersey and Kenneth Blanchard's model called situational leadership. This model recognizes that one size definitely does not fit all in people management; managers have to adapt their approach to where the employee is situated on two dimensions: competence (knowledge and skills) and commitment (motivation and confidence).

_____
First, do no
harm to trust.
_____

But situational leadership is just one framework of many. And as insightful as it is, situational leadership often winds up being useful only after you've gotten over the "do no harm" hump.*

Meanwhile, you are constantly practicing your people management skills in every encounter, every day, whether you like it or not. In this part of the book, we will touch on theories of motivation and share tips on practical things like giving feedback. But frameworks and techniques will come to naught if you undermine someone's trust. Philosopher Alasdair MacIntyre wrote, "The manager represents in his *character* the obliteration of the distinction between manipulative and non-manipulative social relations." No matter how well you understand the management frameworks and how skillfully you apply them, if your direct report thinks that you are deploying them for manipulative purposes, you'll lose trust.

## SETTING EXPECTATIONS

Keeping promises lies at the heart of building trust. We trust that you do not *intentionally* make promises to benefit from breaking them. If you

---

* That situational leadership might be a tad more advanced than new managers need is underscored by Ken Blanchard's own attempt to boil the essence of management down to something managers can perform in one minute. Hence his influential book (along with Spencer Johnson) *The One Minute Manager*.

are that kind of person, then this book—or, really, any good book or the Good Book—won't be of much use to you. For the rest of us, the challenge of keeping promises is to avoid breaking them *unintentionally*. That can happen when, by mistake, we make two promises that are mutually contradictory. For instance, we might promise two direct reports a promotion to the same position. Mistakes like that happen, but there's little universal guidance on how to avoid them. You're on your own there (and so are we)! The interesting and challenging situations occur when we had no intention of

> Building and maintaining trust is ultimately about setting the right expectations and meeting them.

making a promise but our counterpart heard one anyway. You say, "Spencer, I'd like to know what kinds of projects you want to work on," and Spencer hears, "Yay, I get to pick my own projects!"

Of course, we rarely use the phrase "I promise to…" because we wisely reserve it for special occasions. But as we think about and plan our futures, we have to base our assumptions on limited data and make them in the face of uncertainty. Much of the limited data comes from stuff people tell us. We invariably construct sand castles out of our own hopes and dreams and others' casual comments. The things we say set the expectations others have for the future, and we in turn base our expectations on what they say.

Building and maintaining trust is ultimately about setting the right expectations and meeting them. Anything we do and say in a relationship—*including the things we do not do and say*—will contribute to our partner's expectations. In any relationship, setting expectations is a mutual affair. As a manager, you set your reports' expectations, and they set yours. Your job is not only to set their expectations well but also to coach your reports on setting your expectations well. And the best way to do that is to model good expectation-setting behavior.

Imagine you are working with a young man named Jim. In a manager-employee relationship, expectations are set in three major areas:

**The relationship:** When you first interact with Jim, you will shape his expectations about how you will collaborate. Notice we didn't write "you *have to* shape." We wrote "you *will* shape." No matter what you do or don't do, your initial behavior will establish a set of expectations. You can readjust them later, but at considerable effort. So it's best to get started on the right foot. Expectations you set about the relationship concern what behavior you expect of Jim, and that's not just for you to decide. Jim has a say in these expectations as well, and he will have to inform you about what's realistic. The best way to get him to be transparent is to set an example. Tell *him* what to expect from *you*: what kinds of support you can (and cannot) provide, how you communicate best, how you give feedback.

**Tasks:** Day to day, most expectation-setting behavior takes place around tasks. You set expectations about a task's deadlines, specifications, and quality level but also about what resources and support you will provide, what inputs will be provided by other people, and, in turn, what tasks and results depend on Jim's performance. It would be great if Jim set accurate expectations about what he can realistically do. But he will do so only insofar as he (a) trusts you and (b) has had good expectation-setting behavior modeled for him (by you!).

**Development:** Jim has a vision of where his career path will take him and how you can help him realize his ambitions. You will have a vision of what capabilities you'll need in the future and what you think Jim is capable of. Your respective visions may diverge. And even if you have the same vision for Jim, your organization may not. Of course, things are easier if everyone's vision aligns. But this is an area where sand castle expectations form the most easily and where conversations can be the most uncomfortable!

No matter what, expectation-setting always goes in both directions. The key difference between your role as a manager and Jim's as a direct report is that you have to be prepared to take the first step, model good expectation-setting behavior, and coach him on setting expectations as needed.

## INTENT AND IMPACT

Communication theory is an endlessly large and fascinating field of study that tries to describe exactly what goes on when we try to convey information to each other. Let's boil communication theory down to one basic insight and two practical recommendations for expectation-setting as a manager. First, in any communication, even if there is an asymmetrical relationship between a *sender* and a *receiver*, both parties must actively participate in the transmission and must share the responsibility for ensuring that the information arrives intact at its destination. When information—like an expectation—is sent from one person to another, we must **close the loop**: The receiver has to repeat back to the sender what they heard so that the sender can confirm that the message arrived correctly.

This basic communication technique is well established when lives depend on it. In aviation, regulations around the world require pilots to *read back* the instructions from the air traffic control tower. Once the pilot repeats the instructions, air traffic controllers respond with the phrase "readback correct" to establish that the communication has been received correctly.

At least some of the time, that same convention can be useful when we communicate with colleagues (and others). Suppose you inform Jim about the deadline for an important project, and he responds by telling you when he intends to take a vacation. Jim's intent is probably to convey that the deadline is unrealistic given his plans, although he did not say this explicitly. As the manager, you close the loop with Jim by repeating back to him what you understood him to say, both explicitly and implicitly.

That way, Jim can verify that the impact he had on you matches his intent. In this way, you and Jim are addressing the common communication problem of **intent versus impact**.

Conversely, when you convey something to Jim, it would be great if he closed the loop, too, and said back to you what impact he felt, including making explicit anything you left implicit. He may not have learned how to practice this communication technique very well yet. Eventually, by observing the behavior you model or by absorbing the coaching you provide, he will close the loop. But before he's as skilled a communicator as you, you may need to do one simple thing to get him to close the loop: Ask him to close it. Ask him what he heard.

As simple as these two communication techniques—closing the loop yourself and asking your report to do so—are, we* fail to use them, surprisingly often. They are simple techniques, but we have to practice them until they become second nature. By using them routinely, we can avoid building sand castles of expectations that cannot be met. Because fairly or unfairly, unmet expectations erode the foundation of trust on which our relationships rest.

## MUDDLING THROUGH IN A GLOBALIZED WORLD

Setting appropriate expectations by closing the communication loop is a simple idea, but doing so is often easier said than done. On a family vacation in the United Kingdom, one of us and the rest of our family were approached by a couple while we were admiring a scenic Iron Age hill fort: "Would you like us to take a photo of you?"

What a kind and considerate offer! You could take it at face value and answer it with a simple "yes, please" or "no, thank you," which is what the structure and the explicit content of the question demand. But of course, there was a different implicit message in their question. It was a graceful way to ask *us* to take a photo of *them*. It's tempting to interpret closing the

---

* And by "we," we mean all of us as humans, managers of all stripes, and, above all, the two of us personally.

loop as being all about making the implicit things explicit, but you probably know from hard experience that doing so is not always appropriate or useful. We could have closed the loop by responding, "Let's just get this straight. You would like us to take a photo of you, and in return, you are proposing to take a photo of us. Sounds fair, so we accept." That's more likely to produce a mumbled apology and retreat than a mutually beneficial and pleasant exchange!

Our communications are always multilayered in meaning. The explicit message of "Would you like a cup of coffee?" is the tip of the iceberg; beneath the surface could lie any, all, or none of "You look tired," "I find you attractive," or "I accept that my social status is lower than yours." Some of us have brains that are wired to fathom all the deeper levels of meaning, and some are less adept at doing so.

Frankly, whether you're natively good at teasing out implicit meaning or not is becoming increasingly irrelevant. You can make sense of layers of meaning within your own cultural framework, but different languages and cultures have different conventions about what ought to be said explicitly and implicitly. The two of us are, respectively, married to partners from other cultures and are perhaps especially sensitive to the challenges of cross-cultural communications. Organizations and businesses have become increasingly global, and we're all likely to interact with people who bring different assumptions about communication to the table. When it comes to setting expectations and making the implicit explicit in management conversations, we try to stick to two simple principles:

1. Set expectations, and bring to the surface your implicit assumptions about measurable, quantifiable things like times and dates.
2. Always attribute to others the motives you wish they would attribute to you.

These two principles work well outside the workplace, too.

# CHAPTER 12 KEY TAKEAWAYS

Trust is the foundation of any relationship, and in an organization, the basic building block of trust is the manager-employee relationship.

Trust is built up over time by repeatedly setting expectations and meeting them.

Although senders and receivers share the responsibility for setting expectations, managers shoulder the primary responsibility for modeling what good expectation-setting looks like and for setting the tone of communication.

Day to day, the most frequent arena of expectation-setting will be around tasks. Setting expectations around a task should include clarity about several issues:

- What the outcome will look like, and how success will be measured
- When the task needs to be accomplished, and what intermediary steps will be reviewed
- What kind of feedback to expect, and when to expect it
- What support the employee will receive and from whom
- What consequences success and failure will have, individually, for the team, and for the company

Absent contrary evidence, attribute to others the motives you wish they would attribute to you.

Above all, do no harm to trust.

## CHAPTER 13

# Adventures in Feedback

Imagine a scenario with us for a moment. Your manager—let's call him Nate—has assigned you an important task: drafting a report of your team's strategy for the coming year. It's your first time. You complete the report hours before your deadline. You've gone over it nineteen times, and it seems great to you. With trepidation, you click Send. Then you go home to a restless night.

Your first message the next morning is Nate's reply, and you audibly sigh when the first line reads "Fantastic work!" You excitedly speed through the rest of the message—something about some "suggestions" and "constructive feedback"—and open the attached document.

Carnage. It's a bloodbath of angry-red tracked changes. Entire paragraphs are crossed out, and new, unfamiliar text is everywhere. You can count on two hands the words that are still peacefully black on white.

Feelings well up too quickly to count, let alone label. None of them are pleasant. As you read through Nate's "suggestions" your first reaction to many is, "Well, that's just your opinion." With others it's, "He's got a point." Your self-awareness catches up with the emotional spigot and informs you that you feel anger, shame, fear, and…something else. You look up across the office space and see Nate speaking to another colleague.

He glances your way, rearranges his face into what might be called a grin, and signals a ridiculously overwrought thumbs-up. Your onboard emotion monitor produces another reading: confusion, seasoned with a touch of betrayal. "Fantastic work," huh?

> What we say and don't say, do and don't do, communicates something. It can't be helped.

Giving feedback is not something you can choose to either do or not do. Like setting expectations, it's impossible not to give feedback as a manager. Feedback and expectation-setting are communications, and communication theorist Paul Watzlawick had this to say about them: "No matter how one may try, one cannot not communicate. Activity or inactivity, words or silence all have message value: they influence others and these others, in turn, cannot not respond to these communications and are thus themselves communicating."

Nate's approach to feedback had some productive elements, but some important things were entirely counterproductive.

## FEEDBACK: THE BEATING HEART OF PEOPLE MANAGEMENT

Feedback is particularly important because it helps resolve a perennial tension in people management: driving results in the present while building capacity to deliver results in the future. As we saw in Part I, creating value is about both present and future results. When working with a team of direct reports, a manager has to coax great performance out of them now while also maintaining or building their capacity to perform next quarter, next year, and indefinitely. Short- and long-term results often trade off against each other. Employees who never stop rushing once more into the breach on "mission-critical" projects will get exhausted. They will leave the company, taking their valuable expertise with them. Or worse, they'll stay on, disengaged, delivering subpar performance and possibly inspiring others to do likewise. Meanwhile, employees whose time is allocated to capacity-building activities like training and team building have less time to push current projects across the finish line.

In our business we help our clients build long-term capacity by delivering training events that take people out of their real jobs for a few days and then return them to the workplace armed with new concepts and skills. Some major career transition points—like going from individual contributor to manager—force you to look at both yourself and the world from new angles. For those caterpillar-to-butterfly transformations, stepping away from day-to-day business is essential. As important as those metamorphoses are, *most learning goes on between those big transitions*, incrementally improving newly learned skills by applying them daily. But we only improve if we get the right kind of feedback.

> In organizations, we don't always receive rapid and intelligible feedback.

Nobody learns how to ride a bike by attending a lecture. Cycling 101 is taught by Professor Hard Asphalt. Most of what we learn, we learn by trying out a behavior, observing how the environment responds, and adapting our behavior until the environment's response becomes less disagreeable.* The world schools us in what is usually a rapid and clear, if sometimes painful, feedback loop. Organizational life, however, does not always provide feedback that is as rapid and intelligible. Best-selling business author Daniel Pink memorably calls corporations "feedback deserts."

With the workload divided into ever-smaller chunks, it's entirely possible that you never discover whether your particular chunk of work fits together with someone else's. You might never find out whether the combination made it through quality assurance, whether salespeople found a buyer for it, and whether it ultimately delighted or disgusted a customer. If learning to ride a bike were like working in a major corporation, you

---

* That's the principle behind the business and management simulations at the core of The 12-Week MBA program.

might be pedaling furiously in a soft, gray fog, with neither the joy of the wind in your face nor the anguish of a skinned knee. Thanks to the division of labor, both our best and worst performances may meet nothing but silence. And since there is no such thing as no communication, that silence speaks volumes: "Your contribution is worse than bad; it's meaningless. Yours is a bullshit job."*

One of the most important roles of people managers is to fill that awful silence with useful feedback. By doing so, we not only prevent employees from losing sight of their work's meaning—though that's an important objective in its own right—but we also give feedback to highlight the work and behaviors that turned out well and to correct those that didn't. When given skillfully, praise not only makes contributors feel good about themselves but also lights up a North Star to guide future work: "This is good. More, please." When given skillfully, corrections allow us to improve our current work and mark out the shoals to avoid on the next project.

## GOOD AND BAD
## (NOT POSITIVE AND NEGATIVE) FEEDBACK

There are productive and counterproductive ways to deliver both praise and corrections. Let's now look at the characteristics of effective feedback. But first a caveat. There are dozens of feedback models out there, each with its own mnemonic acronym, like STAR, CEDAR, or DESC,† to name just three. There's also little scientific research out there to say which feedback models are more effective, nor is the research that does exist conclusive. In fact, feedback might not lend itself readily to laboratory research.

---

* Yes, we said this is a family book. But in this case, we're referencing legit academic work. In his book *Bullshit Jobs*, David Graeber updates Karl Marx's argument that industrial production alienates workers from their labor. In the twenty-first century, Graeber argues, a huge proportion of jobs are, in fact, meaningless and create no value for anyone. We'd complement that view with the observation that because of the division of labor, many of us fail to receive the feedback that reveals our job's meaning.
† STAR stands for situation/task, action, and result. CEDAR stands for context, examples, diagnosis, actions, and review. DESC stands for description, effect, solution, and conclusion.

In the previous chapter, we cited Alasdair MacIntyre's warning about obliterating the distinction between manipulation and nonmanipulation. Consider the feedback sandwich, the sometimes-useful recommendation to shove corrective feedback between two thick layers of praise. Yes, the praise may help the criticism go down. At first. But if your direct reports recognize the pattern—which isn't terribly hard—they may learn to dismiss or discount the praise. Not only will they learn that praise is just a herald of bad news, but they'll also see the feedback sandwich for what it is: a technique. "People don't like being techniqued" is how one of our collaborators put it.

> "People don't like being techniqued."

Ham-fistedly applying feedback techniques with catchy names may backfire and undermine the foundation of trust.

Most of the models agree that the feedback has to be specific. Or put the other way around, it should not be vague. There are probably many reasons that "Your room is a mess!" does not translate into corrective action from your teenager. But surely one of them is that this general declaration is not very instructive: What specific things are wrong with the room?

Corrective feedback needs to be specific, but so does praise, and that is where many managers fall down. Manager Nate's feedback sandwich we recounted at the beginning was a laundry list of highly specific criticisms between a superlative but vague "Fantastic work!" and an equally vague thumbs-up. What exactly made the work fantastic? What impact will your strategy report have? How will it make a collaborator's work easier or delight a customer? Hearing "Fantastic work!" may give you a sugar high, but it's hardly a road map for the future. Meanwhile, if the only detailed feedback you get is corrective, it will undermine any well-meant generic praise, earned or unearned.* Undermined praise not only ruins

---

* In *Pragmatics of Communication*, Watzlawick cites an example from his couples therapy practice. In the example, one partner is eternally confused and demoralized by the other's incessant compliments, no matter how poorly the meals are cooked.

the intended positive impact on engagement but also undermines the trust in the relationship between manager and employee.

Another common theme among all the different feedback models is *timeliness*. Many organizations require regular performance reviews, often on an annual basis. Whatever merits those reviews may have, saving up your feedback for the next performance review is a bad idea. Feedback is a dish best served hot, whether you are giving feedback on a task performed or on workplace behavior.

**Feedback is a dish best served hot.**

In addition to timing, the setting in which you give the feedback is important. You might choose to praise someone publicly—although public praise does not float everyone's boat—but detailed praise and corrective feedback should be delivered in private.

And speaking of how and where feedback is given, when feedback goes awry, the problem is often due to misaligned expectations, a topic examined in the previous chapter. Independent of the content of the feedback, you and your direct report can jointly define rules around exchanging feedback both for a particular task and more broadly for your working relationship.

For example, when you give someone a stretch assignment—a task just beyond the person's current responsibilities—you can discuss the parameters for the feedback you'll give. That discussion can start quite simply with a question: "What kind of feedback do you think you'll need, and when do you expect to need it?" The answer can help shape the project plan, for instance, with checkpoints at intermediate stages, a set deadline for delivering feedback, and time carved out to address it. In that discussion, you can also set expectations for what kind of feedback you'll give: "Because it's a stretch assignment, I expect that I will be giving you a lot of corrective feedback. That's all part of your development plan."

Beyond individual tasks, you and your report can set general feedback rules, for instance, how frequently you deliver it. Inexperienced employees may both need and want frequent feedback; experienced employees working on routine tasks may neither need nor appreciate it more than once a month.

The all-important issue of expectations sheds some light on one of the misunderstood dimensions of feedback. People tend to think in terms of *positive* and *negative feedback*, terms that are dangerously misleading. That's why both of us have studiously avoided those terms, opting for the terms *praise* and *corrective feedback** instead. Whether it's the feedback sandwich just discussed or Mary Poppins's spoonful of sugar that helps the medicine go down, we all have intuitions about the need for an appropriate balance between kudos and gripes. When psychologist John Gottman's groundbreaking research on durable marriages entered popular consciousness, it seemed to validate something most people had known instinctively all along. We need more kudos than gripes. According to Gottman, the "magic ratio" of positive-to-negative interactions is five to one. Cue the army of management consultants recommending a ratio of five items of praise for each item of criticism!

Leaving aside the fact that a marriage is a very different relationship from an employment contract, much of Gottman's wonderful research hinges on what he means by positive and negative interactions, a highly nuanced and context-dependent notion. Consider these two examples of feedback:

1. "I didn't think you were capable of baking such a tasty cake."
2. "This cake isn't quite up to your usual sky-high standards."

Which one is positive? Which one is negative? Which one would you prefer to hear? Whether the feedback recipient rates the *interaction* as positive or negative has to do with a complex host of factors beyond the *content*. Those factors include the perceived intent, the overall dynamics

---

* The previously mentioned management guru Ken Blanchard uses the terms *praise* and *redirection* in his updated classic, *The New One Minute Manager*. Although we like Blanchard's term *redirection*, we thought the word required too much additional explanation and have opted for *corrective feedback* in this discussion.

and history of the relationship, and specific expectations set around the feedback. Again, independent of the sender's intent, the impact of praise could be positive or negative, and so can the impact of corrective feedback.

In terms of maintaining relationships—including those with employees—Gottman's magic five-to-one ratio is as good a general rule as any. Remember, corrective feedback doesn't have to be a negative interaction. With aligned expectations and a foundation of trust, even the delivery of the most critical feedback can be one of your positive interactions.

## FEEDBACK ON BEHAVIOR (SIGH)

So far, we've only addressed feedback on task performance. Delivering corrective feedback on tasks always entails some risk, especially when expectations are misaligned. Still, most professionals we've had the privilege of working with expect that, yes, it's the manager's role to provide corrective feedback. And while this kind of criticism isn't always pleasant to hear, it is valuable and better than not knowing where you stand. Tell me I could have saved half a day by using pivot tables in my spreadsheet? "Wish you had told me before, but that's great to know for next time."

> Managers aren't therapists. They neither can be nor ought to be.

Far more difficult is delivering feedback on workplace behavior. Want me to clean up after myself in the break room? "Sorry, not in my job description. And are you calling me a slob? How about telling Jane not to chew with her mouth open!" We expect and want corrective feedback on our work. We want to improve! But behavioral feedback often comes as a surprise and involves changes to long-formed habits that may even be part of our self-image.

You will encounter disruptive behavior as a manager. Full stop. You might get lucky, and it will be no more than a person who consistently leaves the break room a mess. But it might be bullying or sexual harassment. You may be able to get good results out of a skilled but disruptive team member in the short term, but failing to address disruptive behavior will degrade your team's capacity to perform in the longer term. We wish we had a simple recipe that would fix every situation. We don't. There are limits to what kinds of behavior change you can hope for. And there are limits—important ones—to what kinds of behavior-changing approaches you can ethically attempt. Managers aren't therapists. They neither can be nor ought to be.

The causes of disruptive behavior are many, including things that the person may not want to change or be able to change even if they did want to. When conflict erupts between people, it's not always clear whose behavior ought to change. Even when disruptions seem to emanate from one person alone, the easier, more productive, and fairer approach may be to give others feedback on how to work with that person. We work with a global insurance company that recently recognized the need to accommodate itself to neurodivergent employees. The company realized it was better to harness their many talents rather than bludgeoning them with feedback about how different they are from the company's idea of neurotypical.

All that said, your best approach to the wild and woolly world of people management uses two simple tools. The first is the principle we already cited in the previous chapter:

*Absent contrary evidence, attribute to others the motives you wish they would attribute to you.*

Although we all tend to share intentions like working toward the same goals and respecting each other, the point is not whether the person you're managing truly has these intentions. But applying this principle sets you up with a mindset that has the best hope for eliciting an open mind in your counterpart. No one likes hearing corrective behavioral feedback; we all react defensively to it. We'll open our defenses only to someone willing to hear our side of the story, someone whom we can trust to assume that our heart was in the right place, even if our actions went awry.

The second tool, called SBI, is a simple coaching and feedback framework developed by the Center for Creative Leadership. Yup, another acronym, this one standing for situation, behavior, impact, and sometimes complemented by a second *I* for intent. SBI(I) gets really, well, specific about what *specific* feedback means. For this reason, it's especially valuable in the minefield of behavioral feedback, although it works well when giving feedback on tasks, too.

Here's what SBI(I) looks like in the Case of the Break Room Slob:

**Situation:** First, you describe the situation in which the behavior occurred. Avoid vague descriptions like "You always…" or "You never…" or "I've seen you do…" Details of time, place, and circumstances are essential: "When you used the break room yesterday afternoon…"

**Behavior:** Next, you describe the behavior with great specificity, avoiding judgmental language: "…I noticed that you left your ~~disgusting smelly dirty half-eaten~~ sandwich and a coffee mug on the floor of the break room ~~like a pig~~."

**Impact:** Here's where things become even more delicate. You want to make sure you convey what impact the behavior had. In most cases, it's best to frame the impact in terms of the effect the actions had on you rather than on others. The behavior may have affected others, but bringing them into the discussion can sow seeds of conflict and usually backfires. At the same time, you have to be as specific with the impact as you were in describing the behavior. For example, "I would not have enjoyed using the break room in that condition, and I would have felt like my time wasn't

168

being respected if I had cleaned it up after someone else. I can imagine others might have felt the same way."

**Intent:** Asking the person about their intentions signals that, deep down, you know that this person is a full-fledged member of the community who simply made a mistake and is not someone who willfully inflicts unpleasantness on coworkers. Admittedly, in the break room example, asking the person about their intentions with the sandwich is a bit of a stretch. You can, however, signal that you don't believe the intent was bad: "I know you didn't mean to disrespect anyone" or "Were you in such a hurry?"

The SBI(I) approach is a relatively safe way to provide behavioral feedback and will likely lead to positive change if a person is willing and able to change. More often than not, people are simply unaware of the impact their behavior is having on others. It's the embarrassment—a truly unpleasant feeling—that leads to a defensive reaction. SBI, a graceful and generous way of giving feedback, can ease the discomfort. It's also a perfectly good way to structure praise and corrective feedback in the context of tasks.

## CLOSING THE LOOP (IN THIS CHAPTER)

Although the name has been cleverly disguised, you may have guessed that the Nate example is based on a true story. Young Nate had gotten some feedback of his own from his manager, let's call him Bill, about low morale on Nate's team. "They only ever hear critical feedback and feel like they are doing terrible jobs," Bill told him. "You need to praise them more."

Naturally, Nate took Bill's feedback with characteristic grace: "What the heck? I say nice stuff all the time!" The feedback seemed unfair to Nate. He had, in fact, been doling out praise. Clearly, though, whatever his intent, his praise was not having the desired impact on the team.

Nate chewed on it for some time and came to some important realizations. His praise was of the vague "Great job!" sort, paired with excruciatingly specific corrective feedback. Nate learned that his praise had to be just as specific, including comments not just on what worked well but also on why it worked well and how to repeat the same high performance in the future.

But perhaps most importantly, Nate learned something about himself and about setting expectations. After a few more stumbles with feedback, he realized that he simply wasn't very good at delivering praise, even when it was both specific and merited. The harder he tried, the less his feedback seemed to land well. He realized that the effort he expended to comment on praiseworthy work was too obvious, making the compliments seem inauthentic and undermining the feedback's credibility. When life gives you lemons, you make lemonade. From then on, when Nate hired a new employee, he would set expectations about feedback: "I am the world champion when it comes to giving corrective feedback. I'm lousy at delivering praise. Because I have to make an effort to praise, it may come across as insincere. It's a personal failing that I hope you will help me overcome."

It was a simple step, though difficult to take, and it made all the difference, establishing many trusting, productive, and joyful working relationships and friendships.

# CHAPTER 13 KEY TAKEAWAYS

People managers strive for twin goals that lie in tension with each other:

- Delivering results in the present
- Building capacity to deliver results in the future

Feedback uses present performance to improve future performance. It should be specific and timely, and it should be delivered in an appropriate (private) environment and an appropriate context.

Both praise and constructive feedback can strengthen the manager-employee relationship and can lead to deeper trust.

A framework for feedback is the Center for Creative Leadership's SBI(I) model:

- Describe the specific *situation* in which the behavior occurred.
- Describe the *behavior* nonjudgmentally.
- Describe the *impact* the behavior had on you or on the organization.
- Ask the person about their *intent* with the behavior.

## CHAPTER 14

# Engagement and Motivation

Every year, the Gallup organization publishes a report titled *State of the Global Workplace*, which summarizes the results of a survey on employee job satisfaction. And every year, the report warns that only around 20 percent are "engaged" at work. Roughly 60 percent are "not engaged," and what's worse, around 20 percent are "actively disengaged."

What's behind those terms? Employees who are not engaged are putting in the time and meeting the expectations set for them, neither more nor less. Engaged employees bring something extra to the table: enthusiasm, in Gallup's words, an "ownership" mindset, a "drive [for] performance and innovation [to] move the organization forward." Meanwhile, the actively disengaged are those whose resentment "threatens to undermine what their engaged coworkers accomplish."

Let's look at two perspectives on Gallup's numbers, two stories of workplace engagement and the people manager's contribution to it. Why two stories? Neither story is wholly correct or wholly wrong, and as is so often the case, we need to look at something from more than one angle to understand it.

## STORY NUMBER ONE: CRISIS AND OPPORTUNITY

Gallup has characterized the results of its surveys as a crisis of **engagement**. *Crisis* is a scary word, and Gallup's annual news is alarming for two reasons. On the one hand, Gallup's own research shows that companies with a higher proportion of engaged employees tend to perform better on many metrics, not just those directly linked to shareholder value creation like profitability and growth. These companies also tend to have lower turnover, fewer industrial accidents, and higher customer loyalty, for example. With low engagement scores overall, the world's organizations are not nearly as productive as they could be. What's more, they are more dangerous psychologically and physically. On the other hand, the whole basis of the survey is how employees *feel* about their jobs. How we feel about something—especially something that takes up a large part of our waking lives—is intrinsically important to us individually. According to the surveys, we're in dual crises of organizational productivity and individual happiness.

> For as long as we've been recognizably human, we've built great and complex things for no other reason than the sheer joy of working together on something awesome.

Crises, however, are also opportunities. The glass-half-full perspective on Gallup's report is to look at all those workers who are not engaged—and even those who are actively disengaged—and see a world of human potential waiting to be unlocked. What fantastic things might we achieve if only we moved even a few of the unenthusiastic middle into the "engaged" column? And the actively disengaged—shouldn't we try to rescue them from a life of bitterness and resentment?

Gallup has detailed recommendations about how to move people into the engaged column, and so do we. We've already discussed the importance of setting expectations and giving feedback in the service

ENGAGEMENT AND MOTIVATION

of development. In this chapter, we'll look deeper into what gets people to do more than phone it in and to exude contagious enthusiasm. Why? We want to create more (shareholder) value—and it's not hard to see how an engaged workforce could contribute to growing the company's sales, increasing its profitability, and building greater confidence in its future. But there's more than that at stake. For as long as our species has been recognizably human, we've built great and complex things, from the prehistoric temple at Göbekli Tepe to the James Webb Space Telescope, often for no other reason than the sheer joy of working together on something awesome.*

It's a joy managers have the opportunity to kindle and protect.

## STORY NUMBER TWO: CRISIS? WHAT CRISIS?

The word *crisis* originates from a Greek word for "decision" and came into use originally as a word for a turning point. In a crisis, change is coming, for better or worse, but the status quo cannot continue. Looked at over time, Gallup's engagement scores have been remarkably stable, with a very slow upward trend among engaged employees and a nearly constant proportion of actively disengaged. Gallup's data is interesting, but does it describe a crisis? Or do the numbers just reflect the nature of work life in the division of labor?

The idea that managerial effort can push people from not engaged to engaged, thereby improving organizations and lives, sounds great to a manager or a management consultant (and we are guilty on both charges). But it's self-flattering. Let's complement our heroic point of view with the down-to-earth perspective of someone with two decades of experience as an individual contributor. Call him Patrick.

*Do I give my all or punch the clock? Am I engaged or not engaged? Listen, life is characterized by cycles. It's not just about good days and*

---

* In the original sense of that overused word!

*bad days. There are life phases when I have a surplus of time and mental energy to throw at my work, but there are also times when my attention is elsewhere: on my kids, on my aging and dying parents, on my partner, on my health. During those times, I can do what my job description tells me to do and I can handle the routine tasks with one hand tied behind my back. That's what makes me an experienced professional. But during those times, you're not going to wring 110 percent of what I'm capable of out of me, not with overtime pay, not with other incentives and perks, and certainly not with an inspirational speech.*

*Meanwhile, if you executives and managers were honest, you'd acknowledge that the organization moves through cycles, too. In different phases of its existence, different functions and teams may move the organization forward with an all-out effort, while others may do nothing more than get in the way by trying to go above and beyond. Over the past three years, I've had five managers, each one coming into my team with a new "mission-critical" initiative that languishes as soon as they get promoted again.\* So how mission-critical was it?*

*And the weird thing is, when the workload is light and I don't have a crisis to deal with on the home front, I can put my energy into some other project, like building a new porch. Guess when the best ideas for my day job pop into my head!*

*As for coworkers who hold us back more than anything, yeah, I've known a few actively disengaged folks. The way I see it, they come in three types: There are those who aren't happy with themselves and can't be made happy anywhere. Then there are those who are just in the wrong job; they do perfectly fine elsewhere once they decide to leave. But the heartbreaking group is the people who kept giving it all, again and again, sacrificing themselves to the company. They burn out when they realize the company can't and won't sacrifice itself in return.*

---

\* Based on a true story.

*I don't know much about these Gallup numbers. For me, when there's an important project that needs 110 percent of my effort, and I don't have conflicting priorities at home, you can count on me. I like a manager who has good judgment about which projects deserve this effort and who knows when I can deliver and when I can't. The manager who compares us to Leonidas and the three hundred Spartans every Friday?\* Sorry, that's just ridiculous. Plus, the Spartans all died, didn't they?*

As managers ourselves, we naturally lean toward the story of crisis and opportunity. In that story, the manager is on a heroic mission of world-historic import. But as managers, we would prefer this narrative, wouldn't we? We find it intrinsically *motivating to us*.

In our own lives, we've worked with a Patrick or two. We see his point. Our individual capacities and inspirations are not pegged at a static level. Life is full of ebbs and flows, and organizations are, too. The remarkable consistency of Gallup's results against the backdrop of all sorts of management fads might just trace and retrace those tidal motions over the slow-moving sand dunes of the human condition. Expecting and demanding total engagement from everyone at all times is unrealistic and unnecessary. Consequently, efforts to force it can be counterproductive.

So where does this leave us as managers? Can we motivate the people whose performance we rely on with our words and actions? Where—if anywhere—can we make a difference as a manager? The answer boils down to two key components in the art and science of motivating employees. First, there is the manager's Hippocratic oath mentioned earlier: Do no harm. Second, understanding the *intrinsic* motivators of individuals can be helpful when we have to decide who to task with extra work, shower with public praise, offer a raise, and pull aside for a heart-to-heart.

---

\* Based on *another* true story.

Jan Jenisch, the previously mentioned CEO of cement manufacturer Holcim, speaks about being aware of what discourages people: "The management gurus talk about motivating people. But actually, first of all, you should not *de*-motivate people." There are a thousand ways to take the wind out of someone's sails, even with the best of intentions. One of the surest ways to thoroughly demotivate people is to violate norms of fairness. If someone perceives that others are being treated better without an explanation, that person's motivation will suffer. Unfortunately, it's not always easy to meet everyone's expectations of what fairness means. That's why managers need to set expectations on how compensation, benefits, perks, and status are awarded.

> One of the surest ways to thoroughly demotivate people is to violate norms of fairness.

## UNDERSTANDING PEOPLE'S INTRINSIC MOTIVATORS

Avoiding demotivation is one thing. But individual life is more glorious, and organizations are more successful, when we work enthusiastically, even passionately, and not just because it pays the bills. Let's look at some of the situations in which a person finds the motivation to go above and beyond. Notice how we placed the onus of motivation on the person, not on their manager. Motivation comes from within; managers cannot create it. But we can try to understand our employees' motivators and then shape the workplace environment, assign tasks, and tailor our words to engage—and, above all, not to sabotage—their intrinsic motivators.

What can intrinsically motivate an employee? Here is a partial list* that can be a good starting point for exploration. Each item on the list includes an example of a person who is motivated by this attribute. Keep in mind that an individual's motivators may shift over time as their life situation changes.

---

* Our friend and collaborator Kate McLagan was instrumental in helping us define this list.

### *Achievement (Angie)*

Angie meticulously keeps task lists and relishes striking through each item on completion. If she completes a task she didn't put on the list, she will retroactively add it and immediately cross it out. On her own, Angie is usually good at breaking down a big, long-term goal into intermediary steps on a list of tasks, but as her manager, you find that she sometimes gets lost when the goal is too big and too abstract. If she's listlessly haunting the corridors or Slack channels, check in to make sure Angie has some next steps she can tick off today.

### *Companionship (Colin and Colleen)*

Humans are social animals, but there is a spectrum of sociability, and Colin is at one end. Giving him opportunities to enjoy companionship may motivate him; depriving him of them will send him into a tailspin. During the Covid-19 lockdowns, while productivity at home soared for many of his colleagues, Colin's productivity cratered so far that under normal circumstances, you would have had to let him go. Others may be at the opposite end of the need for companionship, and companionship is another motivator whose importance can grow and fade. Colin just moved from another city to work at your company. Equally sociable Colleen has deep roots in the area and extended family nearby, and she sings in a choir. Companionship may be one of her most powerful motivators, but she may not appreciate the not-mandatory-but-you-really-should-be-there happy hour.

### *Recognition (Randy and Renata)*

Randy lives for acknowledgments of his contributions, whether for his work or for organizing the holiday party. He likes awards, badges, and being pulled onstage to receive them during company meetings. What works for Randy doesn't work for everyone, though. Renata doesn't crave the limelight and prefers to be recognized in a one-on-one conversation. Like money, recognition is a currency whose value can be debased. While Randy laps up every opportunity for recognition, giving it to him publicly for screwing in a lightbulb devalues the recognition that Renata earned for saving the company $100,000.

### *Status (Sara and Sam)*

Whereas recognition can be doled out to everyone in principle—notwithstanding what we said about debasing its value—status is, by definition, a zero-sum game. It's about one person's rank relative to others. Job titles are one way of marking status, and Sara is always eager to advance through the ranks. Sam cares quite a bit less than Sara does about titles... until Sara gets the promotion to senior associate before Sam does. Then it turns out he cares a lot. We're not all angling to be at the top of the heap, but we don't care to slip down. Because someone else's advance necessarily changes our relative position, promotions are always a fraught event in which motivating one person may demotivate many others.*

### *Security (Steven)*

Some of us feel more anxious, some of us less, about the future. Steven is highly anxious, and that anxiety distracts him from doing his best work. He would never describe himself as motivated by money, but for Steven, money buys peace of mind. He appreciates employment contracts that give him long-term visibility. What he doesn't appreciate is rumors about big changes like mergers and layoffs. If you're working with Steven, avoid idle speculation! Once rumors are in the air, be sure you check in on Steven. You may not be able to guarantee stability—remember what we said about not breaking promises—but simply giving Steven a chance to discuss his anxieties is often helpful. As people's life situation evolves, their need for security may also change. It's far easier to be happy-go-lucky before you have a mortgage and a family to support.

---

* Status games are so compelling that entire theories of performing arts are built around them. Improv theater guru Keith Johnstone places relative status at the heart of any scene; differences in status establish tension, and sudden shifts in status can make for the most riveting performances. It may be polite to pretend we don't care about status. The entertainment world knows otherwise.

## *Mastery (Maria)*

Just honing a skill toward perfection can be deeply satisfying. Sure, Maria gets recognition, status, and a sense of achievement from using and improving her skills. There's more to mastery than those rewards, however; there's a meditative delight in performing your skill and getting better at it, even when nobody's watching. The delight of mastery is not something you can easily give somebody, but managers often take it away inadvertently. With mastery as her motivator, Maria is self-contained as long as she's working at the edge of her current abilities. That's the only way she'll get better. Give her tasks far below her capabilities or, worse, a promotion that takes her out of her beloved domain, and Maria's resignation letter will land on your desk faster than you can say "Niccolò Paganini."

## *Autonomy (Andy)*

What Andy loved about the Covid-19 lockdowns and the move to the home office was the power he gained over his own time. Like Patrick in a previous discussion, Andy is acutely aware of the ebbs and flows of life and business. The old-school 8 a.m. to 5 p.m. office hours had never corresponded to the reality of his work, his night-owl biorhythm, and his unpredictable home life. The pandemic taught many businesses that they could trust people like Andy to do the work on time and up to snuff while giving them flexibility in terms of the when and the how.*

## *Purpose (Bjorn and Nathan)*

In our twenty-odd years of working together, both of us have had opportunities to throw in the towel and try our hands at something other than management training. One thing that has kept us coming back for more is our belief that we are not just building a company—although that's

---

* Giving Andy that autonomy is an act of trust. And trust begets trust. Taking autonomy away again—as many businesses decided to try once the pandemic lockdowns were lifted—sent people like Andy to the exits during the so-called Great Resignation that followed the pandemic.

fun, too! We're doing our part to help managers enable more people to contribute passionately for their own individual benefit and for the world's.

> If your takeaway is that management is all about playing employees' motivators like piano keys, we'll have done you and your team a disservice.

Life should be filled with purpose. But it's a bit much to expect everyone to find theirs in their work. Some people use their work as a means to achieve entirely private purposes, like giving their children more opportunities. And that's OK; these people can be just as productive as those who have found purpose at work. Meanwhile, not every organization offers a purpose that's worth going above and beyond for. Some companies will contort themselves trying to represent their business as deeply meaningful. We don't think trying too hard pays off in the long run.*

This list of motivators is hardly exhaustive. Candidly, as the two of us have worked together, we've discovered that pure ornery opposition has sometimes brought out our best work, if not always our best selves. If you ignore humanity's wilder palette of motivations, you might not be able to make sense of your team members' shifts between different states of engagement. Or your own. The human heart is a complicated thing.

And that's why the issue of motivation is a delicate topic. If your takeaway is that management is about driving your team's performance by playing their motivators like piano keys, we'll have done you and your team a disservice. People don't come with their engagement level and their top three motivators branded on their foreheads.† Will people reveal what moti-

---

* Consider the farce of WeWork, a shared-office-space company that once billed its mission as "elevating the world's consciousness." After being effectively plundered by its founders, the company has yet to turn a profit and has revised its mission to the humbler "Our mission is to empower tomorrow's world at work."
† Although in some of the computer-based simulations we use with our sessions, we do have characters conveniently running around with engagement numbers visible for our player participants to see. It's just one of the many simplifications needed in simulation design.

vates them if you ask them? Only if they are self-aware enough to give you an accurate picture. That's a Texas-sized if. Even then, they'll only be open about motivators if they trust you and the larger management team. And nowhere does the line between manipulation and nonmanipulation get as blurry as when you start looking at employees as instruments to be played.

So what can you do with these perspectives on engagement and motivators? We suggest the following:

- Take the three engagement statuses—engaged, not engaged, actively disengagement—as useful constructs, but think of them as states of mind that a person may cycle through even throughout a single day.

- Recognize that people will sometimes go above and beyond—give "one hundred and thirty-eleven percent," as a friend of ours likes to say—precisely because they sometimes have the leeway to just phone it in.

- Don't assume people move up or down through the states of engagement one step at a time. People are weirdly awesome and awesomely weird, and they may jump from one state of mind to another for reasons that may have nothing—or everything—to do with you. Even when your team member is in a slump for reasons unrelated to anything you've done, you can help the person recognize that it's time to take the foot off the gas pedal before they burn out.

- Remember that a perceived breach of trust can take someone from contagiously chipper straight to actively disengaged. The longer they flounder in that pit, the harder it will be for them to leave it by any other exit than the one that takes them out of the organization entirely.

- Be *present*: Keep in regular and frequent one-on-one contact, even if there is no urgent business priority to collaborate on. Then you'll have a fighting chance to observe shifts from one state to the next.

- When you do observe a shift, use the motivators to come up with a working hypothesis for what caused it; you might discover some patterns and regularities that will help you...
- ...above all, do no harm.

# PRESENCE

The preceding list of recommendations gives short shrift to a deeply important concept: **presence**, our undivided attention to the person we are with in that moment. At one point while writing this book, we wrote that the concept is so simple you can explain it to a three-year-old, but we realized we had that completely backward. Our children have done a far better job teaching us about presence than we ever could, and it's a lesson we've never stopped having to relearn.

We could make all the obvious recommendations about presence: We could recommend carving out time for one-on-ones in your calendar, finding private space for conversations, and silencing phones and closing laptop screens. We could also talk about preparing for a meeting not just in terms of its content, but also by emptying the mind of all other cares, as important and urgent as they may (or may not) be.

But the truth is, being present is not something you can learn from a book, no matter how practical and hands-on its list of Top Ten Presence Tips. It's fundamentally an attitude we have to cultivate through practice *and* reflection. We can remind ourselves—on the many occasions when others aren't as present with us as we'd like them to be—to focus on the mote in our own eyes. We can acknowledge that there are many demands on our attention, most of which are deserving, but that we have to prioritize, sometimes even ruthlessly. And we can recall that our personal lists of life's most precious moments have an odd way of overlapping with our lists of moments when we were truly present with someone.

If we can do all that, then we'll have achieved something more important even than being a good manager. And that's saying a lot.

# THE EMPLOYEE PERSPECTIVE

In 2022, one of the business world's buzzwords du jour was *quiet quitting*. Quiet quitters don't leave their jobs. Instead, they stay put in their positions but without a certain something. What is that something? Drive? Relentless pursuit of excellence? Obsession with customer satisfaction? To us, quiet quitting just sounds exactly like Gallup's "not engaged," a state of mind that half the working population has been in since the turn of the new century, according to the surveys. So is quiet quitting worth all the hand-wringing? Let's turn to our philosopher-employee Patrick for his perspective.

> *The Covid-19 pandemic forced the vast majority of us into a different relationship with our work and our workplaces. Many of us experienced working from home for the first time, for better and worse. We gained autonomy but lost companionship. Some of us relished the moment, and some of us hated it.*
>
> *For a few months, we were starkly reminded that some of us perform "essential" work and that, correspondingly, some of us do not. It turned out that status and recognition, not to mention pay, hadn't always aligned neatly with that distinction. We saw that essential work had a purpose and that many of us gave our all for a very long time. A spell of phoning it in would have been quite welcome in the aftermath. Others had to confront the fact that the survival of the human race did not hinge on their contributions, no matter what their company's onboarding packet said.*
>
> *Some of us worked less or not at all, but the demands at home more than made up for that. Turns out running a day care or a school is harder than office life, and your three-year-old sure as heck doesn't give you recognition, a promotion, or pleasant office banter.*
>
> *Not all of us who delight in the mastery of skills could exercise them, and some people watched in horror as these skills atrophied. And if you had a deep need for security, then the pandemic and its sociopolitical impacts weren't kind to your psyche.*

*The pandemic showed us that our assumptions and expectations about work might be up for grabs. Many of us renegotiated employment contracts in the Great Resignation. But maybe we're also collectively renegotiating what employment means. Where should work occur physically? At what times? And what purpose does work serve in our short, precious time on this earth?*

*If there's anything to it at all, quiet quitting is just another eddy in the universe's great cycles, the waters sweeping back out after a storm tide.*

# CHAPTER 14 KEY TAKEAWAYS

A sometimes-helpful construct is the Gallup organization's categorization of engagement:

- Engaged employees go above and beyond their job descriptions.
- Employees who are not engaged do the minimum required to keep their jobs.
- Actively disengaged employees undermine their organization's goals.

People's intrinsic motivators may keep them engaged or at least not actively disengaged.

To avoid demotivating employees, managers should not assign tasks or create a workplace environment that robs people of their intrinsic motivators.

Managers may be able to use intrinsic motivators to their advantage to drive extraordinary individual performance if they do so with great care and respect.

People's motivation may be influenced by their life situation and other circumstances. Common motivators include achievement, autonomy, companionship, mastery, purpose, recognition, security, and status.

## CHAPTER 15

# Leadership

The manager-employee relationship is asymmetric, with each side wielding different power over the other. That is why the relationship has to be founded on trust. By building that trust, the manager-employee relationship becomes the basic fiber in the network of trust that keeps an organization cohesive.

But organizations that rely only on the bonds of formal authority to coordinate activities may find it difficult to adapt to rapid change. When you're implementing a new process, introducing a new product, or responding to an emerging crisis, you'll have to activate the network of trust while simultaneously rewiring it. As you work across hierarchical and functional boundaries, the toolkit of formal authority may not get you very far. Something else has to come into play, something that we might call *leadership*.

Leadership is an intimidating topic for the two of us. Few concepts in business have generated as great an explosion of words and ideas as the distinction between management and leadership. Heads many times wiser than ours have weighed in, and in spite of their wisdom, neither of us have been fully satisfied with many of the canonical stories about what it means to be a leader.

It doesn't help that many of the most famous illustrations of leadership are speeches like John F. Kennedy's call to put a man on the moon. Sure, even today, JFK's speech can inspire you to drop everything and dedicate your life to space exploration. However, it can also be deflating to use JFK's grand speech as your leadership lodestar: "My oratorical skills can barely get someone to take out the trash. And I wouldn't do myself or the organization any favors by going around promoting audacious goals. I guess I'm not a leader." Do you have to be a brilliant speaker to be an effective leader?

JFK's presidential predecessor, Dwight D. Eisenhower, called leadership "the art of getting someone else to do something that you want done because he wants to do it, not because your position of power can compel him to do it." We like how Ike cut right to the point. An *authority* can make you eat your greens; a *leader* makes you like 'em. But getting someone to want to do something that you want done could just as easily be called *influence* or *persuasion* or, depending on the motives involved, *manipulation*. Is that what leadership boils down to?

Leading and following go together, and they evoke three things: a point of origin, a destination, and a shared journey between them. Are leaders those who select the destination? If so, then leadership ought to be all about wisdom in selecting common goals. But history is chock full of people we would unambiguously call leaders but who led their followers off cliffs.

So, what is leadership, really?

In our early careers, as we quested for leadership's essence, the two of us couldn't help but notice that many books on leadership suffered from a kind of logical fallacy, something that business school professor Phil Rosenzweig dissects in his book *The Halo Effect*. Here's how the halo effect operates: A researcher in organizational behavior assumes that successful organizations must be those with good leadership. This researcher looks at what the people with formal authority in those successful organizations do. Reasoning that those behaviors constitute leadership, the person writes a book about it. The company's success lends its leaders a glowing halo.

Of course, the leadership expert's conclusions reflect the character of the CEOs of whichever companies happen to have a high-flying stock price at that moment. Interestingly, those authors rarely issue a recall for their books when the companies' stock prices fall back to earth. Or lower.

Not all leadership books are short-sighted hagiographies of corporate titans. Some are based on broader research from all types and scales of organizations, taking advantage of thousands of surveys but still starting with case studies of "success." Casting their nets widely, these books haul in a motley catch of so-called leadership behaviors—a catch that includes…every virtue ever recommended to humankind. Are good listening skills important in business? Indubitably. Good listening skills are important in any human relationship. Are they quintessential to anything we might call leadership? Color us skeptical: If everything is leadership, leadership is nothing in particular.

In short, much of what has been written about leadership is simply a projection of our hopes and dreams, dreams about the success all of us aspire to, and hopes about the behavior of those with formal authority over us. We *want* our CEOs and politicians to be virtuous. We *want* their virtue to be the reason they have advanced into their positions. And we *want* to be virtuous ourselves so that we, too, can take the reins and achieve great things.*

Granted, the two of us may be a bit allergic to the term *leadership*. We have deep and complicated ties to Germany, a nation once disastrously enamored of great leaders. Even so, we don't see how defining leadership as "what (currently) successful executives do" or "how we wish our bosses would behave" tells us very much. These definitions fail to tell us what leaders do that mere managers might not. And they don't help us solve the problems we've wrestled with in the organizations we've been a part of.

---

* Do words like *virtue* and *virtuousness* strike you as old-fashioned? Perhaps they left a vacuum when they went out of style, a vacuum that the amorphous definitions of leadership have filled.

So instead of working backward from success stories, let's work forward from a problem. A very real, very ordinary, yet very thorny problem: organizing your kid's school bake sale.

## SOCIAL DILEMMAS

Your own bake sale experience may vary from ours, of course. In our circumstances, there is no formal authority to do the organizing or to reward or penalize individual parents for contributing well, poorly, or not at all. The proceeds of the bake sale will fund extracurricular activities that benefit all the children. But your kid will benefit whether or not you helped organize the bake sale. So why contribute at all? Why not sit back and let the other parents do the work?

Of course, if everyone adopted this attitude, there'd be no bake sale.

Our humble bake sale is an example of a **social dilemma**, a problem of collective action. Social dilemmas permeate life. Many examples are negatively framed because collective action frequently fails. Despite the recognition that overgrazing or overfishing will destroy a valuable natural resource for everyone, it can be very difficult to get individual actors to restrain themselves from exploiting grasslands and fisheries to the fullest.* While we sometimes fail to cooperate—pastures are overgrazed, seas are overfished—we often manage to work together for a common benefit. Obviously. Otherwise, there would be no such things as bake sales, let alone moon shots, labor unions, and companies.

The wonderful thing about us humans is that we (sometimes) overcome social dilemmas even when there is no formal authority to boss us around. In fact, few of us are inveterate freeloaders, willing to sit back and let others do the hard work. Much of the time, we are what behavioral economists call **conditional cooperators**. We're happy to contribute to a collective undertaking *as long as we believe others are doing so, too*. The bake sale gets off the ground because someone steps forward and says,

---

* Common terms used for these types of social dilemmas are the *tragedy of the commons* and the *prisoner's dilemma*.

"I'm in—who's with me?" and you believe not only that this parent is in but that others now believe so, too, and that they will also step up. Only then does the flurry of organizing and baking begin. No sooner.

*Leaders enable collective action by building and nurturing the belief that everyone is working toward a common goal.*

Saying "I'm in—who's with me?" sounds easy, but you probably know from hard experience that it isn't and that words alone rarely have the desired impact. In the next section, we'll look at what types of social dilemmas arise in business. We'll look at how organizations overcome social dilemmas *without* leadership. Then we'll examine specific leadership behaviors that build and nurture the belief that everyone is working toward a common goal. First, though, let's observe how starting with a problem—social dilemmas—helps us as we aspire to be leaders and take concrete action.

> Leaders enable collective action by building and nurturing the belief that everyone is working toward a common goal.

For one thing, the bake sale example shows us that leadership is not tied to any formal role. Overcoming social dilemmas is something anyone can do: From intern to CEO, anyone can be the one to go first and say "I'm in." And come to think of it, what does the word *lead* mean if not "to go first?" Going first in a social dilemma needn't mean contributing an idea for a collective goal or being the one to select the goal for an organization. But by being the first to step up, you may be the one who gets the ball rolling. If that isn't empowering, we don't know what is.

Taking this first step is also empowering without being exclusive. The first follower, the first person to join the movement, is also a leader by demonstrating what following means. The first follower is as important as the leader in getting the ball rolling, and so are many of the next few followers.

Looking at leadership this way also clearly separates the act of leading from an organization's success or the worthiness of its goals. Someone can go first—get the ball rolling—toward a goal that turns out to have been a bad idea. Many of history's saddest episodes occurred at the instigation of people whom we would indisputably call leaders. The fact that leadership is a tool that functions just as well for good and bad purposes should force us all—whether or not we are in roles of formal authority—to think carefully about which goals we pursue and whether they align with our values.

## SOCIAL DILEMMAS IN BUSINESS

Our bake sale example is a great illustration of a social dilemma in its purest form, where there is no formal authority to impose a solution. Organizations usually do have hierarchies. But even within hierarchies, social dilemmas emerge.

Many social dilemmas are instances of withholding *effort*, aka shirking or free-riding. For example, conditional cooperators may be willing to put in extra hours to push a project across the finish line but only if they're confident that others are pulling their weight.

More subtle—and more pernicious—problems arise from withholding information and expertise. Say you're a salesperson who develops a particularly persuasive way to position your company's solutions so that you consistently outsell your colleagues. Do you share your expertise freely? Sure, if you see others doing so, too—if that's part of your team's norm of cooperation. But in an environment in which you can't count on others to return the favor, conditional cooperators might think twice about sharing their expertise.

Other information-based social dilemmas arise when it comes to revealing mistakes and risks instead of sweeping them under the rug. Again, conditional cooperators will be willing to step forward and report problems if they see someone else—especially managers—doing so first.

Social dilemmas arise when individual and collective interests lie in conflict. But it's not all about self-interest versus collective interest. Social dilemmas arise equally frequently between teams in larger organizations. Turf wars and competition for resources may be fought by team leaders who might—as individuals—be as selfless as saints.* When it comes time to lobby for your team's budget, do you base your argument on what your team needs, or do you, ahem, augment your request by 20 percent because you know that the other team leaders are doing the same thing? Leadership overcomes these social dilemmas by defining a common goal and nurturing the belief that everyone is working toward it.

## LEADERSHIP AS A COMPETITIVE ADVANTAGE

Can organizations successfully overcome social dilemmas and achieve great things without leadership as we've just described it? Absolutely. Most organizations use *incentives* like commissions, promotions, and stock options to overcome social dilemmas and align individual and group interests. In fact, one of the main purposes of organizational hierarchy—aka management—is to create and fine-tune incentives to get people to coordinate toward common goals.

Incentive systems, however, are costly and can be gamed in destructive ways.† A case in point is GE. This company went from the world's most valuable company in 2000 to being broken up into parts two decades later. In the 1980s and 1990s, the two decades before GE's zenith, Jack Welch led the company as CEO. His philosophy of management revolved around incentives: carrots and sticks. One of his innovations was stack-ranking managers, with stock options and bonuses lavished on the top 20 percent of performers and the bottom 10 percent being fired. Every year.

You might be reluctant to share your expertise or reveal emergent risks in Welch's "rank-and-yank" regime. Yet while Welch was at the helm, GE's stock rose from around $8 in 1982 to over $400 at its height

---

* The fact that some of the most bitter conflicts are fought not between selfish individuals but by representatives on behalf of groups is one reason the leadership manuals that read like catalogs of individual virtues ring so hollow to us. The truly difficult dilemmas are those in which you, as a manager, feel that you have to reconcile the interests of your own team and those of the wider organization. Admonitions to be virtuous as an individual are frustratingly unhelpful when you are weighing the demands of different groups.

† In *Managerial Dilemmas: The Political Economy of Hierarchy*, Gary J. Miller rigorously collects and demonstrates the analytic and empirical evidence for why reliance on incentives can place companies at a competitive disadvantage. Miller's book helped us recognize the underlying problem—social dilemmas—as the starting point for understanding leadership.

in 2000. Welch's system seemed to be working and was imitated widely in corporate America. He was one of those corporate titans about whom leadership myths were woven.

Not too long after he retired in 2001, however, the Welch myth began to unravel along with GE's fortunes. Much of what had made GE such a valuable company came from the reliability with which it met investors' profit expectations—exactly as we described in Part I. But as it turned out, not all that reliability was due to GE buying low, selling high, keeping customers delighted, and using its assets wisely. Much of its consistency came from clever accounting manipulation that had hidden the volatility in GE's profits and its declining ability to earn them through the core industrial businesses that were facing ever-tougher global competition. The incentives Welch had structured for GE had shaped behaviors in counterproductive ways. Welch and his protégés did well for themselves with the stock-based incentive systems, at least in the short run. Investors, customers, and employees may not have done as well in the long run.

Organizations can do just fine when they consist of individuals with perfectly aligned individual incentives. But given the costs and the risks of incentive-based management, these groups may be outcompeted by an organization with a cooperative culture, one that doesn't rely *purely* on incentives to enable collective action. Leadership builds a culture of cooperation. In such a culture, everyone believes that people are committed to a common goal and to shared success rather than just feathering their own nests.

## LEADERSHIP IN PRACTICE

So, what can you do to contribute toward a cooperative culture? As we noted, just saying "I'm in—who's with me?" is easy. Whether someone believes you and believes that others believe you, too, is another matter. Words are important, don't get us wrong. Still, it takes more than words to convince people that they won't be left organizing the bake sale alone.

The leadership books that characterize every conceivable human virtue as a key leadership competency aren't strictly wrong. *Of course* the people we admire and trust are going to have an easier time making "I'm in!" credible. So, by all means, be your best you! Be a good listener. Be forthright. Be empathetic. Be optimistic. Be vulnerable. Smile at babies, and call your mother on her birthday. Do all those things, and *do them for their own sakes*, not because they make you a better leader.

For our part, we'd like to highlight three behaviors that we believe are particularly effective in building a cooperative culture when practiced by people with formal authority. Let's look at them in detail.

### Communicating the Vision

Leaders speak frequently—even repetitively—about shared goals and shared benefits. The larger the organization and the more complex its division of labor, the more finely the organizational goals have to be broken down into smaller and smaller targets. When you're in the trenches, it's all too easy to lose sight of the big picture as you maximize your local performance metrics. If you've lost sight of the big picture, you've got to assume others have, too. Leaders' constant communication about the overall vision and goals helps you remember them and believe that others also remember and are committed to them.

Does a leader need JFK-level rhetorical skills—not to mention a professional speechwriter—to communicate the vision? No. *Whether* you communicate the vision—not *how* you do it—is what creates the shared belief.

### Role Modeling

Among our many frames of reference for leadership is our stint as chefs in student cooperative housing.* With no prior culinary experience, we led crews of about six people, all of us cooking dinner for around a hundred people in commercial-grade kitchens. In a situation like that, it's all too

---

* If there ever was a place with social dilemmas lurking around every corner, it's a student co-op.

easy to adopt a just-get-it-done attitude. Alternatively, you can strive for a true dining experience.

What did we learn from that crucible? How did we get our unskilled and marginally motivated fellows to cook pasta al dente instead of serving up noodles that could easily be confused with mashed potatoes?* It took expectation-setting, feedback, and the occasional inspirational speech. But a lot of the time, it meant scrubbing the burnt and greasy pot while handing over the more prestigious work—dessert!—to someone else.†

> As a leader, you can't be a show horse. You have to be a workhorse with flair.

Later in our managerial careers, we discovered that acting as role models is not quite as simple as rolling up your sleeves. People must *perceive* you doing so. Working late along with your team to accomplish an important project has both an intrinsic value for the project and the symbolic value of demonstrating your commitment. But if no one sees you working late, well, that symbolic value is lost. Therein lies a paradox: You need to go first visibly, and yet the more effort you put into shaping the perception of your contribution, the less effort goes into your actual contribution. You can't be a show horse; you have to be a workhorse with flair.

The three-way balancing act between (1) plain-old doing, (2) making sure your doing is perceived, and (3) sometimes *not* doing because it's more important to give others the space to step up has been a dominating feature of the leadership roles we've placed in the last two decades. It's a balancing act in which you never stop discovering your own areas of improvement.

### Recognizing Cooperative Behavior

In the previous chapter, we addressed how recognition can motivate a person. It can serve another purpose, too, highlighting that the organization's cooperative culture is alive and well.

---

* True story.
† James Kouzes and Barry Posner call this key leadership practice "model the way" in their groundbreaking book *The Leadership Challenge*.

There is, however, a dark side to spotlighting individual performance to promote a cooperative culture. Especially when recognition-worthy star performers are spotlighted repeatedly, the rest of the organization may come to rely on their outstanding performance. Did you volunteer for the school bake sale once and get applauded for it? Guess what: your fellow parents will only too happily leave that limelight to you next year.*

Although anyone can perform these cooperation-sustaining practices—communicating the vision, being a role model, and recognizing others' cooperative behavior—managers have a wider impact, thanks to the higher visibility of their position. Ultimately, leadership is more of a responsibility that increases with ever-greater levels of formal authority rather than a unique set of skills or character traits.

## LEADERSHIP IN BUSINESS

Our feelings about leadership are highly ambivalent. On the one hand, we are acutely aware of the need for people who say, "I'm in—who's with me?" Acutely enough that we—in our formal roles and in other settings—*will* go first when faced with a social dilemma or go first in following when someone else steps up. On the other hand, we are equally aware of the hazards of relying on individual leadership to organize and motivate collective action. Going first, again and again, requires superhuman effort, which is probably why all of us are so prone to project superhuman virtues onto business leaders.

But none of us are superhumans. We set ourselves up for *disillusionment* when we expect extraordinary effort of ourselves or others. We set ourselves up for *confusion* when we see businesses succeed under the guidance of flamboyant CEOs who are sometimes deeply flawed as individuals. Worse, we risk surrendering our judgments to charlatans who create the appearance of being superhumans and who lead us toward destructive, even self-destructive goals.

---

* You got it: another true story.

We respect, admire, and try to emulate those who go first and lead whenever true social dilemmas present themselves. At the same time, in our experience, business value is more consistently created from the skillful administration of humdrum incentives and the collective efforts of aligned teams rather than from high-minded speeches and superhuman acts of leadership.

That's why the focus in the next chapters lies on the *procedures* we adopt as we coordinate our specialized contributions in the division of labor, and not on the *personalities* of leaders.

# CHAPTER 15 KEY TAKEAWAYS

Leaders enable collective action by actively building and nurturing the belief that everyone is working toward a common goal.

Life in general and business in particular are full of social dilemmas. As contingent cooperators, we're happy to deliver our contribution as long as we believe that others are doing so, too.

Incentive structures are one possible way to overcome social dilemmas, but they can be costly and vulnerable to being gamed by less scrupulous actors. A company whose managers establish norms of cooperation will have a competitive advantage over companies relying solely on incentives.

Anyone can act like a leader, but the more visible you are, the more impact you will have as you

- Communicate the organizational vision
- Model cooperative behavior
- Call attention to and recognize cooperative behavior

## CHAPTER 16

# Collective Action and Decision-Making

Having founded the fitness bike company Peloton and led it to fantastic success during the Covid-19 pandemic, CEO John Foley abruptly resigned in February 2022. Investor group Blackwells Capital had demanded Foley's head. Foley was still the majority shareholder at the time, and he could have put up a fight. But he didn't. What happened? As the pandemic entered its later stages and a widely vaccinated public started to return to offices and gyms, Foley had continued to bet on a bright, growth-driven future. But growth evaporated, leaving warehouses stuffed with bikes, declining subscription sales, and unused manufacturing capacity. Blackwells Capital released a public slide deck that simply shredded Foley's performance. The deck's sixty-five slides outlined in excruciating detail why Foley was not the right man for the job of CEO.

"Peloton Has Been Grossly Mismanaged" was the title of the longest chapter in Blackwells Capital's screed. The major critique? "Poor decision-making" across the board: in strategy, demand forecasting, safety issues, and executive hiring.

From the perspective of January 2022, Foley's bets had, indeed, not paid off. But was it fair to fault him and his executive team for poor decision-making? What makes a good decision good and a bad decision bad? Foley had bet on growth, and growth hadn't materialized. Is good decision-making about having a crystal ball that always correctly forecasts the future? We believe that there's more to decisions than forecasting. When we make decisions under uncertainty—as Peloton did when it planned optimistically—some calls will turn out the way we intended, and some won't. That is what uncertainty means.

> When we make decisions under uncertainty, some calls will turn out as planned, and some won't. That's what uncertainty means.

The central topic of this chapter and the next three is how organizations make decisions. In Chapter 11, we pointed out that the fundamental challenge of management is to coordinate the activities of armies of specialists in the division of labor. There are many dimensions of coordination, for instance, the basic question of which tasks *can be* performed in parallel and which *must be* performed in sequence. Those coordination problems largely fall into the realm of functional expertise; few rules (if any) apply equally well to exercise bike manufacturing, insurance underwriting, and sound engineering. Arguably, though, the most important and the most difficult thing to coordinate across an organization is decision-making. When R&D creates products for individual consumers while marketing develops a brand concept for corporate buyers, something has gone horribly wrong in the organization's decision-making process.

Of course, organizations don't make decisions; people do. As a manager, you will be contributing to decision-making, whether you are proposing options, channeling information to those who make the call, informing your team about what call has been made, or making the call yourself. Perhaps most importantly, you will be shaping the process by which decisions are made.

# THE TEAM AS THE BASIC DECISION-MAKING UNIT

If you and a group of friends have ever had a hard time choosing a restaurant, you know how difficult collective decision-making in a team can be. And if that's hard, how much more difficult must it be to make decisions as a company of thousands, like Peloton, or a company of hundreds of thousands, like Amazon? Big or small, though, organizations have managed to act as one by leveraging the most basic collective unit: the team. Whether a large organization subdivides itself into teams or whether it emerges from the growth and integration of smaller teams doesn't really matter. Organizations with all sorts of purposes—commercial, military, governmental—have structured themselves into smaller groups with some degree of independent judgment, whether this judgment is exercised by the team's leader or by the team as a whole.*

There's no hard-and-fast rule for how large a team ought to be, but most people agree that it should be in the single digits to be effective. Amazon founder Jeff Bezos encourages the **two-pizza rule**: Teams should be no larger than the number of people you can feed with two pizzas.†

You are probably a member of several teams of this size, whether at work or at play. As a manager, you are likely to be a member of at least two teams: the one you lead and the one your manager leads. One of the great insights from Patrick Lencioni's wonderful leadership book *The Five Dysfunctions of a Team* is the distinction in priority he makes between the two: Your manager's team is your **first team**, and the team you lead is your **second team**. Both are important. But the first team commands a higher loyalty. All too often, we think of the social dilemmas described in the previous chapter in terms of conflicts between individuals, or between

---

* Organizations exhibit the property called self-similarity: at any scale, you can recognize similar structures. Zoom into any part and any hierarchical level of an organization, and you'll find small teams wrestling with the same basic challenges of decision-making: discovering and evaluating options, reaching a conclusion, and ensuring that everyone executes in alignment with the decision. We'll explore these challenges in more detail in later chapters. Leadership expert Nick Obolensky explores the deeper significance of organizations' self-similarity in his book *Complex Adaptive Leadership*.

† If you are reading this book outside the United States, keep in mind that American pizzas typically feed three or four people.

individuals and a monolithic collective organization. But complex organizations don't consist of individuals only; they develop structures that are themselves collective entities: divisions, functions, and, ultimately, teams. You can be individually selfless and yet work selflessly toward your second team's goals and not those of the wider organization. By committing fully to your first team, you are more certain to be aligning your area to the overall organizational goals.*

Several factors affect whether a team works well together, and there are several ways to define what constitutes working well together. Does the team achieve specific goals? Does it have fun? Does it stay together? Does it accept new members and part ways with old ones while remaining, in some sense, itself? All of these are fascinating questions. Our focus will be on how you, as a manager and leader, can help structure the team's decision-making to achieve organizational goals.

As a manager, you will be participating in team decision-making processes, and whether you are leading a team of individual contributors or sitting on an executive board, lots of the same basic guidelines apply. You can't learn how to get every decision right, but you can learn how to structure decision-making so that you get things right more often than not. And you can learn how to structure decision-making processes that don't cost as much as the benefit you hope to derive from the choice.

## BUSINESS, GAMES, AND BUSINESS GAMES

In the next chapters, we'll look at what structuring decision-making processes means concretely. Let's first remind ourselves what we mean by a decision. A decision presents itself when at least two different courses of action are possible, leading to potentially different outcomes. In our own business, not only do we decide how to run our company but we're also specialists

---

* Your first team is, of course, your manager's second team, and it's your manager's job to keep that team aligned by resolving social dilemmas with an eye to the goals of the manager's own first team, and so on, up to the board of directors.

in *engineering* decisions. We run our business simulations—computer games—with executives to generate discussions around how to make decisions in the real world. We have been deeply influenced by Sid Meier, the creator of the strategy games *Railroad Tycoon* and *Civilization*. He defined games as a "series of interesting decisions." We think that *business* is a series of interesting decisions.*

What makes a decision interesting is that the options for action are mutually exclusive and the outcomes uncertain. If the options aren't mutually exclusive, you just do both; no decision necessary. And if the outcomes are certain, you just do whatever is obviously better. Again, no decision necessary. Although these observations might sound trivial, they set up the distinction between the decision-making *process* and the decision's *outcome*.

Suppose we proposed the following dice game to you:

- You predict which of two mutually exclusive outcomes of rolling two six-sided dice will occur:
  - *Prediction 1: The total will be between 2 and 8.*
  - *Prediction 2: The total will be between 9 and 12.*
- Roll the dice, and add up their respective results (the total could range from 2 to 12).
- If your chosen prediction comes true, we pay you $1. Otherwise, you pay us $1.

With regular dice, Prediction 1 (a total of 2 to 8) is the better bet: It comes up more frequently. Now suppose you chose Prediction 1 and then rolled a combined 10. You would have "lost" and you would owe us $1. That definitely wasn't your preferred outcome. But in what sense did you choose incorrectly? Would you choose differently if you played again? In light of the available information, we doubt you would. We wouldn't.

---

* You can decide for yourself if business is fun because it's like a game or if games are fun because they are like business.

You might, however, add a step to your decision-making process and first ask to have a close look at the dice. And if you discovered that one of them had a 6 on all six faces, you would choose differently. If you could fault yourself for your loss in the first game, it wasn't because of your choice. It was the assumptions you brought into the game. Conversely, if the dice turn out to be fair, this game doesn't involve an interesting decision. Then the important thing is not which bet you place but persuading us to play the game with you as often as possible!

> Good decision-making is about having a process that uncovers false assumptions, that delivers good results more often than not, and whose costs don't exceed the benefits of any of the options.

Let's make it one step more complicated: Suppose we agreed to show you the dice before rolling but charged you $0.05 for every face we revealed. How many revelations would you pay for before making a final choice?

Modeling decisions in terms of outcomes and probabilities—as discussed in Part I—is an extremely important dimension of decision-making. But gathering the data to inform that model is itself a cost—in time, effort, and cash—that has to factor into the decision. There's an old story about a donkey who sits midway between two equally attractive piles of hay and starves to death. The animal got stuck in a decision-making loop because it couldn't find a rational reason to prefer one haystack over the other. It's the kind of absurd edge case philosophers love, but it illustrates an important point. Real-world donkeys—as well as people—have internal decision-making processes that halt themselves before the costs of running them exceed the benefits of any available alternative. Organizations need to replicate that halting mechanism. Good decision-making is about having a process that uncovers false assumptions, that delivers good results more often than not, and whose costs don't exceed the benefits of any of the options on the table.

Later in this chapter, we'll look at a simple framework that can help us identify the structural decision-making errors that teams make and the mechanisms they can put in place to avoid them. But first...

## THE CONTENT TRAP

It would be nice if we could just rattle off a framework with a catchy acronym to explain to teams how to make good collective decisions. But even when they have learned and bought into a framework, teams often throw every best practice overboard once they face an actual decision.

We know this because we've watched it happen thousands of times. Our business simulations are little laboratories for observing team behavior. We've observed teams in over fifty countries, from small start-ups to executive teams at some of the world's largest companies. We see the same things time and again.

Imagine you're on a five-person team in one of our simulations. You are put in charge of a virtual company, competing against three similar teams. Your first task is to choose which of three market segments your team will target. You have all the data you need: market size, preferences, prices, investment costs, and operating costs. We, as game designers, have engineered this decision to be much like the poor donkey's dilemma. The three market segments are equally attractive haystacks. Which segment your team chooses isn't important. What's important is that you make a choice. Otherwise, you'll spread your resources too thin or, worse, work at cross-purposes within the team.

We typically give the teams around thirty minutes to make their decision. But it really doesn't matter how much time they get. In some of our programs, we set the competition up in the afternoon and let the teams work on their strategy over dinner, only to find them at the bar at 11 p.m., still arguing! What are they arguing about? Given enough time, just about anything. They'll pick apart every bit of data we give them and come up with stories about the economics of the virtual world we've designed for them. The stories are far more complex than anything we would dare to code.

The one thing they will not have discussed? *How* they will make the decision as a team. It's a question they rarely turn to at all. Consequently, they argue in circles about the relative merits of the segments until the clock runs down, leaving them no time to discuss what execution will look like. Team performance suffers accordingly.*

Truthfully, we set our simulation teams up for this failure. We don't hint that they should first figure out *how* to make decisions. So, we're not being quite fair. To make amends, we stop the game after a round of execution and reveal our trickery. We make it clear that defining and following the decision-making *process* must precede the decision itself. And we share our observation that the teams that win the competition are usually those that take this lesson to heart. We send the teams off for another round of planning with the explicit instruction to discuss how they will work together as a team. Then we sit back and watch.

Someone will start the discussion with something like this: "That was an interesting insight from Bjorn. What worked and what didn't in our decision-making process?" To which, within seconds, someone else will almost invariably reply, "I think we need to lower our prices this round..." And the circus begins again.

Why do teams find it so difficult to discuss how they work together and so easy to talk about what they are doing?

Our answer is, that's how we roll. Faced with a challenge, we like to tackle it head-on. We like to get into the weeds, find a solution, start executing. Psychologists speak of an **action bias**. We just can't sit still when there's a problem to solve, even when doing nothing is a plausible—and possibly the best—response. Whether action bias is a strength or a vulnerability (it's both), let's take for granted that we are individually biased

---

* Fortunately, the struggle happens consistently enough that teams don't go off the rails right at the beginning, simply because their competitors are doing no better! Roughly a third of the way through the exercise, the teams that more quickly find effective decision-making processes pull ahead of the dysfunctional teams.

toward action. What's more, people who aspire to become managers, have already been promoted, or have decided to launch a business—that means you, dear reader!—are probably more action biased than the average person. And we all know from experience that although our action bias sometimes gets us into trouble, our accomplishments have come from seizing moments rather than watching them drift by.

The problem with individual action bias is that it can paralyze collective action. Put simply, five people working together need to agree on who speaks when and how conflict-

> Individual action bias can paralyze collective action.

ing views are resolved into a single course of action. Without that prior agreement—a team's constitution—a team discussion is nothing more than an intellectual brawl. To step back and create the rules of engagement, we have to overcome our own bias toward tackling the matter at hand. Overcoming this bias is hard. The content of our decision exerts a truly seductive attraction.

Our friend and collaborator, leadership expert Nick Obolensky, calls this the **content trap**.* We're attracted to the decision's content like moths to a flame. We focus on what we will decide without giving much thought to how we should make the decision. After all, contributing good ideas and insights, making compelling arguments—that's what earns us respect. Talking about processes isn't nearly as exciting. At least initially, it can be downright drab.

So before we dive into frameworks and best practices of collective decision-making, it's good to pause for a moment and reflect on the content trap. Think of your own experiences in any sort of team, including personal relationships. What conflicts are you trying—and unable—to resolve? How much time have you spent arguing about the content of

---

* One of our favorite professors at Harvard Business School, Bharat Anand, also wrote a fascinating book called *The Content Trap*. We recommend it highly as a discussion of how content providers like newspapers can survive in the digital age, but Anand's is a very different content trap.

your disagreement? How much time have you devoted to shaping the process by which you argue and come to a conclusion? We'd be willing to bet that you—like us—are often stuck in the content trap. The first step out of this trap is to recognize it.

Newly formed teams—like those in our simulation-based training programs—have the most work to do when it comes to creating working processes for collaboration. Although they have their work cut out for them, they also more easily become aware of the content trap. It's just too obvious to ignore. Psychologist Bruce Tuckman described the process of team development with the memorably rhyming **forming, storming, norming, performing** model. It's pretty self-explanatory: After a team joins forces (forming), frictions emerge among the members (storming). Teams don't reach the final stage where they successfully reach their goals (performing) until they first learn how to manage conflict productively by establishing rules of engagement (norming). Forming, storming, norming, performing is pretty much the plot summary of every movie about a sports team.

Existing teams may have established rules of engagement. Some of those rules will be consciously chosen. Many more will be tacitly adopted. In a sense, teams with established norms face a deeper risk than do new teams. They feel safe jumping into the content because they trust their process. But their assumptions about how well they work together leave them unaware of the possibility that they could be collaborating even more effectively. They also fail to realize that their environment may have evolved so much that what worked in the past no longer does. For these teams—and for the two of us as twenty-year collaborators—the content trap is all the trappier for being less obvious.

## A SIMPLE MODEL FOR DECISION-MAKING

We may eventually run out of rare earth elements, fossil fuels, and—heaven forbid—clean air and water, but for the foreseeable future, there will be no shortage of decision-making frameworks. We'll refrain from adding another forced acronym to the crowded space and simply observe that most decision-making processes have three distinct phases: We *define* the decision. We *deliberate* toward a conclusion. Then we *execute*.

## *Define*

Most of the effort of decision-making goes into recognizing when we face a true decision point, identifying the options for action, and evaluating the likely outcomes and their probabilities. These structural errors are common:

- Mistakenly ignoring important decisions on the one hand and making mountains out of molehills on the other
- Seeing an either/or where in fact we have a both/and situation; conversely, locking ourselves into a limited range of obvious options before considering some less obvious but potentially more attractive ones
- Going off half-cocked with bad assumptions about costs, benefits, and probabilities; conversely, analyzing until the world has moved on without us

## *Deliberate*

Even when we've defined the options and have evaluated them, reasonable people may disagree about what course of action to take. When we can't agree on a course of action, we need to at least agree on a process for halting the weighing of pros and cons and picking one option.

## *Execute*

It's one thing to say "I've decided to go on a diet." It's another thing to follow through and execute.

The next chapters explore these three phases of collective decision-making in detail.

# CHAPTER 16 KEY TAKEAWAYS

One of the most important and difficult dimensions of coordinating individual activity is collective decision-making.

Organizations structure themselves into interlocking small teams, and these teams form the basic decision-making units.

Under uncertainty, the quality of a decision's outcome is not necessarily an indicator of the quality of the decision-making process.

Good decision-making is about having a process that uncovers false assumptions, that delivers good results more often than not, and whose costs don't exceed the benefits of any option on the table.

Action bias leads teams into the content trap, where they focus on the content of the decision before considering the decision-making process.

Common structural errors in decision-making include

- Misidentifying which decisions are important
- Exploring either too few or too many options
- Failing to aggregate relevant data; spending too much time aggregating data
- Failing to define the mechanism by which the decision is made
- Failing to execute: to follow through with aligned downstream decisions

## CHAPTER 17

# Defining the Decision

In the previous chapter, we broke down the *define* phase of decision-making into three main tasks: recognizing the need to make a decision, discovering the options, and gathering information to compare them. It might be tempting to interpret these tasks as a logical sequence of their own, but beware! Decision-making is often an iterative process. In practice, you'll uncover some of the best (and unexpected) options while evaluating the obvious ones. Or, after many days of research, you'll discover that the decision wasn't really one in the first place, that there was, in hindsight, an obvious single option. In some cases, you'll even find that the most attractive option is to short-circuit the definition task and jump straight into execution in a small, revocable way to generate data to inform a bigger, irrevocable decision.*

---

* In some of our more advanced workshops with executives, we introduce a systems analysis framework called Cynefin. It distinguishes between ordered systems, in which cause-and-effect relationships are known (so we can make valid predictions of the impacts of our choices) and complex and chaotic systems, in which cause-and-effect relationships are unclear. In complex systems, quickly interacting with the system in a limited way (probing) may get you somewhere, whereas no amount of prior analysis will do so.

Similar ideas have shaped the agile approach to software development. Agile development has many dimensions, of which a crucial one is its emphasis on flexibility—the willingness to revise prior decisions as new information arises—during the development process. Of course, a software developer's capacity for agility is not the same as, say, a nuclear power plant operator's!

In this chapter, we'll look at structural solutions to the kinds of structural errors that teams are prone to make as they define the decision. We'll begin by looking at how we can make sure we're tackling relevant decisions in the first place and some ways to limit the number of options to a manageable few.

## CONSTRAINING DECISIONS THROUGH STRATEGY

How many decisions do we make every day? Search online—always a dangerous proposition—and you'll find an amazingly wide range of answers. Seventy. Thirty-five thousand. It all comes down to how you define a decision. What's clear, though, is that an awful lot of decision-making must go on unconsciously.

Consider your teeth. We presume you brush them. You could also choose not to (which we don't recommend). In what sense do you make a choice? Your choice is made by force of habit, outside of your conscious awareness. But if asked, you can easily account for why you brush your teeth. It's a ritual that connects to deeper choices about how you would like to live your life: healthily, and with some people willing to come within a foot of your face. Brushing twice daily is just the execution of a larger, longer-term—dare we say strategic?—decision. Whenever we zig when we might have zagged, we are usually operating on autopilot, guided (hopefully) by a greater plan for navigating life. And that's good. Imagine that every evening, you analyzed whether there might be an even more important use of those three minutes than toothbrushing.

Organizations make many more decisions than individuals do. Clearly, organizations also need to do something analogous to automating their smaller-scale decisions. Automation is useful, not because these small decisions are unimportant—brushing your teeth is important. But it would be enormously costly to devote time and attention to every single smaller decision. People have overarching guiding principles and life plans that help clear the jungle of possibilities they face, and organizations have...well, what exactly?

Let's look at a decision made by an organization in the widest sense of the word: the nation of Sweden in 1967. In what is called, charmingly, the *Högertrafikomläggningen*, Sweden switched from driving on the left side of the road to the right. The nation had some reasons for making the switch.* In general, though, there are neither moral nor practical reasons to prefer one convention over the other. You can't say with a straight face, "Driving on the right side of the road—brilliant idea!" It simply doesn't matter what side of the road you drive on *as long as everyone chooses the same side*. The alternative is pure mayhem.

*Högertrafikomläggningen* (feel free to linger on that word!) illustrates something important. Overarching decisions that simplify routine decisions can be, literally, matters of life and death and yet can be completely arbitrary in content. We're going to look at one mechanism companies use to provide some guardrails for decision-making: strategy.

Few words are as overused in business as *strategy*. There are many fascinating concepts and models of strategy we might have discussed in a longer book: game theory, Porter's five forces, the resource-based view. It's great stuff, all of it. Most of the ideas are focused on how companies choose which markets to compete in and how they position themselves in those markets. The truth is, even executive teams make those kinds of decisions relatively rarely.

Whether the business press winds up fawning over a company's brilliant strategy or ridiculing its failure often hinges on how well the strategy was executed, not on how smart or stupid the strategy was. That's why we've chosen to focus on strategy as a guide to decision-making, a mechanism for aligning and coordinating decisions made in every team at every level and in every function of the business. Yes, there may be some brilliance and stupidity to the selection of markets. But the first test of strategy is whether it succeeds at getting everyone to drive on the same side of the road. Strategy can be about complex moves in a game of 3D

---

* Prompting the decision were Sweden's land borders with right-side-driving nations and the high percentage of cars with the driver's seat on the left.

chess with competitors, customers, and suppliers. But strategy is also a convention to help us from running into each other.

For business school professor Roger L. Martin, strategy "cascades" through the organization like a white-water river of choice. He offers the following example. Suppose a bank's executive team chooses to focus on retail banking—instead of investment banking—as a strategy. That's a great starting place, and it probably guides some decisions about how to allocate capital for investment. But what does this choice of strategy mean concretely? The head of retail banking might conclude that successful retail banking is all about having the best customer service. Again, what does that decision mean? The customer service head might conclude that great customer service is all about hiring the right people as tellers and then training them appropriately. That decision guides each branch's hiring decisions as well as the training design and delivery choices made by the HR team. Ultimately, even individual tellers need to exercise their judgment, for instance, in choosing how to meet the particular needs of any one customer.

Martin's key point is that thinking in terms of a strategy-versus-execution distinction, in which executives at the top of the organization make choices and people in the lower ranks simply execute them, is dangerously misleading. Decisions have to be made *at all levels*. Execution is not about following orders. It's about making downstream decisions in a way that aligns with the decisions at the top and with decisions being made across the business.

Is strategy necessarily something that originates at the top and flows downward? In fact, you might be able to tell the same banking strategy story the other way around. Maybe a teller—Mary—identifies three categories of customers, each with different needs and expectations. She adopts different approaches for each group and finds that she works faster and with more smiles all round. At the water cooler, she shares her perceptions with colleagues. They like her ideas and begin implementing them, too. The branch's performance metrics improve rapidly, and at an annual branch manager retreat, Mary's branch gets singled out for being exemplary. The head of retail banking investigates, discovers the best practices pioneered by Mary, and rolls them out across all branches. A banking industry magazine honors Mary's bank with the prestigious Best Customer Service Award, outscoring all competitors. The bank's executives realize that they seem to have a competitive advantage in retail banking and decide to invest more in the retail side of the business. The CEO announces a strategy called "Winning in Retail," watches the company stock price go up for five years, and then retires to write a best-selling memoir, *Pure Courage: Leading a Business from the Front*.

> A clearly formulated strategy drastically reduces the cost of decision-making processes by limiting available choices.

Whether it originates in a brilliant insight from an enlightened top or comes from the top's belated acknowledgment of realities welling up from below, strategy constrains the range of decisions for each level. Using strategy as a constraint in decision-making empowers teams. With too many options open, the choice becomes paralyzing in the same way that two dozen brands of butter bewilder us at the supermarket. A common way to visualize decisions is the *decision tree*, with ever-forking branches. Strategy prunes the branches and puts the organization on autopilot. A clearly formulated strategy drastically reduces the cost of decision-making processes by limiting available choices.

### Visions, Values, and Policy Manuals

A company's vision and mission statements also constrain the range of choices and help teams at all levels of the organization arrive at better decisions, faster. Another important set of guardrails for decisions is a company's values—provided they are genuine and lived by all members of the organization, and the values statements are not just fig leaves hiding corporate malfeasance. Indeed, business professors Jim Collins and Jerry

Porras have elevated vision and values to causal elements in a company's abilities to enjoy enduring success.

And of course, companies deploy other branch-pruning mechanisms to deal with specific routine situations. These less lofty and less inspirational tools, such as corporate policy manuals, are nevertheless similarly effective ways to tame the number of choices.

## THE RISKS OF RUNNING ON AUTOPILOT

Have you been wondering whether Sweden benefited from *Högertrafikomläggningen*? Did the change reduce traffic fatalities? The consensus appears to be that it had no noticeable long-term impact, underscoring the fact that the choice between left or right is truly arbitrary. But looking into the details reveals something quite interesting about automated decision-making. After Sweden's switch, the first few days involved some traffic jams and a slightly higher rate of accidents. Then the early kinks were followed by a period of lower-than-normal accident numbers. It looked as if the switch was working as hoped for. By 1969, however, rates had climbed back to where they were before the change. What happened?

The dip and the return to the undesirable normal are attributed to the increased caution with which people drove as they got used to the new rule and the return to less cautious behavior once the new rule became second nature. The ultimate results of the Swedish transition illustrate the hazards of automated decision-making. When we rely on automated behaviors, subtle changes in the environment may escape our attention and we become more vulnerable to disastrous risks. Sweden's shift in traffic policy temporarily broke the automation and riveted drivers' attention back on the road, where it belongs when you're guiding two tons of steel along a road at sixty-five miles per hour.

How do we cope with the downsides of running on autopilot as individuals? The title of Daniel Kahneman's best-selling book captures one of the essential insights of behavioral economics: *Thinking, Fast and Slow.* He proposes that we have two systems of thinking, a fast one and a slow one. The fast one is extremely good at making split-second judgments about most of the challenges our natural environment throws at us, like whether the person we're facing is angry. It's less good—downright bad—at things like evaluating statistics. The slow thinking system is better at stats, but because it consumes a lot of energy, it can't be bothered to get out of bed unless it's important.

It's tempting to beat up on the fast thinking system. Quick and dirty overviews of behavioral economics—what we're doing right now!—leave the impression that we are irrational creatures, riddled with debilitating biases that we need to work day and night to overcome. But the fast system's biases are bugs *and* features. They are mechanisms to prevent us from losing precious moments analyzing whether that longish, grayish thing in the grass is a snake or a stick. Our onboard decision-making mechanisms may not be designed for the world of mortgages and marketing campaigns. But just because those mechanisms are not always suited to today's challenges does not mean that it's easy to overrule them or that we always should.

The real takeaway from behavioral economics is that you need a good switching mechanism, one that knows when to engage the slow system and when to let the fast system run with it, not *in spite of* but *because of* the fast system's biases.

Does something similar apply to organizations? Yes it does, and we have to structure our team decision-making processes to intentionally halt the organization's strategy-constrained, automated decision-making under certain circumstances. Which ones?

Individually, our lives involve three basic challenges:

1. Survive by dealing with routine decisions in the here and now.
2. Thrive by planning and preparing for the long term.
3. Respond to the flaming dumpsters the world likes to roll into our paths.

Organizations face the same three challenges. A company uses strategy and values to simplify and accelerate routine decisions that tend to have immediate costs and benefits, like what prices to charge, when to run promotions, which marketing activities to pursue, and what cost structure to maintain.

When it comes to decisions with longer-term impacts, though, it becomes harder and harder to foresee outcomes and probabilities, as we saw in Part I. Those decisions include developing the strategy itself, such as the company-wide strategy chosen by executives and the team-level implementation of the strategy.

Invariably, as teams decide how to shape the future, they uncover conflicting views about what it may bring. And those views should conflict, because knowable truths about the future are rare. When conflict and dissent emerge, the team needs to halt the automated process. Chapter 18 looks at the mechanisms that teams can use to move forward together in spite of conflict.

Although conflict sounds like something to resolve or avoid, a very real problem in teams is that conflict and dissent may remain submerged when they need to be surfaced. The conflict is often ignored when unanticipated—even "unanticipatable"—threats to the organization first appear on the horizon. In Chapter 19, we'll turn to some best practices for using dissent to halt automation, especially in times of crisis. For now, having discussed how we automate the decisions that don't require our conscious effort, we'll turn to the techniques that help us identify and evaluate our options when we're faced with decisions that do require our attention.

## EXPLORING OPTIONS AND GATHERING DATA

What options you consider, where you look for data, how much time and money you spend to get them, and how exactly you use them is highly specific to the situation you're addressing: Booking holiday parties, setting internal project deadlines, or hiring new research scientists all require different areas of expertise, a topic that lies beyond the scope of this book. But there are structural things that go wrong when we discover the options available and try to evaluate their outcomes and probabilities.

> There's no correlation between the importance of a person's contribution and the enthusiasm and sheer volume with which they express it.

Teams may fail to uncover all the options or all the data to inform the decision because someone on the team withholds important information. A team member might believe divulging it would be personally disadvantageous or might hurt their team. That's a case of a social dilemma, as we explored in Chapter 15.

But even when everyone is on their most team-oriented behavior, teams regularly fail to take advantage of all the ideas and information their members could contribute. Let's face it: Some people participate easily in discussions; others, less so. Most of us fall somewhere on a spectrum between showboats and wallflowers, and wallflowers have a harder time getting their input heard. Even when quieter team members do share their thoughts, they are frequently crowded out by well-meaning but louder colleagues. That effect tends to be self-reinforcing: When your ideas don't have an impact, you may start to doubt their value and become less and less confident in sharing them.

There's no correlation between the importance of a person's contribution and the enthusiasm and sheer volume with which they express it. So how can teams fully use their collective potential? One approach is to place the onus on wallflowers to change their individual behavior, offering them training or coaching on how to be more assertive. Although training may help in some cases, this approach may just as easily backfire.

People are often perceived as less assertive because of factors beyond their control, including physical attributes like the timbre of their voices.

What's more, one of the reasons some people hold back from conversations is that they are busy exercising other skills, including active listening and reflection, skills that enable them to deliver deep insights and creative ideas, if only those insights and ideas could be heard. Finally, we can change our behaviors through conscious practice. But our communication habits are arguably a large part of what makes us *us*, and when we push ourselves to behave against our grains, we risk coming across as inauthentic. People who come across as inauthentic have a hard time gaining trust.

That's why we favor procedural approaches to using a team's full capacity rather than personal approaches. What does a procedural approach look like? When teams define and deliberate about decisions, the discussion is often unstructured. Such free-form discussions can be useful for brainstorming, when insights and ideas collide with each other in unexpected ways to create new possibilities. But when discussions are not structured, the loudest, most assertive voices will take the conversation ball and run with it, leaving no space for those who prefer to step back and reflect. As a procedural fix, dedicating time to a highly structured, even ritualized format can work wonders.

We have watched many real-world teams come up with their own creative—sometimes highly creative—and effective rituals. Some of these can be quite simple: As a standard part of any decision-making meeting, many teams make each participant—showboat or wallflower—take the floor for a set length of time and in a completely arbitrary but strictly enforced order. The teams might go around the room in a clockwise fashion, giving each person two minutes to share their perspective on the matter at hand, without—and this is important—anyone else butting in. This process is sometimes referred to as a **round robin**.

The idea of subjecting decision-making to predefined rules and procedures—independent of either the content of the decision or the personalities of the people involved—is a very old one. It is the foundation of modern nations that define themselves as ruled by laws. Nations use constitutions to define the set of rules for political decisions. Legislative bodies adopt parliamentary rules to lend structure to their deliberations and decision-making, for example the (in)famous filibuster of the US Senate. A wide variety of organizations, such as housing co-ops, trade unions, parent-teacher associations, and corporate boards, may use Robert's Rules of Order* to structure their discussions.

Adopting a comprehensive charter like Robert's Rules may be overkill for the typical team in a business. But using a few mechanisms and procedures like the round robin can help a team do more than just use all its members' ideas and insights.

---

* *Robert's Rules of Order* is a handbook of parliamentary procedures created by Henry Martyn Robert, a US Army officer, in the nineteenth century.

# CHAPTER 17 KEY TAKEAWAYS

Many organizational coordination problems are similar to getting everyone to drive on the same side of the road: It doesn't matter which side you choose, as long as everyone makes the same choice.

Externally, a company's strategy may help it navigate competitive relationships, but internally, a strategy serves to get everyone driving on the same side of the road. It constrains the number of options for decisions at all levels of the organization.

As teams explore options and predict outcomes, they often fail to take advantage of the ideas and insights of all their members. Rather than find fault with less outspoken team members, teams may be far more productive if they institute procedural solutions to make sure all voices are heard.

Lending a formal structure to a discussion through simple and effective methods like the round robin can ensure that the loudest voices aren't drowning out equally useful but quieter ones.

## CHAPTER 18

# Deliberating and Executing

When teams of managers play our training simulations, they often fail to define a procedure for ending the discussion and choosing a single clear outcome. When the selection process is not well defined in advance, teams lose precious time as they debate in circles, even to the point that the world passes them by and makes the choice for them. Although many closing mechanisms, or ways to conclude a decision, are possible, we'll focus on three broad types: **consensus**, **majority rule**, and the **sole decider**.

> Without a clear deliberation process, teams may debate in circles until the world makes the decision for them.

These mechanisms have their respective advantages and vulnerabilities, but how should we compare them? As we consider the three decision-making procedures, we'll ask ourselves the following:

- How costly is the selection process in terms of both time and other resources?
- How committed to the decision will the team members be?
- Is there accountability? To what degree can the team learn from the decision's outcome?

## *Consensus*

In our leadership training simulations, the participant teams often describe their decision-making as consensus driven, even when we observe otherwise! This misrepresentation demonstrates how consensus is often assumed to be an ideal to strive toward even if it might be hard and slow to achieve in practice. With agreement all around, shouldn't the chosen path be the best alternative, given the available information, and shouldn't everyone be fully committed to it?

Though it may look like an attractive if difficult ideal, consensus decision-making has its dark side. Consensus decision-making generates social dilemmas: Because any single person can derail the consensus-building process, successful options are often cluttered with concessions to each individual. These concessions may be costly, irrelevant, or even actively detrimental: "OK, we'll go with Jane's strategic plan, but only if Tom's department gets a 10 percent budget increase, Dick gets a promotion, and Harriet gets to implement *her* strategic plan next year." Consensus-building can move at a glacial pace and yet result in a grab bag of giveaways that nobody is enthusiastic about.

A team's leadership culture can help it avoid costly horse-trading. But even then, teams may only reach consensus by tackling the least controversial decisions, those whose outcomes and probabilities are known. Their need to come to consensus may prevent them from tackling more interesting and consequential decisions, like launching new products or hiring someone with an unconventional background.

Finally, if a team operating by consensus consistently makes decisions that don't play out as hoped for, what can it learn from those failures? Who can be held accountable, coached toward better performance, and removed from the decision-making process if necessary? Consensus—far from being a (hard-to-achieve) ideal—harbors its own risks even when implemented "successfully."

## *Majority Rule*

As a selection process, majority rule can short-circuit the consensus-building process, reducing both the horse-trading inefficiencies and the time to reach a conclusion. The most interesting decisions are often those whose outcomes and probabilities are hard to quantify and where different people will bring different beliefs to the table. Faced with deep uncertainty, team members may simply have to agree to disagree. Instead of getting stuck in analysis paralysis, searching endlessly for more data, a majority vote can push the team into action. The resulting decision is one that at least a majority are committed to. That's definitely better than one that a majority oppose!

But as with consensus, it's not quite clear who should take responsibility if the decision goes south with majority rule. When a situation is irreducibly uncertain, it may make little sense to pinpoint responsibility on any one person. But when used for routine decisions, majority rule leaves unclear who should be held accountable for repeated bad choices.

## *Sole Decider*

The time-honored—though not always beloved—decision-making procedure of having a single person make the call addresses the issue of accountability. When decision-making authority is assigned to one person, that person can be targeted for both praise and remedial action, including removal from responsibility.

Are members of a team whose leader calls all the shots disempowered? In some ways yes, in others no. Sometimes, when a team's role is to propose options but not participate in the decision, it can be empowering not to bear the weight of accountability. When you won't be held accountable for the decision, you may be less likely to self-censor, liberating yourself to contribute more outlandish ideas. Just suggesting them may drag the deliberation into new and fruitful territory, even as your initial suggestion gets vetoed by the sole decider.

Accountability is the main argument in favor of the sole decider model, and it's the reason that most organizations tend to deploy it. There is a common perception that voting and consensus-based procedures are slower than sole deciders. It's a central theme in the Star Wars prequel trilogy, where Emperor Palpatine's pitch is that he will bring peace and order without the endless bickering and inaction of the Galactic Senate.* But sole deciders aren't necessarily more efficient or decisive than majority-rule teams. An up-or-down vote needn't take a lot of time as a concluding procedure. Meanwhile, we've known some very indecisive senior executives. But indecisive leaders can be held accountable when dithering leads to bad outcomes.

Either way, it's the definition phase—when options are mooted and information is gathered—that takes time. And it can take the same amount of time under a team's chief decider. This person might seem to save time by cutting short the definition phase and issuing a decree. But will the leader get much commitment out of the team? The decider will likely have to spend just as much time explaining their reasoning. Sole deciders may struggle to get the team to execute in a coordinated way if they haven't involved the team just as intimately as the members would have been in a consensus or majority-rule procedure.

## ALIGNING TO EXECUTE

Like individuals, organizations can fail at execution because downstream decisions do not align well with the initial decision or with each other. Achieving *alignment* is what the execution phase is all about, and alignment becomes more and more challenging the larger the organization.

Communicating decisions downstream to the next team is the first challenge, of course. It's where you can flex your loop-closing muscles from Chapter 12. But beyond the bedeviling difficulties of communicating

---

* To bring order to the galaxy, Palpatine just had to murder people with his finger lightning, launching a messy rebellion in the process and ultimately failing...but we digress.

with your fellow human beings, it's just plain hard to put your back into executing a decision that you disagree with.

In all three of our decision procedures, we couldn't be sure everyone was on board with the decision. In majority rule, a minority is—by definition—not in agreement. A sole decider may face majority opposition. Even consensus may have been achieved through compromises that no one is really committed to. Lack of commitment can lead to difficulties executing even within the team. A typical large company has to coordinate the actions of many teams: One team may make a decision that another has to execute with little to no say in the matter. How do organizations overcome the problem of executing across many interlocked teams?

First, a helpful model to keep in mind is the **agreement versus alignment** distinction.* You and two friends may never be able to *agree* on a restaurant you all like. But you've probably resolved conflicts like this with a round of Rock, Paper, Scissors or a flipped coin. As long as you all agree that the outcome is binding, you can *align* your behaviors, all show up at the same place, and have a rip-roaring good time. Agreement may remain forever out of reach, but alignment is realistic. So how do organizations get to alignment?

Naively, organizations work through incentives, that is, carrots and sticks. Who cares if you agree or disagree with a decision? You get paid for executing. You get fired for not executing. End of story. Things aren't quite that simple, of course. Even if it were possible to buy people's enthusiasm for things they don't agree with† or fire everyone who disagreed, doing so would be enormously costly for the organization. As we mentioned earlier in the book, companies that get everyone to align around a common goal without a costly incentive scheme have a competitive advantage.

Getting to alignment is yet another reason decision rules and procedures are so important, and it relates to the political concept of **legitimacy**.

---

* We're indebted to our friend and collaborator Jerome Bigara for this helpful distinction between agreement and alignment.
† Pro tip: Don't bother.

People recognize decisions as binding—regardless of how they feel about the matter personally—if they believe the decision was made legitimately.

What makes for a legitimate decision? Sociologist Max Weber identified three sources of legitimacy: charisma, tradition, and procedure. *Charismatic* leaders may enjoy legitimacy; people will execute charismatic leaders' decisions willingly by the sheer force of the leader's personality ("I'll do it to please you"). Even uncharismatic leaders or committees may enjoy legitimacy by virtue of *tradition* ("I'll do it because, hey, who am I to reject the wisdom of our forebears?"). But in the last few centuries, organizations—both public and private—have tended to base legitimacy on procedural grounds. A decision is recognized as binding if it has emerged from a *procedure* that everyone knows about in advance and that is defined independently of the decision's content or the people involved in making it.

Hiring is an important decision at all organizational levels, most visibly so at the highest level. Even when there is an obvious candidate for an executive position, though, organizations will often go through a rigorous, standardized hiring process. One of us sat on the board of a nonprofit organization that had fired its managing director. The obvious replacement was Alan, the CFO. Alan had been with the organization for over a decade and enjoyed the board's and the staff's trust. We still painstakingly searched for and evaluated two other candidates. We subjected Alan to the same interview and evaluation process as the others. Ultimately, we chose Alan. Did that make the process a waste of time? We'd argue that it was essential. Getting the procedure right ensured that everyone—the board, the staff, and the organization's members—believed that the decision was legitimate. Alan was effective as he implemented some uncomfortable organizational changes because no one doubted he was the right person for the job.

Contrast that with exercise bike maker Peloton, where one of the hiring decisions that eroded the shareholders' confidence in CEO John Foley—and reportedly eroded internal confidence as well—was Foley's decision to put his own wife in charge of Peloton's branded-apparel division. This hiring decision was neither based on a procedure nor independent of the options and personalities involved. Correspondingly, it did not enjoy legitimacy.

When teams make decisions according to a rule-based process, it's not just the team members themselves who will accept the decision as binding, even if they individually have reservations. Others outside of the decision-making process are likely to as well.

## COMPARING DECISION PROCEDURES

So, is any decision-making procedure better than the others? First, the most important takeaway is to establish a clear decision-making process. Almost any process is better than none at all. Without a process, teams are unlikely to collect and share the available information, come up with a range of options (including less obvious and more creative ones), arrive at a clear outcome, and execute it with discipline.

Whether consensus, majority rule, or sole decider works for your team is based on many factors, including your broader organizational culture and even your national culture. We've worked with many global companies, and something they struggle with is clashing decision-making norms when their teams are composed of people from around the world.

One thing is for certain, though: Teams encounter different types of decisions. There are many ways to categorize decisions. In our training simulations, we engineer decisions around the three basic challenges we mentioned earlier:

1. Surviving to fight another day by making routine decisions in the here and now
2. Thriving by setting long-term goals and establishing norms and procedures around how to achieve them
3. Dealing with unexpected crises and opportunities

Different selection processes may be more or less helpful in these different scenarios. For example, when we make routine decisions, by definition, we ought to have some data to work with. A marketing team may have to routinely decide which industry conferences to attend. In the division of labor, someone will develop more expertise in that area than will other members of the team. Although this "conference expert" may seek input from others, this person is in the best position to make the decision on their own.

In contrast, for alignment to happen when agreement can't be found, teams must have unanimously agreed on a legitimate process. When establishing or amending a team's constitution, consensus may be the only way to ensure that future decisions—even those made by sole deciders—are accepted as legitimate.

Finally, in an unexpected crisis, outcomes and probabilities may be unknown and unknowable—that's precisely why the crisis wasn't expected. A majority decision may be the quickest way to come to a conclusion that engages all the participants and commits them to move forward as one.

## THE PROCESS GUARDIAN

At this point, you may have forgotten about the content trap. Exactly. That's why it is a trap. Team members can play many formal and informal roles on teams: sole decider, co-decider, cheerleader, agenda setter. An additional and often-overlooked role is the **process guardian**. This person observes the team and its individual and collective behavior, calls a time-out when the team is deviating from the commitments it has made to itself, and lifts it back out of the content trap into which it will, inevitably, fall. The process guardian role can be split into several subroles, none of which have to be played by the same person. Nor do any of them have to be played by the team lead. Those roles include the *timekeeper*, who makes sure meetings stay on track, and the *moderator*, who manages the flow of the discussion, including enforcing strict procedural rules in rituals like the round robin.

The process guardian can be helpful in another procedural approach our own leadership team likes to use to structure discussions. Before each meeting starts, we classify each agenda item according to its purpose: Is it meant to inform the team, are we supposed to discuss an issue without reaching a conclusion during the meeting, or should we decide finally in the meeting? Exercising this discipline helps us accomplish our meeting goals. Items meant to inform don't blow up into time-consuming discussions, and neither the "inform" nor "discuss" items spiral out of control into half-cocked, premature decisions.

We'll be blunt: The process guardian role can be a thankless one. Everyone feels at home in the content trap, and the process guardian relentlessly pushes people out of their comfort zone. The guardian politely asks showboats to pipe down and pressures wallflowers into the limelight. Some may play this role better than others do, but even when you play it well, you can get bummed out being the narc at the party. Three techniques can help a process guardian be more effective:

1. **Designate the roles formally:** When people perform the guardian role(s) as offices, neither they nor their colleagues will take their interventions personally.
2. **Express appreciation:** These roles can be emotionally taxing. Not only the team lead but each individual member needs to take responsibility for supporting the people who shoulder the burden.
3. **Rotate the roles:** Again, some people may assume these roles more naturally. But there's no better way to learn to appreciate the roles and the people who play them than to step into their shoes from time to time.

Because it can be a thankless role, and because the existing relationships and interpersonal dynamics can make it difficult for any team member to play the process guardian role effectively, it can sometimes be helpful to introduce an outside moderator who has not been part of prior discussions to play that role.

# CHAPTER 18 KEY TAKEAWAYS

Three representative concluding mechanisms for a collective decision are consensus, majority rule, and sole decider.

Each mechanism has its strengths and weaknesses with respect to cost (time and resources), commitment, and accountability.

Different types of decisions may require different decision-making procedures:

- Routine decisions
- Decisions about setting team norms (including decision-making rules!)
- Decisions in the face of unexpected crises and opportunities

When decisions are made according to the established norms, they enjoy legitimacy and team members are more likely to execute the decision with alignment even when they individually disagree with it.

It can be helpful to designate someone as a process guardian to ensure that the team sticks to its norms. That role can be divided and rotated, or it can be assigned to someone from outside the regular team.

# CHAPTER 19

# The Power of Dissent

During one of our training simulations, we ask the participant teams early on to take stock of their performance using a simple tool, the **plus/delta exercise**. We place two columns on a whiteboard, one column for things that are going well (pluses) and one for things to change (deltas). Then we ask the groups for their thoughts on both in a free-form discussion. Almost invariably, someone will share as a plus: "I think we're communicating well as a team." Many heads around the table (or webinar screen) nod quickly in agreement. Pressing for explanations of what "communicating well" looks like, we'll hear a lot about how consensus is reached quickly, how the atmosphere is friendly and collegial. Words like *harmonious* and *respectful* come up.

It's rare that someone steps up and says, "I don't think we're communicating effectively." Left to themselves, teams will continue to claim that their teamwork was great, right through the end of the exercise, even when every objective measure shows their final results are awful. Good team communications don't guarantee good results, though. Maybe these teams are highly functional and they've just been cursed with bad luck or better competitors?

Then we impose the round robin structure on the plus/delta exercise, going around the room in a strict order. Crucially, we insist that each person share both a plus and a delta. This exercise often destroys the happy illusion of harmony. The people who initially vaunted "good communication" and "consensus" were the ones who had been dominating the conversation all along. Of course, *they* thought communication was smooth! It turns out that, especially among their less assertive colleagues, not everyone thought that the team was communicating well. In fact, many had misgivings about the decisions the team had made, misgivings that never emerged during the defining and deliberating phases of the decision-making process.

What happened during the *unstructured* plus/delta exercise illustrates exactly what goes wrong in our simulation teams and in real-world teams. It's called **groupthink**, a term popularized by research psychologist Irving Janis in the 1970s. One hypothesis—"We're communicating well!"—gets voiced early in a team discussion, and an easy consensus emerges around it. It's not exactly a consensus. It's more like the absence of opposition. Nobody wants to rock the boat. And in this state of apparent harmony, teams are at their most vulnerable to making costly mistakes.

Imagine a situation similar to the one we described earlier: A team has to hire a new member, and there is an immediately available candidate, Orson the Obvious. One person's mindset that aggregates into groupthink looks something like this: "I understand all the arguments in Orson's favor. Nice guy. Personally, I've seen him exercise poor judgment on a few occasions. But what do I know? I'm not in Orson's field. My misgivings are kind of vague. Everyone else thinks he's an all-star, and they must know him better. If I pipe up, it'll only slow us down right when we need to be accelerating."*

Sound familiar? We'd be willing to bet you've experienced a thought process like this yourself at some point. Notice the important remark at the end about speed. One of the downsides of consensus-based decision-making is that it can take too long. But when consensus comes

---

* Based on true events! The real-world Orson turned out to be a conspiracy theorist who embarrassed the organization in front of its clients. He was let go after two months.

naturally and early, it may seem as if the team has hit on the best of all worlds: efficiency, clarity, and legitimacy.

Since the 1970s, the groupthink concept has been investigated thoroughly, and the resulting picture has—inevitably—become much more nuanced than Janis's original view. Nevertheless, we're going to use groupthink to describe the general situation that emerged in our simulation laboratories and in our own teams. We will identify some strategies that teams can use to nurture dissent rather than skirt it or even try

> Teams need a certain amount of friction to generate better information and better options and to execute effectively.

to stamp it out. Alignment is essential once a decision has been made and needs to be executed, but agreement often comes too quickly during a team's deliberation.

Teams need a certain amount of friction to generate better information and better options and to execute effectively. A team that agrees unanimously in the face of every decision is probably not trying hard enough to identify truly interesting decisions.

## THE DEVIL'S ADVOCATE

For better and worse, some teams may be endowed with a formal leader who rules through love or fear or both: A pied piper who will lead you dancing off a cliff. A tyrant who credibly threatens, "When I'm done with you, you'll never work in this industry again!" Most managers are neither prophet nor tyrant. Nor are most team members starry-eyed fans or cringing bootlickers. Still, the views of formal leaders inevitably get more attention, and these people risk generating easy, early consensus before all the facts are in and all the alternatives are explored. Once the leader's preference gains a certain amount of approval from the group—sincere or insincere—it can be hard to raise a voice in opposition individually. No one wants to become the group's killjoy or draw the ire of a temperamental boss.

A possible structural technique to counteract a leader's structural advantage is to hold at least one meeting without the leader. Teams—or at least subsets of teams—will do this informally anyway. Instituting it formally ensures that whatever insights are generated are easier to uncover, because they emerged as part of an agreed-on decision-making process.

Famous cases of groupthink come from corporate boardrooms or the political sphere. Practically by necessity, these prominent cases involve high-status executive groups with team members who genuinely risk their careers or worse if they register opposition.* However, groups may seek out easy consensus to avoid confrontation, even without a glorious leader to cower from or to suck up to.

A case in point is our training simulations. They are populated with arbitrarily chosen pretend CEOs who have no mechanisms for sanctioning or promoting anyone in the simulation, let alone in the real world. And still, we routinely watch groupthink emerge just for the sake of maintaining a collegial atmosphere.

Disagreement is never comfortable, and we all know from hard experience that small disagreements can spiral out of control and jeopardize relationships. Nevertheless, the mark of a high-performing team is not that it politely avoids conflict. Instead, a high-performing team achieves its goals and uses dissenting voices to its advantage without blowing up its relationships beyond repair.

An easy consensus can emerge when everyone's individual short-term interests align around one course of action, but this consensus is made at the expense of collective long-term interests. That's a classic example

---

* Janis's most famous examples are President John F. Kennedy's handling of the Bay of Pigs fiasco and President Lyndon B. Johnson's escalation of the Vietnam War. A more recent example is Vladimir Putin's decision to invade Ukraine, a nation of 43 million, with an army of merely 150,000, and what in retrospect has proved to be poor training, poor equipment, and poor...well, just about everything else. And we don't want to think about where opposing groupthink in Putin's cabinet gets you.

of a social dilemma as described in Chapter 15, and an unusual type of leadership is needed to overcome these dilemmas: the **devil's advocate**.* This person argues against the easy, popular consensus, for instance highlighting a low-probability but deeply impactful risk. A fun example of such a risk—and of the devil's advocate strategy deployed against it—is in the film *World War Z*. (Fun, that is, if you're into zombies.) In the movie, only one nation, Israel, takes steps to prepare for the zombie apocalypse, applying the tenth-person principle, a kind of devil's advocate procedure. If nine people unanimously agree on an interpretation of the data, it is the tenth person's job to produce an alternative interpretation. In the movie, nine security analysts, interpreting intercepted military communications of a foreign nation, concluded that the word *zombie* was code for "terrorist." The tenth man asked, "What if they really mean *zombies*?"

The **innovator's dilemma** is another example. When a company has an existing solution that performs well in the market, the arguments *against* investing in an innovative product can be quite powerful. Sales and marketing won't have figured out how to position it in the marketplace. The production process won't be optimized, so costs will be high. And—most importantly—when the innovation starts gaining traction in the market, it will often cannibalize sales from existing, beloved, and profitable solutions. Although the value of the innovation might be acknowledged by all, any individual functional area's performance might look bad in the short term before the kinks get worked out. It's not hard to imagine an executive team developing an easy, early consensus against an innovation. As described in an earlier chapter, Nokia developed a touchscreen internet-enabled smartphone years before Apple released the iPhone, but Nokia chose to bury it.

---

* The term comes from the Catholic Church, whose deliberative process—canonization—for creating saints also created a kind of social dilemma. For any *individual* candidate, why should the church—always vulnerable to sectarian splintering—risk an argument that might blow up into an all-out schism? Wouldn't it be simpler and safer to just wave a new saint through the pearly gates? But then everyone would try to get their grandparents canonized. And if everyone is a saint, nobody is. Consequently, the church appointed someone to the office of the promoter of the faith—*devil's advocate* is just a popular term—whose job was to systematically oppose what would otherwise turn into a runaway train. The office no longer plays this role in the Catholic canonization process, although contrary testimony is still sought out.

The devil's advocate institutionalizes dissent. But designating one person as the official devil's advocate may not always be helpful, neither for the person nor for the organization. Even the orneriest contrarian risks burning out from carrying the burden of opposition alone. Meanwhile, from the organizational point of view, teams will gradually come to discount the predictions of Chicken Littles. It's better to create a climate and processes that allow dissent to emerge.

We already described one technique for sharing the devil's advocate role: using the round robin to require each team member to come up with both arguments for and, importantly, against the prevailing consensus, regardless of personal preference. Because of the team lead's outsized influence, it makes sense for the leader to take on, at best, a facilitating role in that discussion and to abstain from sharing their own views until a later point. Alternatively, as we already suggested, the leader can stay out of the discussion entirely until dissenting views have emerged.

For everyday team decisions—where the team *isn't* led by a sociopathic dictator or contemplating the zombie apocalypse—a simple technique can identify whether an emerging consensus is the result of groupthink: the **fist of five**. On the count of three, team members simultaneously raise their hands for all to see, showing the number of fingers corresponding to how enthusiastically they support a proposal. No fingers up means complete opposition; five fingers means you're willing to be its champion.

By making people raise their hands simultaneously, the fist of five exercise overcomes a vulnerability of the round robin, namely, that earlier voices tend to prejudice later ones. By indicating the degree of enthusiasm, the exercise can lead to better, more targeted deliberations. For example, suppose everyone agrees with the proposal, but nobody is enthusiastic. This unanimous but tepid response could be a sign the team is asking the wrong question: the proposal might be a great solution to an irrelevant problem. Meanwhile, people who struggle to articulate their misgivings can register the strength of their opposition, and then the team can help the more reticent colleagues express themselves. And if the team members unanimously express five-fingered enthusiasm for the proposal, then they should realize they may have succumbed to groupthink and need to make a concerted effort to come up with a contrary position.

When a team's decision hinges on forecasting using quantitative data, a more sophisticated approach similar to fist of five can be quite powerful: individually using the data to make private forecasts, then aggregating the results and measuring both the average forecast and the variance between individual forecasts. Our favorite professor at Harvard Business School, Jan Hammond, pioneered this approach when working with the CEO of sporting goods company Sport Obermeyer. Hammond observed that in meetings where market forecasters had to predict the upcoming season's color preferences for sporting goods, the dominant voices consistently skewed the consensus forecast. The fix was to let team members write down their forecast privately—without discussion—and then average the opinions.

This approach significantly improved the accuracy of the forecast. Moreover, statistically minded team members were now able to use the standard deviation—a simple measure of how far apart the forecasts were from each other—to attach a level of confidence to the forecast. Tightly clustered forecasts indicated higher confidence; more dispersed forecasts indicated lower confidence. Measures like these can help teams recognize when it might make sense to gather more data before making an irrevocable decision.

## DIVERSITY

It's easy enough for a devil's advocate to yell, "I oppose!" Opposition isn't valuable, though, until it provides counterarguments, new data to inform the decision, and concrete alternatives. The opposition has to bring a fresh perspective. Teams that have worked together for a long time may have great rapport, but their members will also start to look at the world through remarkably similar lenses.

What's more, in many organizations, teams will be composed of people with similar backgrounds. The members will have similar educational and professional experiences just by virtue of the industry they are in. To top that off, when we hire people, most of us tend to choose people we think we'll get along with. In practice, that means we often hire people to whom we related quickly during an interview. We consequently wind up working with people who look, speak, think, and behave an awful lot like ourselves.

Our tendency to flock together with birds of a feather means that, historically, many people have been excluded from professions and positions of power for reasons that have nothing to do with their abilities. This exclusion has come at great cost to the people rejected, their communities, and society at large. How organizations today should include people from backgrounds that have been historically excluded is an important political question, one of the most important of our time.

In addition to the all-important issues of fairness, we have often seen firsthand that teams need **cognitive diversity** to collectively generate interesting new ideas, interesting new solutions to problems, and interesting new problems to begin with. Social scientist Scott Page defines **cognitive diversity** in four dimensions:

1. **Diverse perspectives:** different ways of representing situations and problems
2. **Diverse interpretations:** different ways of categorizing or partitioning perspectives
3. **Diverse heuristics:** different ways of generating solutions to problems
4. **Diverse predictive models:** different ways of inferring cause and effect

In his book *The Difference*, Page shows how teams that exhibit cognitive diversity are better at solving certain types—though not all types—of problems. By combining different approaches to problem-solving—in fact, different understandings of what constitutes a problem—cognitively diverse teams are better at dealing with precisely the kinds of decisions we've characterized as interesting: those whose outcomes and probabilities are difficult to estimate.

Cognitive diversity is not the same thing as identity diversity, but as Page points out, hiring for identity diversity may help bring cognitive diversity into the team as well. In addition, hiring people with different educational backgrounds and from different fields will also diversify the cognitive range of the team. Forming a diverse team helps ensure that it can come up with divergent ideas and solutions.

> Forming diverse teams helps ensure that innovative ideas and solutions emerge.

It may still take some of the procedural approaches we've suggested in this chapter to ensure that those viewpoints get voiced and get attention. A high-performing team achieves its goals by using dissent, not by avoiding it or sweeping it under the carpet.

## CHAPTER 19 KEY TAKEAWAYS

Teams that come to consensus quickly and frequently may be suffering from groupthink. In a state of groupthink, dissenting views on a decision are withheld by people who are afraid of repercussions or simply don't want to disrupt team harmony.

Teams need a certain amount of friction to generate better information and better options and, in the long term, to maintain credibility, internally and externally.

Institutionalizing dissent may help protect teams from groupthink. The devil's advocate is a famous example; in practice, teams are better off sharing responsibility for raising dissent so that no single person faces reputational risk and so that the team doesn't form the habit of discounting that one person's dissent.

Building teams with cognitive diversity helps ensure that diverging views emerge. Hiring for identity diversity—itself a worthwhile goal—may also increase cognitive diversity.

# CONCLUSION

# CHAPTER 20

# Embracing Responsibility

On April 9, 2017, United Airlines personnel at Chicago O'Hare International faced a difficult but routine situation. Flight 3411, the last one flying to Louisville, Kentucky, for that day, was sold out and fully boarded. However, because of an unrelated delay, UA 3411 was the only way a United crew could get to Louisville in time to staff another flight the following morning. If the crew didn't make it to Kentucky, hundreds of travelers would experience delays the next day. Following procedure, local United staff tried to recruit volunteers for rebooking, and when they were unsuccessful, they took the next step. They selected four paying passengers—already seated—to be deboarded and rebooked involuntarily.

The decision to deboard customers wasn't really made at O'Hare on April 9. It had been made elsewhere and long before as a matter of corporate policy, a classic example of automated decision-making. And from the airline's perspective, the calculus of customer satisfaction is pretty simple: Hundreds of inconvenienced passengers outweigh four. But when you're one of the four whose priorities are sacrificed, you tend to see things a bit differently.

One of the four nonvolunteers was David Dao, a sixty-nine-year-old doctor who had patients to treat in Louisville the next day. He refused to leave the plane. The local United supervisor boarded the aircraft and threatened to have Dao removed by airport security officers. When Dao remained in his seat, the supervisor made good on her threat. In a dramatic collision of the numbers and people perspectives on business, Dao—struggling against his removal by security—sustained bloody injuries, including a broken nose and the loss of two front teeth.

All of this was filmed by other passengers on smartphones, videos that were soon uploaded to social media. Where, of course, they went viral.

United's CEO, Oscar Munoz, quickly responded the next day. Munoz had won trade magazine *PRWeek*'s Communicator of the Year award just weeks previously, so United shareholders might have hoped he'd make the best of what had become a public relations disaster in addition to a human disaster. They were sorely disappointed. Munoz euphemistically apologized for "reaccommodating" the four passengers. On top of that, he sent an internal email in which he not only affirmed his support for employees but also described Dao—whose face had just been reaccommodated to the shape of an armrest—as "disruptive and belligerent."

Internal emails are always just a click away from reaching the public. Within twenty-four hours, negative media attention was ubiquitous and customers were threatening boycotts. As you might expect after reading Part I, investor confidence in United's future cash flows plummeted. United Airlines saw its market value drop by nearly $1 billion.

On April 11, Munoz apologized for the email, and the next day, the CEO took a first public interview on *Good Morning America*, where he apologized directly to Dao. It was too little, too late. Munoz had been slated for a promotion to executive chair of the board, a promotion that was scuttled on April 21. Among the hundreds of news articles condemning United Airlines, one was in *PRWeek*, the very same publication that had named Munoz Communicator of the Year just weeks earlier. Editor in chief Steve Barrett wrote, "In time, the episode and subsequent response will be quoted in textbooks as an example of how not to respond in a crisis."

Although there are public relations lessons to be learned here, there's still more to be learned by looking deeper. How did Munoz go from Communicator of the Year to PR disaster in just a couple of weeks? Under what circumstances did United's Munoz write the email that seemed to place the responsibility for the incident on Dao?

United had merged with rival Continental Airlines in 2010. Mergers and acquisitions build on the kinds of shareholder value business cases we explored in Part I, but as often happens in mergers, the airline executives underestimated how difficult it would be to integrate the two workforces and management cultures. To realize the value-creation argument that had justified the merger, United's management focused on profitability in the years following the merger by cutting costs. Famously, even coffee cups were removed from break rooms. Thanks to the cultural integration difficulties and the ham-fisted cost cutting after the merger, United consistently ranked toward the bottom of US airlines when it came to employee satisfaction.

When he took the reins in 2015, Munoz was an airline industry outsider. He knew perfectly well that he lacked the expertise to solve all of United's many problems. One urgent and important problem, though, was employee morale. He believed that disengaged employees could not possibly bring smiles to customers' faces. To address the airline-specific problems, Munoz hired executives with complementary expertise and entrusted them with decision-making authority in areas like pricing and operations. Then he threw his own energy into employee well-being. The move paid off. Within months, he had helped resolve a key union negotiation.* These efforts are what had earned him the Communicator of the Year award.

When the Flight 3411 incident hit, Munoz had a choice: Join the outraged public, or choose the role of employee advocate. Publicly condemning the O'Hare team—the course of action that PR experts might have suggested—could have undone years of trust building with his team.

---

* He also brought back the coffee cups.

Although he took a drubbing in the press and United's stock value took one in the days after the incident, United did turn itself around in the long run. The stock price recovered, and Munoz eventually received the promotion to executive chair of the board of directors.*

Did his first instinct—to stick by the employees even at the cost of his public reputation—send the signal that finally welded the staff of United and Continental into one engaged workforce? Did Munoz ultimately thread the needle when it came to balancing the claims of all of United's stakeholders? Did he preserve or destroy shareholder value? What about stakeholder value?

> A company is a system of interlocking stakeholder interests. Sometimes those interests coincide, and sometimes they conflict.

We wish we could resolve questions like these conclusively, but in business, final answers will eternally evade us. Business is often compared to sports, and movements in a company's stock price are often framed in terms of winning and losing. But business is much more complex than a win-lose competition. A company is a system of interlocking stakeholder interests. Sometimes those interests coincide, and sometimes they conflict. The system is too complex, the uncertainty too unfathomable, to follow hard-and-fast rules of the game. Nor is there ever an endpoint at which you can declare a winner even if you wanted to.

## RESPONSIBILITY AVERSION

Perhaps the most difficult thing about managing a business is that managers have to make decisions on behalf of others. These decisions involve not just trade-offs between different stakeholders but also trade-offs between the present and the future.

---

* Munoz retired in 2021.

Individually, we're all capable of imagining the future and making painful choices today to realize our goals tomorrow. Choosing present pain for long-term gain is all well and good when you alone face the pain and reap the gain. But when your decisions impose costs on others, things get harder. Managers very often make choices whose consequences they don't bear themselves. The consequences are borne by the employee let go, the supplier squeezed, or the pension fund whose dividends dry up. Pains and gains cannot always be shared equally in an organization. As managers, we search for win-win solutions. Sometimes they are not on offer.

This challenge points to a necessary capability for managers: the willingness to make tough decisions on others' behalf. Recent research hints that we are, as humans, *responsibility averse*, that is, reluctant to make decisions that impose burdens on others. Imposing a burden exacts a psychological toll on us. The same research indicates that some people may be less averse to responsibility, more willing to make decisions that impose costs on others. These less responsibility-averse people naturally self-select into leadership positions. One might conclude that only people with certain psychological profiles are suited to management positions, and perhaps not the most attractive profiles. Here's where you can cue the media hysterics about psychopathic and narcissistic CEOs, incapable of empathy!

## MANAGEMENT IS A CALLING

We suggest a different approach. Do not limit your career ambitions because you are averse to imposing costs on others. If you don't embrace responsibility, someone else will. That someone might not understand that management is about building trust and keeping promises, about overcoming the social dilemmas that prevent us from achieving moon shots and bake sales, about structuring decision-making so that it leads to aligned action, and about creating sustainable value for all stakeholders.

The world is full of problems and opportunities that cannot be addressed without pooling our resources, our knowledge, and our diverse and quirky talents. As managers, we not only help solve problems and create delightful things. We also shape the workplace environment where we spend a good portion of our lives, making it a place where we can all experience the sheer joy of collaboration and build deeply meaningful relationships.

For the global companies we've served and for the thousands of managers we've had the privilege of training, the limiting factor is rarely their expertise in sales, marketing, production, delivery, research, HR, legal, or any other functional specialization dictated by the division of labor's relentless logic. The limiting factor is the ability to see the forest for the trees and to see it both as a collection of measurable resources—the numbers—and as a web of relationships—the people—at one and the same time.

Management is challenging, at times frustrating, but ultimately one of the most rewarding callings we can answer. More than anything else, we hope the ideas presented in this book will encourage you to take the next rung up the management ladder with both humility and confidence.

# NEXT STEPS

*Practice Your Skills at www.12weekmba.com*

**C**ongratulations: You've reached the end of the book! So... Now what?

As authors, we know that "mastery" of "business administration" only comes with practice in the real-world and not from a book or a two-year academic program. We learn by doing and, ultimately, that means learning from mistakes. A whole career's worth of trial, error, and, eventually, success.

Wouldn't it be nice to accelerate that process by running some of those trials in a safe laboratory environment before experimenting in the workplace?

This book's *content* is based on The 12-Week MBA by Abilitie, the leadership development company we founded in 2015. At the core of that program is the idea of a learning laboratory. In the lab, you get to apply all the "numbers" and "people" concepts discussed in the book. Specifically, participants in The 12-Week MBA will:

- exchange ideas and experiences with a group of **peers**,
- explore concepts with **faculty** who have a real-world business background,
- test-drive insights in business **simulations** that are both competitive and collaborative,
- practice management conversations using **ground-breaking generative AI**,

- connect with an active and growing **alumni network**, and
- take away insights, skills, and tools to demonstrate **readiness to lead** in a business.

The 12-Week MBA takes place online in webinars, workshops, and discussion groups, and it is supplemented with self-study resources. The core experience is run across—you guessed it—twelve weeks, but there are options to stitch together different modules to fit the constraints of your schedule.

Check out the details at **www.12weekmba.com**, and accelerate your learning journey!

# APPENDIX

## *Food Truck Financial Statements*

**C**hapters 5 and 6 used hypothetical figures for two years of operations of our grilled cheese food truck. The numbers were selected for simplicity, not for realism! Other simplifications include the omission of taxation (convenient but highly unrealistic) and research and development expenses (probably realistic for your garden-variety food truck business).

All figures are in US dollars.*

| Profit and Loss Statement | | |
|---|---|---|
| | Y1 | Y2 |
| Net sales | 240,000 | 540,000 |
| Cost of sales | 60,000 | 120,000 |
| SG&A | 60,000 | 120,000 |
| Depreciation | 2,000 | 4,000 |
| Interest | 2,500 | 2,500 |
| **Net profit** | **115,500** | **293,500** |

---

* Abbreviations: A/P = accounts payable; A/R = accounts receivable; PP&E = plants, property, and equipment; SG&A = selling, general, and administrative expenses.

| Balance Sheet | | |
|---|---|---|
| | **Y1** | **Y2** |
| **Current assets** | **70,000** | **210,000** |
| Cash | 65,000 | 175,000 |
| Inventory | 5,000 | 10,000 |
| A/R | 0 | 25,000 |
| **Noncurrent assets** | **38,000** | **74,000** |
| PP&E | 40,000 | 80,000 |
| Cumulative depreciation | −2,000 | −6,000 |
| **Total assets** | **108,000** | **284,000** |
| **Current liabilities** | **7,500** | **12,500** |
| A/P | 5,000 | 10,000 |
| Current portion of loan | 2,500 | 2,500 |
| **Noncurrent liabilities** | **20,000** | **17,500** |
| Bank loan | 20,000 | 17,500 |
| **Shareholders' equity** | **80,500** | **254,000** |
| Paid-in capital | 25,000 | 25,000 |
| Retained earnings | 55,500 | 229,000 |
| **Total liabilities & equity** | **108,000** | **284,000** |

| Cash Flow Statement | | |
|---|---:|---:|
| | Y1 | Y2 |
| **Operating cash flow** | **117,500** | **272,500** |
| Net profit | 115,500 | 293,500 |
| Depreciation | 2,000 | 4,000 |
| Change in A/R | 0 | −25,000 |
| Change in inventory | −5,000 | −5,000 |
| Change in A/P | 5,000 | 5,000 |
| **Investment cash flow** | **−40,000** | **−40,000** |
| Capital expenditures | −40,000 | −40,000 |
| **Financing cash flow** | **−12,500** | **−122,500** |
| Debt issued/repaid | 22,500 | −2,500 |
| Equity issued | 25,000 | 0 |
| Dividends | −60,000 | −120,000 |
| **Beginning cash** | **0** | **65,000** |
| **Net cash flow** | **65,000** | **110,000** |
| **End cash** | **65,000** | **175,000** |

# GLOSSARY

**accounts payable:** The value of payments to suppliers outstanding based on goods or services delivered and invoiced. Accounts payable are recorded on the balance sheet among the current liabilities.

**accounts receivable:** The value of customer payments outstanding based on goods or services delivered and invoiced. Accounts receivable are recorded on the balance sheet among the current assets.

**accrual accounting:** An accounting method whereby sales and operating expenses are recognized and recorded in a P&L statement; it is based on when customers receive the goods or services, or when the expenses were incurred, not on when cash payments were made.

**action bias:** A preference for undertaking externally visible action in situations characterized by uncertainty, as opposed to taking no action or observing and reflecting while waiting for further action-guiding data.

**agreement versus alignment:** In a decision-making context, two or more parties are in agreement when they all prefer the same course of action; in contrast, they are aligned when they all commit to supporting or executing the course of action selected, regardless of their own individual preferences. Usually, to achieve alignment, the parties have to universally agree that the decision-making process is legitimate.

**amortization:** The systematic allocation of the acquisition cost of an intangible asset over its useful life. It is an expense recorded in the P&L statement, although it may be attributed to the main expense categories, depending on the use of the asset. The rate of amortization will typically be determined by an accounting standard for the type of asset.

**assets:** Resources that are owned by an individual or organization and that have a monetary value and can be used to generate future benefits. Assets are recorded in a company's balance sheet and constitute one side of the balance.

**assets, intangible:** Nonphysical resources held by a company for the purposes of generating future benefits. Intangible assets include patents, licenses, and rights.

**assets, tangible:** Physical resources held by a company for the purposes of generating future benefits. These assets include real estate, equipment, and tools.

**balance sheet:** One of the three main financial reports that publicly traded companies must release to shareholders and file with regulators (e.g., the US Securities and Exchange Commission). The balance sheet (sometimes referred to as the statement of financial position) lists a company's assets on one side and the claims that others have on those assets on the other side, either as liabilities (for creditors) or equity (for ownership claims).

**bankruptcy:** The legal process whereby individuals or businesses unable to fulfill their financial obligations to creditors can seek relief while allowing creditors to recover as much of their claim as possible. In bankruptcy proceedings, the debtor's assets are liquidated to pay off as much outstanding debt as possible. In a company bankruptcy, any proceeds of the asset liquidation exceeding the claims of creditors are retained by the company's owners.

**breakeven analysis:** A quantitative business tool used to determine the sales volume required to exactly cover both fixed and variable costs. At the breakeven point, sales and total expenses are exactly in balance; profit is zero. Below the breakeven point, the company generates a loss; above it, a profit. Breakeven analysis helps entrepreneurs determine the commercial viability of an offering and its pricing strategy.

**bundle:** To sell two or more products or services as a package with a single price to provide greater customer value and to increase sales.

**cannibalization (business):** The result of competition between a single company's products, one of which is a lower-priced, lower-margin offering that reduces the company's overall sales and profits by outperforming a higher-priced, higher-margin offering.

**capital (financial):** Financial resources provided by investors to a company to fund assets that provide a future stream of benefits.

**cash-based accounting:** A simple accounting method that reports only cash transactions. Cash-based accounting is used by some small business with simple business models. It may provide a misleading picture of a company's financial health when a business model involves significant disjoints between the timings of economic activities—such as delivery of goods and services to customers, payments to suppliers, and consumption of assets—and the timings of cash flows.

**cash flow model:** A description of the monetary impacts of a business project that reports cash flow benefits and cash expenditures and the times at which they occur. A cash flow model is usually created on a spreadsheet and can be used to calculate a project's NPV, to communicate with stakeholders, and to plan financing.

**cash flow statement:** One of the three main financial reports that publicly traded companies must release to shareholders and file with regulators (e.g., the US Securities and Exchange Commission). The cash flow statement reports what cash payments have flowed into and out of the company's accounts over a specific period, usually a quarter or a year.

**closing the loop:** A procedure in communications whereby the sender and receiver of a message jointly ensure that the sender's intent was conveyed accurately to the receiver by having the receiver report the impact back to the sender.

**cognitive diversity:** Intragroup differences in perspectives, interpretations, problem-solving approaches, and predictive modeling approaches.

**common-sizing:** Transforming currency-denominated financial results (such as gross profit in US dollars) into percentages relative to a common base amount (such as sales in US dollars). Common-sizing allows for better comparability between different products or business units, or between companies, over time. P&L statement line items are usually common-sized relative to the sales figure, for example, gross margin (gross profit per sales).

**conditional cooperators:** People who, in a social dilemma, are willing to forgo individual short-term advantage in the interest of collective goals only if they believe that all other interaction partners are doing likewise, that is, that no interaction partners are pursuing individual advantage at the expense of the collective goals.

**consensus:** A collective decision-making process that selects a course of action other than a default or status quo option only if all participants formally agree with that course of action.

**content trap:** A group behavioral preference for focusing on the content of a decision—the options, the impacts, the probabilities—before and even to the exclusion of focusing on the process by which the decision will be made.

**continuing value:** An asset's value at a future date; the value is based on an estimation of the future net cash flows it will generate beyond that date. The continuing value takes into account the future net cash flow, the rate at which it is expected to grow, and the cost of capital.

**contribution margin:** The difference between the unit price of an offering and its unit variable cost. When the contribution margin is positive—when the price is higher than the variable cost—it is at least theoretically possible to sell an adequate volume to cover fixed costs. If the contribution margin is negative, no volume of sales will generate a profit.

**cost of capital:** The minimum return on investment required by investors to compensate them for the risk inherent in the investment and the time value of money.

**cost of sales:** Direct costs involved in producing and delivering whatever the company sells to its customers, whether that be a good or service. Cost of sales includes raw materials, labor, and production or delivery-related fixed costs. It is used to calculate a company's gross profit and gross margin and is a component of operating expenses. Companies whose main business involves selling goods may call this expense the cost of goods sold, and those selling services, the cost of services.

**cost structure:** The relative weighting of fixed and variable costs in a company's business model. Cost structure determines how variability in sales leads to variability in profitability. A higher proportion of variable costs allows a business to control costs as sales volumes decrease or when they are difficult to predict. A higher proportion of variable costs allows a business to increase profitability as sales volumes increase, but can lead to higher losses when sales volumes fall short of expectations.

**current assets:** Resources that a company expects to convert into cash or to consume within one year or one operating cycle, whichever is longer. Current assets include cash itself, accounts receivable, inventories, and short-term debt securities held by the company. Current assets represent the company's ability to meet its short-term obligations and cash flow needs. They are reported in the company's balance sheet.

**current liabilities:** Debt and other liabilities that a company expects to have to repay in the coming twelve months. Current liabilities include accounts payable, short-term debt, and the current portion of long-term debt. They are reported in the company's balance sheet.

**current portion of long-term debt:** Contractually scheduled repayments of the principal of long-term debt in the following twelve months. Some portion of long-term debt may be current either because the principal is amortized over the course of the loan or because the repayment deadline of what was originally a long-term loan is now less than twelve months off.

**customer payment terms:** The contractually agreed-on conditions for how and when a company's customer will pay for goods and services provided by the company. Typical payment terms allow for the customer to pay net 15 (fifteen days after the invoice date) or net 30, net 60, or net 90.

**customer segmentation:** A marketing strategy in which a given customer group is subdivided into smaller segments according to common needs and preferences to tailor offerings and marketing messages more precisely to the needs of each segment.

**debt:** Financial obligations of an individual or a company toward creditors. Debt is usually defined by its principal (the amount to be repaid), its duration (the period over which repayment must be completed), and a rate of interest to compensate the creditor for the time value of money and the risk-free rate forgone.

**default:** The situation in which a borrower is unable to meet its contractual obligations to creditors, usually by failing to make a payment of either principal or interest or both on a contractually defined date.

**depreciation:** The systematic allocation of the acquisition cost of a tangible asset over its useful life. It is an expense recorded in the P&L statement, although it may be attributed to the main expense categories, depending on the use of the asset. The rate of depreciation will typically be determined by an accounting standard for the type of asset.

**devil's advocate:** In collective decision-making, a procedural approach to ensure that early, easy, and biased consensus views (groupthink) are challenged with dissenting perspectives and interpretations. The devil's advocate institutionalizes dissent by investing responsibility for dissent in a particular person, in a subgroup, or even in the entire decision-making body.

Glossary

**discounted cash flow (DCF) analysis:** A tool of financial mathematics used to value uncertain future flows of cash to make investment decisions. DCF analysis involves projecting net cash flows over a finite or infinite horizon and discounting those cash flows to their present value using the cost of capital.

**discounting (financial):** Recognizing that, because of the cost of capital, today's value of a future cash flow must be lower than that future cash flow's nominal value.

**disruption (in business):** A rapid and profound change in market dynamics; often incited by technological or business model innovation. Disruption is usually characterized by significant change in customer behavior and changes in market share, often in favor of new market entrants and at the expense of incumbents.

**dividend:** A cash payment distributed to a company's owners; usually funded by the company's operating cash flows. The amount and timing of dividend payments is usually decided by a company's board of directors, who represent shareholder interests or are shareholders themselves.

**dumping (in business):** The business practice of selling a product or service at a loss to gain market share and drive competitors out of the market, at which point prices can be increased to profitable levels. In the case of exporting companies attempting to drive domestic companies out of their home markets, dumping may be prohibited by law or international trade agreement.

**engagement:** An employee's willingness to deploy discretionary effort toward achieving organizational goals, over and above what is spelled out in a job description. The Gallup organization distinguishes between three broad categories of engagement: "Engaged" employees are willing to deploy discretionary effort. Employees who are "not engaged" comply with the minimum formal standards demanded of them. "Actively disengaged" employees hinder the achievement of organizational goals.

**equity (financial):** Broadly speaking, an ownership interest in a company or an asset. On the balance sheet, equity refers to the residual value of a company to its owners if its assets are sold off and the proceeds are used to extinguish creditor claims. The term *equities* is also used to refer to the investment asset class of shares (or stocks) of corporations.

**expected value:** The long-run average value of the outcome of a probabilistic event; calculated by multiplying each mutually exclusive outcome by its probability of occurrence and adding up the results.

**expenses:** Resources consumed by a company over a period; includes materials, labor, cash, and the partial consumption of long-term tangible and intangible assets.

**factoring:** A financial service in which a nonfinancial company sells its accounts receivable to a financial services company at a discount to rapidly generate cash and avoid the risk of customer nonpayment.

**first team, second team:** A framework described by Patrick Lencioni; distinguishes between the team you lead and the team your manager leads. The collective interests of your first and second teams may conflict; organizations with a culture in which managers consistently prioritize the pursuit of their first-team goals over those of their second teams will be better able to achieve global organizational goals and avoid internal conflicts such as turf wars.

**fist of five:** A basic tool of collective decision-making in which individuals signal their degree of support for a proposed course of action

271

by simultaneously displaying a number of fingers on a single hand. No fingers displayed indicates strict opposition; five fingers displayed indicates the willingness to be a champion for the proposal.

**fixed costs:** Expenses that do not vary with changes in production or sales levels in a given period. Examples include rental fees for equipment or real estate and salaries.

**forming, storming, norming, performing:** A model of team development described by Bruce Tuckman. As teams first begin collaborating (forming), conflicts emerge (storming). Teams that introduce rules of engagement to manage conflict (norming) can eventually take advantage of their individual strengths, coordinate action, and use disagreement productively (performing).

**free cash flow:** Cash available to a company after it has made good on all its commitments to employees, suppliers, creditors, and tax authorities and has invested in any capital necessary to maintain its current level of business. Free cash flow can then be distributed to shareholders, used to pay down debt, or deployed to pursue growth opportunities.

**gross margin:** The ratio of a company's gross profit to its sales in a given period. The gross margin is expressed as a percentage.

**gross profit:** The value of a company's sales over a given period less the value of its cost of sales.

**groupthink:** A group behavior phenomenon in which groups reach apparent consensus on a proposed course of action not because all participants agree but because each individual person believes that the others agree with the proposal, and no one wants to be the person who destroys the harmonious collaboration by voicing dissent. First named and described by Irving Janis.

**growth, inorganic:** Increases in a company's sales volumes achieved solely by incorporating the sales of another business acquired or merged into the company.

**growth, organic:** Increases in a company's sales volumes achieved by attracting new customers, convincing existing customers to buy more, or releasing new offerings developed in-house.

**inflation:** The decline in the purchasing power of a given unit of national currency over time. This expected decline is one reason investors will prefer present cash to future cash; hence, inflation is an input to the cost of capital.

**innovator's dilemma:** A concept in innovation. Described by Clayton Christensen, the innovator's dilemma explains why established incumbent companies are often unable to introduce groundbreaking innovations or respond to those of upstart challengers. Incumbents are slow to introduce truly groundbreaking (as opposed to incremental) innovations, because in the short term, their existing customer base is not interested in the innovation and because its introduction would only replace existing, profitable, and reliable sales with less profitable and more uncertain sales.

**intent versus impact:** In communication theory, the observation that a message a person sends to another may have an impact that the first person neither intended nor anticipated.

**interest:** The compensation paid to lenders for the use of financial resources (the principal), usually over a specific time and at a specific rate of interest. The rate of interest, or interest rate (usually expressed as a percentage), is applied to the principal amount of a loan to determine the interest paid by a borrower to a lender. The rate is in proportion to the perceived risk of the borrower's defaulting on the loan.

**intrinsic value:** The value of any asset, including shares of a company. It is based on the expected net cash flows the asset will earn over its useful life, even if that life is indefinitely long. Intrinsic value is based only on the asset's projected cash flows and not on speculation about how others might value the asset in the future.

**inventory:** A company's raw materials, unfinished goods, and finished goods not yet delivered to a customer. Inventory's monetary value is reported on a company's balance sheet as a current asset and may also be referred to as stock.

**investments:** The commitment of financial resources to a less liquid tangible or intangible asset for the purpose of generating a stream of future benefits.

**investor:** A person making an investment. Investors may be lenders who provide funds in a specific amount, for a specific time, and with a defined rate of interest. Alternatively, they may be equity investors (owners) who invest to extract cash flows, funded either by profits or by the resale of the investment asset to another equity investor.

**legitimacy (political):** A property of systems of authority; authorities that enjoy legitimacy can be reasonably confident that their decisions will be executed by their subordinates regardless of whether the subordinates share the authority's preferences. Sociologist Max Weber distinguished between charismatic, traditional, and legal (procedural) foundations of legitimate authority.

**liabilities:** Financial obligations or debt owed by an individual or organization to a creditor. Liabilities may or may not be interest-bearing. They are recorded on a company's balance sheet.

**majority rule:** A collective decision-making procedure in which participants individually select their preferred course of action, and the group agrees to abide by the most frequently preferred outcome. Majority rule can encompass many different voting procedures, including simple majority, supermajority, plurality, and ranked-choice voting.

**mergers and acquisitions (M&A):** Changes in the ownership structure of two companies. In a merger, two legal entities merge governance and operations into a new, combined entity. In an acquisition, one company takes control of another's assets and assumes responsibility for its liabilities. M&A activity is premised on the assumption that the new whole will create greater value for its shareholders than the sum of its parts, for example, by eliminating redundant expenses, increasing market power with respect to customers and suppliers, or providing greater predictability of results by integrating complementary business models.

**net cash flow:** The sum of all cash flows into and out of a company over a specific time.

**net margin:** The ratio of a company's net profit to its sales in a given period. The net margin is expressed as a percentage.

**net present value (NPV):** The sum of the present values of all of the present and expected future cash flows associated with an investment.

**net profit:** The value of a company's sales minus all its expenses over a period.

**noncurrent assets:** Company assets that are not among its current assets. That is, noncurrent assets are not expected to be converted into cash over the next twelve months or the company's operating cycle, whichever is longer. Noncurrent assets include plants, property, and equipment, as well as intangible assets such as patents, licenses, and rights.

**noncurrent liabilities:** Company liabilities that are not among its current liabilities. That is, the holder of the claim on which the liability is based cannot demand realization of that claim within the next twelve months. The primary examples are debt for which principal payments are not due in the next twelve months, and equity, which usually does not involve a contractually defined payment schedule.

**operating expenses:** The value of all resources consumed in the standard operations of a company over a period. Operating expenses include all expenses except for interest payments, taxes, and extraordinary losses.

**operating margin:** The ratio of a company's operating profit to its sales in a given period. The operating margin is expressed as a percentage.

**operating profit:** The value of a company's sales minus its operating expenses over a period.

**option value:** The value that a decision-maker sees in retaining the opportunity to take a future action without the obligation to do so. Possession of cash affords the opportunity to take a near-infinite range of future actions, including both investments and consumption. The option to choose among these opportunities is lost when a single one of those opportunities is chosen. This loss of option value is one reason investors prefer present cash over future cash, and so option value is one of the inputs to the cost of capital.

**overhead:** Business expenses unrelated to the production or delivery of any individual product or service in a business's portfolio.

**paid-in capital:** Financial and other resources invested in a company by its owners when the company is first incorporated. Paid-in capital appears on the balance sheet as a contributor to equity. When a company raises additional resources from equity investors after its initial incorporation, this may appear in the balance sheet as additional paid-in capital.

**perpetuity:** An investment that promises a fixed, regular cash payment that continues to flow indefinitely.

**plants, property, and equipment (PP&E):** Physical assets (including real estate) that a company owns and deploys over a long time horizon to create its goods and services. The monetary value of PP&E is reported as an asset on a company's balance sheet and is depreciated over the useful life of each asset.

**plus/delta exercise:** A simple group reflection exercise used to appraise a group's effectiveness and to discover areas of improvement for collective action. Each member of the group is invited to contribute something they think the team is currently doing well and should do more of (a *plus*) and something the team ought to do differently in the future (a *delta*). Pluses and deltas are listed in columns on a whiteboard by a moderator and are referred to later to determine whether progress has occurred.

**presence:** The mental state of focus on, and awareness of, one's immediate surroundings in the present, including especially the people with whom one is interacting in the moment; as opposed to a mental state in which one is preoccupied with reviewing past events or projecting future ones.

**present value:** The value of a future cash flow discounted to today's terms in proportion to the cost of capital.

**process guardian:** A (usually informal) role dedicated to observing the team's behavior and calling attention to deviations from the team's agreed-on norms and procedures. Timekeeping, moderation of group exercises, and facilitation of discussions are examples of tasks done by the process guardian.

**profit:** Generally, the difference between the value of a company's sales and the value of the resources consumed over a period.

**profit and loss statement (P&L):** One of the three main financial reports that publicly traded companies must release to shareholders and file with regulators (e.g., the US Securities and Exchange Commission). The P&L statement (sometimes referred to as the income statement) displays a company's sales and expenses over a specific period, usually a quarter or a year.

**public goods:** Goods and services that are nonexcludable (nobody can be prevented from using them) and nonrivalrous (one person's use of them does not reduce the availability or quality of the goods for other people). Examples include air and water, public spaces, defense and public safety. Public goods are usually funded by governments through taxation.

**razor blade model:** A business model in which a company sells a long-lived product that locks the customer into buying additional accessory products or services to maintain the product's usefulness. The initial product is often sold at a price close to its production cost, and the accessories are sold at a substantial profit margin. The business model is named after the example in which customers buy a razor and then have to buy the replacement razor blades from the same provider.

**research and development (R&D):** A company's activities directed toward creating new offerings or improving existing ones, from the perspective of enhancing their customer value or reducing production costs, or both. The monetary value of the resources (including materials and labor) consumed in R&D is frequently reported as a separate line item among the operating expenses in the P&L statement.

**retained earnings:** A company's cumulative net profits that have not yet been distributed to its investors. Retained earnings are a contributor to equity on a corporate balance sheet.

**return on investment:** The ratio of the net benefit an investor earns from an investment to the monetary value of the up-front investment. The return on investment is usually expressed as a percentage.

**round robin:** A group exercise designed to elicit ideas and information from all members of the group, including those who less readily share their thoughts in larger gatherings. Each team member is given a set amount of time to speak, without interruption, in a specific order and without interruption from anyone outside of that order. The round robin works both by eliciting input from those who hold back their thoughts and by restraining those who otherwise tend to dominate the conversation.

**sales:** Goods and services sold to customers, or the value thereof in monetary terms.

**selling, general, and administrative expenses (SG&A):** The value of resources consumed in convincing customers to choose a company's good or service (selling and marketing expenses) and in running the business irrespective of either production or selling activities (general and administrative expenses). SG&A is a component of operating expenses.

**shareholder:** A person or an organization that owns one or more shares of stock in a company.

**shareholder value:** The value created by a company for its owners through the expectation of future cash flows from either dividends or from a future sale of the ownership stake to another investor. Shareholder value originates in a company's discounted future net cash flows.

**short-term debt:** Interest-bearing loans with maturities of twelve months or less. Short-term debt is reported as a current liability in a company's balance sheet.

**social dilemma:** An interaction in which two or more parties can coordinate their actions to achieve a beneficial outcome for the collectivity, but in which the individual parties may jeopardize that collective benefit by pursuing narrower individual goals. Examples include the provision of public goods and the conservation of scarce resources. These examples are also known under the terms *tragedy of the commons* and the *prisoner's dilemma*. In the most pernicious social dilemmas, individual parties pursue their own goals not because the parties are self-regarding but because they fear that others are and they know that the collective goal can only be achieved if everyone contributes to it. Social dilemmas can be overcome by altering the individual outcomes through incentives (both rewards and penalties) to better align collective and individual interests. Alternatively, they can be overcome through acts of leadership that instill the belief that all parties will work to achieve the collective benefit.

**sole decider:** A collective decision-making procedure in which a single person retains decision-making rights; it is a collective procedure insofar as the members of the group recognize the sole decider's decision as legitimate and binding even if they individually disagree with it.

**taxes:** Payments made by individuals or organizations to governments of the jurisdictions in which they reside or in which they are economically active. Taxes are among the nonoperating expenses of a company.

**time value of money:** The fundamental idea that cash held in the present is more valuable than the same amount held in the future, attributed to the fact that there are usually risk-free savings options that return some level of interest.

**trade working capital:** The amount of capital a company requires to fund its day-to-day operations of buying from suppliers and selling to customers. Trade working capital is defined as the combined value of a company's accounts receivable and inventory minus its accounts payable.

**two-pizza rule:** A general rule for team size attributed to Amazon's Jeff Bezos, namely, that no team should be so large that it takes more than two (American-sized) pizzas to feed it.

**variable cost:** A business expense that changes in direct proportion to an underlying target quantity, usually a production or sales volume. Examples include raw materials, direct labor expenses, and sales commissions.

**working capital:** The difference between the monetary values of a company's current assets and its current liabilities.

**zero-sum game:** A strategic interaction in which one interaction partner's gain is exactly offset by the total losses of all the other partners in the interaction. Competition for market share in a static or shrinking market is an example of a zero-sum game.

# NOTES

## PREFACE

xi     **hundreds of thousands of smart, ambitious people enroll in MBA programs annually:** The number of master's degrees conferred in the United States in 2018–2019 was 197,089 (National Center for Educational Statistics, "Digest of Education Statistics").

xiv     **When Harvard established the first MBA class in 1908:** See Cruikshank, *Delicate Experiment.*


## INTRODUCTION

xix     **they split the iconic US conglomerate into three companies:** See General Electric Company, "GE Plans to Form Three Public Companies."


## CHAPTER 1: VALUE

3     **both the "biggest" and the "dumbest" idea in business:** For the "biggest," see "Analyse This," *Economist.* For the "dumbest," see Denning, "Shareholder Value, 'the World's Dumbest Idea.'"

4n     **In 1998, their fund—Long-Term Capital Management—famously went belly-up and nearly dragged the whole financial system with it:** Lowenstein, *When Genius Failed,* is an excellent account of the debacle, whose effects reverberated all the way into the great financial crisis of 2007–2008.

6n     **Whether stockholders of a publicly traded company are truly its owners in the same sense that you might own your house or your phone is a matter of some controversy:** For an insightful discussion about how property rights, including ownership of shares in corporations, have been encoded in law, see Pistor, *The Code of Capital.*

9     **In its 2007 annual report, Nokia summarized what looked like a spectacular year:** See Nokia Corporation, *Nokia in 2007.*

## CHAPTER 3: GROWTH

**28n** **Whether share buybacks or dividends are more advantageous, and for whom, is a matter of some controversy:** See, for example, Ritholtz, "Fans and Foes of Buybacks."

**31** **The Pet Rock phenomenon in 1975:** See Woo, "Gary Dahl Dies at 78."

**33** **In 2004, Nokia pondered these questions as it evaluated something its R&D labs had created: a touchscreen, internet-ready phone:** See O'Brien, "Nokia's New Chief."

**35** **Holcim's 2020 annual report has a helpful discussion by the CEO Jan Jenisch, framed as an interview:** See LafargeHolcim, Ltd., *Integrated Annual Report 2020*, 8–9.

**36** **Cement manufacturing is a notoriously carbon-intensive process, by itself accounting for 8 percent of global greenhouse gas emissions:** See Lehne and Preston, *Making Concrete Change.*

## CHAPTER 4: RISK

**41n** **interpreting what probability *means* is a remarkably controversial subject:** See Gillies, *Philosophical Theories of Probability*, whose title alone signals that the idea of a probability can't be quite as simple as we'd like.

**49** **"The sense in which I am using the term is that in which the prospect of a European war is uncertain":** From Keynes, "General Theory of Employment," 213–214.

## CHAPTER 5: THE BALANCE SHEET

**51n** **John Coates's book:** Coates, *The Hour Between Dog and Wolf.*

**52** **Company P is Palantir Technologies, a US data analytics company that sports over $1 billion in annual sales but has never made a profit in its roughly two-decade existence:** See Palantir Technologies, *Annual Report 2021.*

**55** **In fact, our loan contract exercises an enormous amount of pressure on us to get to work:** Surprisingly, economists do not agree on what causes economic growth. What makes us work so diligently to collectively produce more and more goods and services every year? In their book *Ownership Economics*, Gunnar Heinsohn and Otto Steiger argue that the root cause of growth lies in the pressure felt by those who borrow. To keep their promises, borrowers simply have to produce more than they consume. The incessant pressure to keep promises generates a steady surplus that enriches the economy as a whole.

**64** **AT&T's 2021 balance sheet:** See AT&T Inc., *2021 Annual Report.*

## CHAPTER 6: CASH FLOW BASICS

**74n** **Many famous accounting scandals boil down to company accountants stretching the rules around sales and expense recognition to the breaking point and beyond:** See, for example, McLean and Elkind, *Smartest Guys in the Room.*

## CHAPTER 7: CASH FLOW AND WORKING CAPITAL

**86** **Netflix operated a website and a subscription service:** Based on Mayfield, "NetFlix .com, Inc."

**89** **Some retailers like Amazon can benefit from negative trade working capital:** In its 2021 annual report, Amazon reported inventories of $23,795 million, accounts receivable of $24,542 million, and accounts payable of $72,539 million, resulting in negative trade working capital of $24,202 million. That's over $24 billion of funding Amazon did *not* have to raise from investors! See Amazon.com, *Annual Report 2021.*

90    **The computer company Dell got started when Michael Dell took orders and credit card payments over the phone:** For a first-person account of the Dell story, see Dell, *Play Nice but Win.*

## CHAPTER 8: COST STRUCTURES

93    **"We expect our operating expenses to increase significantly in the foreseeable future":** Uber Technologies, Inc., *2021 Annual Report.*

96    **Josh Barro pointed out that the customer loyalty discounts Uber kept sending him must have driven the prices he was paying below the variable costs:** See Barro, "Congestion Pricing."

105    **Game console makers like Sony and Microsoft sell their consoles at low margins, sometimes even at prices below the production costs:** CEO of Microsoft Gaming, Phil Spencer, reported that "consoles are actually sold at a loss in the market. So when someone goes in to buy an Xbox at a local retailer, we're subsidizing that purchase somewhere between $100 to $200" (Spencer, "WSJ Interview").

106    **makers of (cheap) razors and their (expensive and very profitable) replacement blades:** Although the invention of the razor blade business model is attributed to Gillette, apparently its rivals first deployed this model, and only after Gillette's patents expired did it adopt the model itself. See Picker, "Razors-and-Blades Myth(s)."

106    **"We have to make sure the *unit economics* work before we go big":** Our emphasis added. The content of the internal email was reported on CNBC. See Bosa and Browne, "Uber Tells Staff."

106    **the $32 billion reported for 2022:** See 2022 annual report from Uber Technologies, Inc.: https://s23.q4cdn.com/407969754/files/doc_financials/2023/ar/2022-annual-report.pdf.

106    **a nominal profit midway through 2023:** See 2023 press release from Uber Technologies, Inc.: https://s23.q4cdn.com/407969754/files/doc_earnings/2023/q2/earnings-result/Uber-Q2-23-Earnings-Press-Release.pdf.

## CHAPTER 9: VALUATION FOUNDATIONS

109    **On April 19, 2022, the entertainment streaming service Netflix announced that for the first time ever, its subscriber base had declined:** See Netflix, Inc., "First Quarter 2022 Earnings."

110n    **The right book is *Valuation*:** See Koller et al., *Valuation.*

113n    **"recommend using a synthetic risk-free rate":** Koller et al., *Valuation,* 329.

## CHAPTER 10: CREATING VALUE

130    **When Netflix announced the loss of two hundred thousand subscribers on April 19, 2022, it also warned about the potential future loss of two million more:** See Netflix, Inc., "First Quarter 2022 Earnings," 4.

130    the previous forecast (issued on January 10 in the report for the last quarter of 2021) had been for the *growth* of 2.5 million subscribers for the first quarter: See Netflix, Inc., "Fourth Quarter 2021 Earnings," 2.

## CHAPTER 11: JOY AND FRUSTRATION

143    **Adam Smith's *Wealth of Nations* famously opens with the example of a pin factory:** See Smith, *Nature and Causes of the Wealth*, 12.

144    **It's exhilarating and terrifying:** For an exhilarating and terrifying look at exactly how exhilarating and terrifying our global division of labor is, check out Seabright, *Company of Strangers*.

145    ***theory of the firm:*** One of the most important papers on this subject was written by Roger Coase, winner of the Nobel Memorial Prize in Economic Sciences in 1937; his essay, its historical antecedents, and further development of the theory of the firm can be found in Putterman and Kroszner, *Economic Nature of the Firm*.

## CHAPTER 12: TRUST AND EXPECTATIONS

151    **Wiser heads than ours have written many books on delegation and trust:** A standard work about trust in the business world is Covey, *Speed of Trust*.

151    **As Thomas Hobbes suggested, society is at risk:** The classic quote from Hobbes's "Leviathan" that many have heard is that, in the state of nature in which we are all at war with each other, life is "nasty, brutish, and short." But more insightful is his portrait of our psychology that explains why we make war, not love: "So that in the nature of man we find three principal causes of quarrel: first, competition; secondly, diffidence [distrust]; thirdly, glory" (Hobbes, "Leviathan," 490).

151    **As famed investor Warren Buffett supposedly put it:** The quote "It takes twenty years to build a reputation and five minutes to ruin it" is widely attributed to Warren Buffett on the internet. Ah, the internet. The closest we've come to confirming the attribution is a video of a speech Buffett gave at the University of Nebraska in 2003, in which he shared that *Fortune* had recently ranked his company, Berkshire Hathaway, as the third-most-admired company in the United States and that "it took us thirty-seven years to get there but we could lose it in thirty-seven minutes," continuing that "you can lose it a lot faster than that; you can lose it in five minutes" (Buffett, "Warren Buffett Lecture"). The sentiment stands even if the legendary quote is not quite the same.

152    **Paul Hersey and Kenneth Blanchard's model called situational leadership:** See Hersey et al., *Management of Organizational Behavior*.

152n   ***The One Minute Manager:*** Blanchard and Johnson have updated their classic for the twenty-first century: *The New One Minute Manager*.

152    **"The manager represents in his *character* the obliteration of the distinction between manipulative and non-manipulative social relations":** MacIntyre, *After Virtue*. Italics in original.

## CHAPTER 13: ADVENTURES IN FEEDBACK

160    **"No matter how one may try, one cannot not communicate":** Watzlawick et al., *Pragmatics of Human Communication*.

161 **"feedback deserts":** Graeber, *Bullshit Jobs.*

162n **his book *Bullshit Jobs*:** Graeber, "What's the Point?"

162 **nor is the research that does exist conclusive:** See Lipnevich and Panadero, "Feedback Models and Theories," for a meta-analysis, albeit primarily in academic contexts.

163 **"People don't like being techniqued":** We got this expression from leadership coach Tom Hughes, with whom one of us codelivered an executive leadership program. When we reached out to Tom, though, he graciously refused to take credit, as he himself was quoting James Flaherty of New Ventures West Coaching.

163n **Watzlawick cites an example from his couples therapy:** Watzlawick et al., *Pragmatics of Human Communication*, 98.

165 **According to Gottman, the "magic ratio" of positive-to-negative interactions is five to one:** Gottman's multidecade research to this effect was summarized in Gottman, *What Predicts Divorce?* (first published in 1994).

165 **Cue the army of management consultants recommending a ratio of five items of praise for each item of criticism!:** Illustrating how difficult it is to make any simple statements about human interactions, Zenger and Folkman, "Ideal Praise-to-Criticism Ratio," cited a research paper that independently came up with something very close to Gottman's ratio for business teams: 5.6 to 1. That research (Losada and Heaphy, "Positivity and Connectivity") has since been discredited and retracted by the journal in which it was published. The currently available revised version of Zenger and Folkman's article now concludes with "Like many others, we were distressed to learn of the incorrect data in the Heaphy and Losada research and we immediately ceased our citations upon learning that the study wasn't correct. But we do believe the basic assumption and premise that leaders should provide more positive than negative feedback is correct."

168 **The second tool, called SBI, is a simple coaching and feedback framework developed by the Center for Creative Leadership:** Our company works in partnership with the Center for Creative Leadership, and their framework is open source. See Center for Creative Leadership, *Feedback That Works.*

## CHAPTER 14: ENGAGEMENT AND MOTIVATION

173 **in Gallup's words, an "ownership" mindset, a "drive [for] performance and innovation [to] move the organization forward":** Gallup, Inc., "Global Workplace 2022," 164. The Global Workplace Report gets updated annually, and the 2022 report on which we based this chapter is no longer available as of this book's publication. However, the latest report available (2023) has not substantively changed this language.

174 **a crisis of engagement:** As Gallup puts it dramatically, "The U.S.—and the world at large—is in the midst of an employee engagement crisis" (Gallup, Inc. "State of the American Workplace Report," 61). See previous note about the report.

174 **These companies also tend to have lower turnover, fewer industrial accidents, and higher customer loyalty:** Harter et al., "The Relationship Between Engagement at Work and Organizational Outcomes."

175 **the sheer joy of working together on something awesome:** For a fascinating discussion of play as an intrinsic good and fundamental driver of human (and animal) behavior, see Graeber, "What's the Point?"

175 **a very slow upward trend among engaged employees and a nearly constant proportion of actively disengaged:** See Gallup's own data, in which the percentage of engaged employees went from 26 percent in 2000 to 32 percent in 2022, with a high of 36 percent in 2020. Meanwhile, the actively disengaged proportion started at 18 percent in 2000 and was at 17 percent in 2022, with a high of 20 percent in 2008 and a low of 13 percent in 2018 (Harter, "Slump Continues").

178 **"The management gurus talk about motivating people":** Jenisch and Manzoni, "Become a Buddha."

180n **Improv theater guru Keith Johnstone places relative status at the heart of any scene:** Johnstone, *Impro.*

182n **"elevating the world's consciousness":** We Company, "Registration Statement," 127. For a highly entertaining—and also quite disturbing—dramatized rendition of WeWork's history, watch Apple TV's series *WeCrashed*, created by Drew Crevello and Lee Eisenberg.

182n **"Our mission is to empower tomorrow's world at work":** WeWork, Inc., *2021 Annual Report*, 5.

185 **one of the business world's buzzwords du jour was *quiet quitting*:** Our own company's leadership team had a discussion about the significance of quiet quitting, in light of Telford, "'Quiet Quitting.'"


## CHAPTER 15: LEADERSHIP

190 **John F. Kennedy's call to put a man on the moon:** We're referring to the famous 1962 speech at Rice University, in which he said, "We choose to go to the moon in this decade and do the other things, not because they are easy, but because they are hard." See Kennedy, "Rice University."

190 **"the art of getting someone else to do something that you want done because he wants to do it, not because your position of power can compel him to do it":** Eisenhower, "Remarks."

190 **something that business school professor Phil Rosenzweig dissects in his book *The Halo Effect*:** Rosenzweig, *Halo Effect.*

192 **social dilemma:** The concept of social dilemmas in game theory and behavioral economics has influenced our thinking about management and business to a degree that we simply cannot overstate. Perhaps the fact that our learning methodology is based on business games has something to do with that! In addition to the aforementioned Seabright, *Company of Strangers* and works we'll mention later in this chapter, Binmore, *Natural Justice*; Bowles, *Moral Economy*; Gintis, *Bounds of Reason*; Green, *Moral Tribes*; and Nida-Rümelin, *Die Optimierungsfalle* are all excellent resources and have left their mark on this book in too many ways to count.

192 **we are what behavioral economists call conditional cooperators:** In a highly influential laboratory study, behavioral economists Urs Fischbacher and Ernst Fehr found that, in a public goods game—an interaction designed to create a social dilemma—50 percent of test subjects behaved according to the conditional cooperation model, contributing more to the public good the more other participants did as well (Fischbacher et al., "Are People Conditionally Cooperative?").

195 **A case in point is GE:** The full story of the Welch years and GE's subsequent decline under its later CEOs is a story too complex to cover in just half a page. Our short ac-

count builds partly on David Gelles's extremely harsh verdict in Gelles, *The Man Who Broke Capitalism*, as well as two decades of news coverage such as Ritholtz, "Jeff Immelt Versus Jack Welch."

195n **Miller's book helped us recognize the underlying problem—social dilemmas:** See Miller, *Managerial Dilemmas*.

198n **their groundbreaking book *The Leadership Challenge:*** Kouzes and Posner, *The Leadership Challenge*.

199 **There is, however, a dark side to spotlighting individual performance to promote a cooperative culture:** Special thanks to our friend and collaborator Steven Tomlinson for this point. Steven's influence on our thinking, on our company, and on this book cannot be overstated.

## CHAPTER 16: COLLECTIVE ACTION AND DECISION-MAKING

203 **Blackwells Capital released a public slide deck:** Blackwells Capital, "Peloton: A Call for Action."

205 **Amazon CEO Jeff Bezos encourages the two-pizza rule:** As reported by Amazon Web Services in one of its white papers (Amazon Web Services [AWS], "Introduction to DevOps on AWS"). And who are we to question its reliability?

205n **Leadership expert Nick Obolensky explores the deeper significance of organizations' self-similarity:** See Obolensky, *Complex Adaptive Leadership*.

205 **Patrick Lencioni's wonderful leadership book *The Five Dysfunctions of a Team*:** See Lencioni, *Five Dysfunctions*, particularly 135–138.

207 **"series of interesting decisions":** Sid Meier gave a talk at the Game Developers Conference 2012. He attributed this definition ("a series of interesting decisions"), which had become popular on the internet, to an earlier talk he had given at the 1989 Game Developers Conference. See Meier, "Interesting Decisions."

211n **Bharat Anand, also wrote a fascinating book:** See Anand, *Content Trap*.

212 **forming, storming, norming, performing:** Tuckman, "Developmental Sequence."

## CHAPTER 17: DEFINING THE DECISION

215n **In some of our more advanced workshops with executives, we introduce a systems analysis framework called Cynefin:** For a brief overview of the Cynefin framework by its originator, David J. Snowden, and his collaborator Mary E. Boone, see Snowden and Boone, "A Leader's Framework." Snowden presents the core ideas in a nine-minute video as well; see Snowden, "Cynefin Framework."

215 **jump straight into execution in a small, revocable way to generate data to inform a bigger, irrevocable decision:** The basic ideas and method of asset valuation introduced in Part I have been further elaborated and applied to this very simple concept of getting your toes wet under the heading of so-called real option valuation. Those valuation methods can be used to measure the information value gained when a smaller initial investment sheds light on the probability of success of a larger, more uncertain investment. Morel, *Real Option Analysis*, provides a deep dive into real option valuation and its application to the global climate crisis. The book is interesting, profound, but not for the fainthearted!

217 *Högertrafikomläggningen*: Savage, "A 'Thrilling' Mission."

217    **game theory:** Gintis, *Bounds of Reason*, is as good a book as any you will find on introductory game theory and how game theory helps us understand the human condition.

217    **Porter's five forces:** To get it from the horse's mouth, see Porter, "Five Competitive Forces." In a nutshell, Porter suggests we look at the strategic interactions between a company and its customers, its suppliers, and three types of competitors (current competitors, potential new entrants, and substitute solutions). By analyzing the structure of those interactions, we can anticipate whether a given market provides opportunities to create value for shareholders. However, for a truly scathing takedown of Porter's ideas and his bankrupted consultancy Monitor Group, see Denning, "What Killed Michael Porter's Monitor Group?"

217    **the resource-based view:** Penrose, *Growth of the Firm*, is neither the hardest nor the easiest of reads, but there's an insight on pretty much every page. Broadly speaking, according to the resource-based view, companies need to look inward and identify the resources that give them a competitive advantage. The organization has to become "self-aware," so to speak, just like an individual, and understand what native strengths and weaknesses it brings to the table. Advantageous resources include obvious ones like access to natural resources, geographic location, and intellectual property rights but also include "resources" that are more people-oriented. These can include trusting relationships, for example, with customers, suppliers, and capital markets but also the ineffable qualities of a smoothly running leadership team.

218    **For business school professor Roger L. Martin, strategy "cascades" through the organization:** Martin, "Execution Trap."

219    **Jim Collins and Jerry Porras have elevated vision and values to causal elements in a company's abilities to enjoy enduring success:** Collins and Porras, "Building Your Company's Vision," the authors make this case in brief; their classic *Built to Last* features a discussion of their meticulous and voluminous research methodology in addition to their insights. As influential as Collins and Porras have been, however, they've also received an arguably very fair share of criticism. Business professor Phil Rosenzweig's brilliant dissection of the business world's obsession with success formulas (Rosenzweig, *Halo Effect*) cites nine pervasive delusions in business literature, finding fault in Collins and Porras, *Built to Last*, on at least four counts of delusion, most tellingly, the "Delusion of Rigorous Research."

220    **By 1969, however, rates had climbed back to where they were before the change:** Flock, "Dagen H."

220    **The title of Daniel Kahneman's best-selling book:** Kahneman, *Thinking, Fast and Slow*.

225    **Robert's Rules of Order:** See Robert et al., *Robert's Rules of Order*.

## CHAPTER 18: DELIBERATING AND EXECUTING

231    **the political concept of legitimacy:** For an excellent overview of the concept of political legitimacy, see Peter, "Political Legitimacy."

232    **Contrast that with exercise bike maker Peloton:** Blackwells Capital, "Peloton: A Call for Action," 34.

## CHAPTER 19: THE POWER OF DISSENT

240 **popularized by research psychologist Irving Janis in the 1970s:** Janis, *Victims of Groupthink.*

243 **The tenth man asked, "What if they really mean *zombies*?":** Forster, *World War Z.* The film's tenth-person principle is loosely based on an institutional and procedural response Israeli military planners adopted in the wake of the near-disastrous 1973 Yom Kippur War, when military intelligence had failed to correctly interpret the evidence that Israel's neighbors were preparing a coordinated attack. Israel's Military Intelligence Directorate deploys an entire devil's advocate unit, tasked with formulating interpretations and strategies contrary to those of the main research division. Crucially, the results of these analyses are funneled straight to top decision-makers. See Kuperwasser, "Israel's Intelligence Reforms."

243 **innovator's dilemma:** The term was coined and the phenomenon described by Christensen, *Innovator's Dilemma.*

245 **Hammond observed that in meetings where market forecasters had to predict the upcoming season's color preferences for sporting goods, the dominant voices consistently skewed the consensus forecast:** Fisher et al., "Making Supply Meet Demand."

246 **In his book *The Difference*, Page shows how teams that exhibit cognitive diversity:** Page, *The Difference.*

## CHAPTER 20: EMBRACING RESPONSIBILITY

251 **United Airlines personnel at Chicago O'Hare International faced a difficult but routine situation:** Our account of the United Airlines Flight 3411 incident draws on multiple sources, including United Airlines, Inc., "United Express Flight 3411 Review"; McLaughlin, "Man Dragged Off United Flight"; and Barrett, "United Airlines Needs to Do Better."

255 **Recent research hints that we are, as humans, *responsibility averse*:** Edelson et al., "Computational and Neurobiological Foundations."

255 **can cue the media hysterics about psychopathic and narcissistic CEOs:** See, for example, Croom, "Psychopaths."

# BIBLIOGRAPHY

Amazon.com. *Annual Report 2021*. Amazon.com, Inc., January 24, 2022. Available at https://s2.q4cdn.com/299287126/files/doc_financials/2022 /ar/Amazon-2021-Annual-Report.pdf.

Amazon Web Services (AWS). "Introduction to DevOps on AWS." AWS white paper. Amazon Web Services, Inc., 2023. Available at https:// docs.aws.amazon.com/pdfs/whitepapers/latest/introduction-devops-aws /introduction-devops-aws.pdf#two-pizza-teams.

"Analyse This: The Enduring Power of the Biggest Idea in Business." *Economist*, March 31, 2016. Available at https://amp.economist.com/business /2016/03/31/analyse-this.

Anand, Bharat. *The Content Trap: A Strategist's Guide to Digital Change*. New York: Random House, 2016.

AT&T Inc. *2021 Annual Report*. AT&T Inc., February 17, 2022. Available at https://investors.att.com/~/media/Files/A/ATT-IR-V2/financial-reports /annual-reports/2021/complete-2021-annual-report.pdf.

Barrett, Steve. "United Airlines Needs to Do Better. The Airline's Communications Response to Flight 3411 So Far Is Tone Deaf and Is Doing Nothing to Resolve the Situation." *PRWeek*, April 11, 2017. Available at www.prweek.com/article/1430341/united-airlines-needs-better.

Barro, Josh. "Congestion Pricing Only Works If Rideshare Companies Care About Losing Money." *New York Magazine*, May 21, 2019. Available at https://nymag.com/intelligencer/2019/05/ubers-irrational-pricing-is-a-problem-for-policymakers.html.

Binmore, Ken. *Natural Justice*. Oxford: Oxford University Press, 2011.

Blackwells Capital. "Peloton: A Call for Action." Blackwells Capital, 2022. Available at https://www.blackwellscap.com/wp-content/uploads/2022/02/BW_Peloton_Presentation_Feb072022.pdf.

Blanchard, Kenneth H., and Spencer Johnson. *The New One Minute Manager*. New York: William Morrow, 2015.

Bosa, Deirdre, and Ryan Browne. "Uber CEO Tells Staff Company Will Cut Down on Costs, Treat Hiring as a 'Privilege.'" CNBC, May 9, 2022. Available at www.cnbc.com/2022/05/09/uber-to-cut-down-on-costs-treat-hiring-as-a-privilege-ceo-email.html.

Bowles, Samuel. *The Moral Economy: Why Good Incentives Are No Substitute for Good Citizens*. New Haven, London: Yale University Press, 2017.

Buffett, Warren. "Warren Buffet Speech at University of Nebraska 2003." YouTube video, posted by Zero2one Investing, November 29, 2020. Available at https://www.youtube.com/watch?v=SVlJdHGMl4Q.

Center for Creative Leadership. *Feedback That Works: How to Build and Deliver Your Message*. Greensboro, NC: Center for Creative Leadership, 2019.

Christensen, Clayton M. *The Innovator's Dilemma: When New Technologies Cause Great Firms to Fail*. Boston: Harvard Business School Press, 2016.

Coates, John. *The Hour Between Dog and Wolf: How Risk Taking Transforms Us, Body and Mind*. New York: Penguin Group, 2013.

Collins, James C., and Jerry I. Porras. *Built to Last: Successful Habits of Visionary Companies*. New York: Harper Business, 2004.

———. "Building Your Company's Vision." In *On Strategy*, edited by Harvard Business Review, 106–141. Boston: Harvard Business School, 2011.

Covey, Stephen M. R. *The Speed of Trust*. New York: Free Press, 2008.

Crevello, Drew, and Lee Eisenberg. *WeCrashed*. Online series, Apple TV+, 2022.

Croom, Simon. "12 Percent of Corporate Leaders Are Psychopaths. It's Time to Take This Problem Seriously." *Forbes*, June 6, 2021. Available at https://fortune.com/2021/06/06/corporate-psychopaths-business-leadership-csr/.

Cruikshank, Jeffrey L. *A Delicate Experiment: The Harvard Business School 1908–1945*. Boston: Harvard Business School Press, 1987.

Dell, Michael. *Play Nice but Win: A CEO's Journey from Founder to Leader*. New York: Portfolio/Penguin, 2021.

Denning, Steve. "What Killed Michael Porter's Monitor Group? The One Force That Really Matters." *Forbes*, November 20, 2012. Available at www.forbes.com/sites/stevedenning/2012/11/20/what-killed-michael-porters-monitor-group-the-one-force-that-really-matters.

———. "Making Sense of Shareholder Value: 'The World's Dumbest Idea.'" *Forbes*, July 17, 2017. Available at www.forbes.com/sites/stevedenning/2017/07/17/making-sense-of-shareholder-value-the-worlds-dumbest-idea/#479e45682a7e.

Edelson, Micah G., Rafael Polania, Christian C. Ruff, Ernst Fehr, and Todd A. Hare. "Computational and Neurobiological Foundations of Leadership Decisions." *Science* 361, no. 6401 (2018). DOI: 10.1126/science.aat0036.

Eisenhower, Dwight D. "Remarks at the Annual Conference of the Society for Personnel Administration," May 12, 1954. The American Presidency Project, University of California at Santa Barbara. Available at www.presidency.ucsb.edu/documents/remarks-the-annual-conference-the-society-for-personnel-administration.

Fischbacher, Urs, Simon Gächter, and Ernst Fehr. "Are People Conditionally Cooperative? Evidence from a Public Goods Experiment." *Economics Letters* 71, no. 3 (2001): 397–404. DOI: 10.1016/S0165-1765(01)00394-9.

Fisher, Marshall, Jan Hammond, Walter R. Obermeyer, and Ananth Raman. "Making Supply Meet Demand in an Uncertain World." *Harvard*

*Business Review*, May–June 1994. Available at https://hbr.org/1994/05/making-supply-meet-demand-in-an-uncertain-world.

Flock, Elizabeth. "Dagen H: The Day Sweden Switched Sides of the Road." *Washington Post*, February 17, 2012. Available at www.washingtonpost.com/blogs/blogpost/post/dagen-h-the-day-sweden-switched-sides-of-the-road-photo/2012/02/17/gIQAOwFVKR_blog.html.

Forster, Marc, director. *World War Z*. Paramount Pictures, 2013.

Gallup, Inc. "State of the American Workplace Report." Gallup, 2017. Available at www.gallup.com/workplace/238085/state-american-workplace-report-2017.aspx.

———. "State of the Global Workplace 2022 Report: The Voice of the World's Employees." Gallup, 2022. Available at www.gallup.com/workplace/349484/state-of-the-global-workplace-2022-report.aspx.

Gelles, David. *The Man Who Broke Capitalism: How Jack Welch Gutted the Heartland and Crushed the Soul of Corporate America—and How to Undo His Legacy*. New York: Simon & Schuster, 2022.

General Electric Company. "GE Plans to Form Three Public Companies Focused on Growth Sectors of Aviation, Healthcare, and Energy." Press release, November 9, 2021. Available at www.ge.com/news/press-releases/ge-plans-to-form-three-pulic-companies-focused-on-growth-sectors-of-aviation.

Gillies, Donald. *Philosophical Theories of Probability*. London: Routledge, Philosophical Issues in Science, reprint 2010.

Gintis, Herbert. *The Bounds of Reason: Game Theory and the Unification of the Behavioral Sciences*. Princeton, NJ: Princeton University Press, 2014.

Gottman, John Mordechai. *What Predicts Divorce? The Relationship Between Marital Processes and Marital Outcomes*. New York and London: Psychology Press, 2013.

Graeber, David. "What's the Point If We Can't Have Fun?" *Baffler*, January 2014. Available at https://thebaffler.com/salvos/whats-the-point-if-we-cant-have-fun.

———. *Bullshit Jobs: The Rise of Pointless Work, and What We Can Do About It*. London: Penguin Books, 2019.

Greene, Joshua David. *Moral Tribes: Emotion, Reason, and the Gap Between Us and Them*. New York: Atlantic Books, 2014.

Harter, James K. "U.S. Employee Engagement Slump Continues." Gallup, April 25, 2022. Available at www.gallup.com/workplace/391922/employee-engagement-slump-continues.aspx.

Harter, James K., Frank L. Schmidt, Sangeeta Agrawal, Anthony Blue, Stephanie K. Plowman, Patrick Josh, and Jim Asplund. "The Relationship Between Engagement at Work and Organizational Outcomes." 2020 Q12 Meta-Analysis. Gallup, 2020. Available at www.gallup.com/workplace/321725/gallup-q12-meta-analysis-report.aspx.

Heinsohn, Gunnar, and Otto Steiger, with Frank Decker, translator. *Ownership Economics: On the Foundations of Interest, Money, Markets, Business Cycles and Economic Development*. Milton Park, Abingdon, Oxon: Routledge, 2012.

Hersey, Paul, Kenneth H. Blanchard, and Dewey E. Johnson. *Management of Organizational Behavior: Leading Human Resources*. Boston: Pearson, 2013.

Hobbes, Thomas. "Leviathan." In *Classics of Western Philosophy*, 4th ed., edited by Steven M. Cahn, 473–532. Indianapolis: Hackett Publishing, 1995.

Janis, Irving L. *Victims of Groupthink: A Psychological Study of Foreign-Policy Decisions and Fiascoes*. Boston: Houghton Mifflin, 1972.

Jenisch, Jan, and Jean François Manzoni. "Become a Buddha to Drive Sustainable Transformation." Video, CEO Dialogue Series, International Institute for Management Development, September 20, 2022. Available at www.imd.org/ibyimd/videos/ceo-dialogue-series/become-a-buddha-to-drive-sustainable-transformation/#.

Johnstone, Keith. *Impro: Improvisation and the Theatre*. London: Bloomsbury Academic, 2021.

Kahneman, Daniel. *Thinking, Fast and Slow*. New York: Farrar, Straus and Giroux, 2011.

Kennedy, John F. "Rice University, 12 September 1962." Video USG-15-29 -2, National Archives and Records Administration, John F. Kennedy Presidential Library and Museum, September 12, 1962. Available at www .jfklibrary.org/asset-viewer/archives/USG/USG-15-29-2/USG-15-29-2.

Keynes, J. M. "The General Theory of Employment." *Quarterly Journal of Economics* 51, no. 2 (1937): 209–223. DOI: 10.2307/1882087.

Koller, Tim, Marc Goedhart, and David Wessels. *Valuation: Measuring and Managing the Value of Companies*. 7th ed. Hoboken, NJ: Wiley, 2020.

Kouzes, James M., and Barry Z. Posner. *The Leadership Challenge: How to Make Extraordinary Things Happen in Organizations*. Hoboken, NJ: Wiley, 2023.

Kuperwasser, Yosef. "Lessons from Israel's Intelligence Reforms." Washington, DC: The Saban Center for Middle East Policy at The Brookings Institution, 2007. Available at www.brookings.edu/wp-content/uploads /2016/06/10_intelligence_kuperwasser.pdf.

LafargeHolcim, Ltd. *Integrated Annual Report 2020*. LafargeHolcim, 2021. Available at https://www.holcim.com/sites/holcim/files/2022-04/2602 2021-finance-lafageholcim_fy_2020_report-full-en.pdf.

Lehne, Johanna, and Felix Preston. *Making Concrete Change: Innovation in Low-Carbon Cement and Concrete*. London: Chatham House, 2018. Available at www.chathamhouse.org/2018/06/making-concrete-change -innovation-low-carbon-cement-and-concrete.

Lencioni, Patrick. *The Five Dysfunctions of a Team: A Leadership Fable*. San Francisco: Jossey-Bass, 2002.

Lipnevich, Anastasiya A., and Ernesto Panadero. "A Review of Feedback Models and Theories: Descriptions, Definitions, and Conclusions." *Frontiers in Education* 6 (December 31, 2021), 720195. DOI: 10.3389 /feduc.2021.720195.

Losada, Marcial, and Emily Heaphy. "The Role of Positivity and Connectivity in the Performance of Business Teams." *American Behavioral Scientist* 47, no. 6 (2004): 740–765. DOI: 10.1177/0002764203260208.

Lowenstein, Roger. *When Genius Failed: The Rise and Fall of Long-Term Capital Management.* New York: Random House, 2001.

MacIntyre, Alasdair C. *After Virtue: A Study in Moral Theory.* South Bend, IN: University of Notre Dame Press, 2007.

Martin, Roger L. "The Execution Trap." *Harvard Business Review*, July 2010. Available at https://hbr.org/2010/07/the-execution-trap.

Mayfield, E. Scott. "NetFlix.com, Inc." Case 9-201-037. Boston: Harvard Business School Publishing, 2006.

McLaughlin, Eliott C. "Man Dragged Off United Flight Has Concussion, Will File Suit, Lawyer Says." *CNN*, April 14, 2017. Available at http://edition.cnn.com/2017/04/13/travel/united-passenger-pulled-off-flight-lawsuit-family-attorney-speak/index.html.

McLean, Bethany, and Peter Elkind. *The Smartest Guys in the Room: The Amazing Rise and Scandalous Fall of Enron.* New York: Portfolio, 2012.

Meier, Sid. "Interesting Decisions: Presentation at Game Developers Conference 2012." Video posted by Informa PLC, 2012. Available at www.gdcvault.com/play/1015756/Interesting.

Miller, Gary J. *Managerial Dilemmas: The Political Economy of Hierarchy.* Cambridge: Cambridge University Press, 2006.

Morel, Benoit. *Real Option Analysis and Climate Change: A New Framework for Environmental Policy Analysis.* Basel: Springer International Publishing, 2020.

National Center for Education Statistics. "Digest of Education Statistics," table 318.20: "Bachelor's, Master's, and Doctor's Degrees Conferred by Postsecondary Institutions, by Field of Study: Selected Years, 1970–71 through 2018–19." Washington, DC, 2020. Available at https://nces.ed.gov/programs/digest/d20/tables/dt20_318.20.asp?current=yes.

Netflix, Inc. "Fourth Quarter 2021 Earnings Interview. Letter to Share-holders." Netflix, January 20, 2022. Available at https://s22.q4cdn.com /959853165/files/doc_financials/2021/q4/FINAL-Q4-21-Shareholder -Letter.pdf.

———. "First Quarter 2022 Earnings Interview. Letter to Shareholders." Netflix, April 19, 2022. Available at https://s22.q4cdn.com/959853165 /files/doc_financials/2022/q1/FINAL-Q1-22-Shareholder-Letter.pdf.

Nida-Rümelin, Julian. *Die Optimierungsfalle: Philosophie einer humanen Ökonomie*. München (Munich): Btb, 2015.

Nokia Corporation. *Nokia in 2007: Review by the Board of Directors and Nokia Annual Accounts 2007*. Nokia, 2008. Available at www.nokia .com/system/files/files/request-nokia-in-2007-pdf.pdf.

Obolensky, Nick. *Complex Adaptive Leadership: Embracing Paradox and Uncertainty*. London: Routledge, 2016.

O'Brien, Kevin J. "Nokia's New Chief Faces Culture of Complacency." *New York Times*, September 20, 2010. Available at www.nytimes .com/2010/09/27/technology/27nokia.html.

Page, Scott E. *The Difference: How the Power of Diversity Creates Better Groups, Firms, Schools, and Societies*. Princeton, NJ: Princeton University Press, 2008.

Palantir Technologies. *Annual Report 2021*. Palantir Technologies, February 24, 2022. Available at https://d18rn0p25nwr6d.cloudfront.net/CIK -0001321655/85556454-0b81-40e2-ae70-440ae58aa622.pdf.

Penrose, Edith T. *The Theory of the Growth of the Firm*. Mansfield Centre, CT: Martino Publishing, 2013.

Peter, Fabienne. "Political Legitimacy." In *The Stanford Encyclopedia of Philosophy*, edited by Edward N. Zalta. Stanford, CA: Metaphysics Research Lab, Philosophy Department, Stanford University, 2017. Available at https://plato.stanford.edu/archives/sum2017/entries/legitimacy/.

Picker, Randal C. "The Razors-and-Blades Myth(s)." *SSRN Journal*, September 13, 2010. DOI: 10.2139/ssrn.1676444.

Pink, Daniel H. *Drive: The Surprising Truth About What Motivates Us*. New York: Penguin, 2011.

Pistor, Katharina. *The Code of Capital: How the Law Creates Wealth and Inequality*. Princeton, NJ: Princeton University Press, 2020.

Porter, Michael E. "The Five Competitive Forces That Shape Strategy." In *On Strategy*, edited by Harvard Business Review, 56–105. Boston: Harvard Business School, 2011.

Putterman, Louis, and Randy Kroszner, eds. *The Economic Nature of the Firm: A Reader*. 3rd ed. Cambridge: Cambridge University Press, 2009.

Ritholtz, Barry. "Judging GE's Jeff Immelt Versus Jack Welch: The Two Chief Executives of General Electric Co. Were Dealt Very Different Hands." *Bloomberg News*, June 12, 2017. Available at www.bloomberg.com /opinion/articles/2017-06-12/judging-ge-s-jeff-immelt-versus-jack -welch#xj4y7vzkg.

———. "Fans and Foes of Buybacks Aren't in Disagreement." *Bloomberg News*, November 30, 2018. Available at www.bloomberg.com/opinion /articles/2018-11-30/fans-and-foes-of-buybacks-aren-t-in-disagreement.

Robert, Henry M., William J. Evans, Daniel H. Honemann, Thomas J. Balch, Daniel E. Seabold, and Shmuel Gerber. *Robert's Rules of Order* (newly revised in brief; updated to accord with the 12th ed. of the complete manual). New York: PublicAffairs, 2020.

Rosenzweig, Philip M. *The Halo Effect…and the Eight Other Business Delusions That Deceive Managers*. London: Simon & Schuster, 2014.

Savage, Maddy. "A 'Thrilling' Mission to Get the Swedish to Change Overnight." *BBC Worklife*, April 18, 2018. Available at www.bbc.com/work life/article/20180417-a-thrilling-mission-to-get-the-swedish-to-change -overnight.

Seabright, Paul. *The Company of Strangers: A Natural History of Economic Life*. Princeton, NJ: Princeton University Press, 2010.

Smith, Adam. *An Inquiry into the Nature and Causes of the Wealth of Nations*. Edited and with an introduction by Kathryn Sutherland. Oxford: Oxford University Press, 2008.

Snowden, David J. "The Cynefin Framework." YouTube video posted by CognitiveEdge, July 11, 2010. Available at www.youtube.com /watch?v=N7oz366X0-8.

Snowden, David J., and Mary E. Boone. "A Leader's Framework for Decision Making." *Harvard Business Review*, November 2007. Available at https://hbr.org/2007/11/a-leaders-framework-for-decision-making?registration=success.

Spencer, Phil. "WSJ Interview: The Future of Gaming." Interview of Phil Spencer by Sarah Needleman. YouTube video posted by XboxBG, October 30, 2022. Available at www.youtube.com/watch?v=ZvsAwfgl6zs.

Telford, Taylor. "'Quiet Quitting' Isn't Really About Quitting. Here Are the Signs." *Washington Post*, August 21, 2022. Available at www.washington post.com/business/2022/08/21/quiet-quitting-what-to-know/.

Tuckman, B. W. "Developmental Sequence in Small Groups." *Psychological Bulletin* 63, no. 6 (1965): 384–399. DOI: 10.1037/h0022100.

Uber Technologies, Inc. "Uber Announces Results for Second Quarter 2023" press release. Uber Technologies, August 1, 2023. Available at https:// s23.q4cdn.com/407969754/files/doc_earnings/2023/q2/earnings -result/Uber-Q2-23-Earnings-Press-Release.pdf.

Uber Technologies, Inc. *2022 Annual Report*. Uber Technologies, February 21, 2023. Available at https://s23.q4cdn.com/407969754/files/doc _financials/2023/ar/2022-annual-report.pdf.

United Airlines, Inc. "United Express Flight 3411 Review and Action Report." United Airlines, April 27, 2017. Available at https://s3.amazonaws.com /unitedhub/United+Flight+3411+Review+and+Action+Report.pdf.

Watzlawick, Paul, Janet Beavin Bavelas, and Don D. Jackson. *Pragmatics of Human Communication: A Study of Interactional Patterns, Pathologies, and Paradoxes*. New York: W. W. Norton, 2014.

We Company. "Form S-1: Registration Statement Under the Securities Act of 1933." We Company, August 14, 2019. Available at www.sec.gov /Archives/edgar/data/1533523/000119312519220499/d781982ds1 .htm.

WeWork, Inc. *2021 Annual Report.* WeWork, March 17, 2022. Available at https://d18rn0p25nwr6d.cloudfront.net/CIK-0001813756/2e2e2e66 -6dfc-4a67-a399-e3dcd367f452.pdf.

Woo, Elaine. "Gary Dahl Dies at 78; Creator of Pet Rock, 1970s Pop Culture Icon." *Los Angeles Times*, April 1, 2015. Available at www.latimes.com /local/obituaries/la-me-gary-ross-dahl-20150401-story.html.

Zenger, Jack, and Joseph Folkman. "The Ideal Praise-to-Criticism Ratio." *Harvard Business Review*, March 15, 2013. Available at https://hbr .org/2013/03/the-ideal-praise-to-criticism.

# INDEX

accountability for decisions, 227
  consensus decision and, 228
  majority rule and, 229
  sole decider and, 229–230
accounting
  accrual, 73–75
  cash-based, 71–73
  double-entry bookkeeping, 54
  economics *vs.*, 94–97
accounting identity, 68
accounts payable, 58–63
  trade working capital and, 88–89
accounts receivable, 61–63, 82–84
  factoring and, 106
  growth in, 85–87
  trade working capital and, 88–89
accrual accounting, 73–75
accrued expenses, cash flow *vs.*, 81
achievement, as intrinsic motivator,
  179
action bias, 210–211, 214
agile approach to software development,
  215n
agreement, alignment *vs.*, 231
alignment, 230–233
  agreement *vs.*, 231

legitimacy and, 231–232
  using incentives to achieve, 231
Amazon
  logistics and, 100
  negative trade working capital
    and, 89
  Prime membership, 105
  subscription offerings, 66
  team size at, 205
Amazon Prime, 131
amortization, 17
Anand, Bharat, 211n
annual reports, past performance and
  future expectations in, 35–37
Apple iPhone, 5–6, 9–10, 243
applicability of fixed-*vs.* variable expenses,
  95
appreciation, process guardian and
  expression of, 235
assets
  balance sheet, 55, 57–63
  current, 62–63, 62n
  intangible, 17
  life of, 17
  noncurrent, 62–63
  tangible, 17

AT&T
   attracting debt capital, 52
   balance sheet example, 64–67
   Lucent and, 86
Austin (Texas), market growth in, 29
authority, leadership and, 189, 190, 191
automation of decision-making, 216,
   220–222, 251
autonomy, as intrinsic motivator, 181,
   181n
autopilot, decision-making and, 216,
   220–222, 251

balance sheet, 48, 51–68
   analysis of AT&T's, 64–67
   constructing a, 53–64
   defined, 54, 68
   relationship to other financial
     statements, 70, 76
bankruptcy, 42, 52
Barrett, Steve, 252
Barro, Josh, 96
behavioral economics, 220–222
benchmarking performance, 22
Bezos, Jeff, 205
bias
   action, 210–211, 214
   fasting thinking and, 221
Bigara, Jerome, 231n
*The Big Short* (film), 122n
Black-Scholes model of option value, 4,
   4n
Blackwells Capital, 203
Blanchard, Ken, 152, 152n, 165n
Boeing, cash flow at, 72–73, 74
brainstorming, 224
brand, predictability of sales and,
   104–105
breakeven analysis, 97–99
breakeven formula, 98, 107
breakeven point, 97–99
bridge loan, 75

bubble, 122n
Buffett, Warren, 151
*Bullshit Jobs* (Graeber), 162n
bundle, 25
business, defined, 207
business models, sales, predictability, and,
   104–106, 107
business simulations, 206–212
buybacks, 28n

cannibalizing sales, 33
capital, 19
   cost of, 119–122, 127
   debt, 51–52
   equity, 53–63
   investor perspective on business
     outcomes and, 43–47
   paid-in, 56–63
   working, 87–91
career development, expectation-setting
   behavior and, 154
Carell, Steve, 149
cash
   balance sheet, 54–63
   creditor claims on, 27, 28
   option values, 112n
   shareholder claims on, 28
cash-based accounting, 71–73
cash flow
   accrual accounting and, 73–75
   accrued expenses *vs.*, 81
   company promises and, 41, 42, 50
   from investments, 71, 76
   from operating activities, 71–73
   P&L statement and operating, 77–85
   profit, timing issues, and, 71–73,
     74–75, 76, 77
   profits *vs.*, 8, 69, 76
   shareholder value and discounted future
     net, 5, 6–8, 11
cash flow model, 115–116
cash flow statement, 48

constructing simplified, 70–73
defined, 71
P&L statement and, 84–85
relationship to other financial
statements, 70, 76
CEDAR (context, examples, diagnosis,
actions, and review) feedback model,
162, 162n
Center for Creative Leadership, 168, 171
CEOs, leadership and, 190–191. *See also*
executives
CFOs
cost of capital and, 119–120
valuation and, 132n
*See also* executives
chaotic systems, ordered systems *vs.*, 215n
charisma, legitimacy and, 232
*Civilization* (game), 207
closing the loop, 155–157
feedback and, 169–170
Coates, John, 51n
cognitive diversity, 246–247, 248
Cold War, 13
collective action
decision-making and, 203–214
social dilemmas and, 192–194
Collins, Jim, 219–220
commitment to carrying out decision,
227, 230–233
common-sizing, 22, 26
communication
closing the loop and, 155–157,
169–170
of decisions, 230–231
feedback and, 159–160, 171
globalized world and, 156–157
intent *vs.* impact, 156
layers of meaning in, 157
of the organization's vision, 197, 201
communication habits, decision-making
and, 223–224
communication theory, 155

companionship, as intrinsic motivator, 179
company
defined, 41
intrinsic value of, 117–119, 126,
127–128
purpose of, 3, 11
value of, 3–4, 11
competitive advantage, leadership as,
195–196
*Complex Adaptive Leadership* (Obolensky),
205n
computer chips, supply chain disruption
and, 90
conditional cooperators, 192–193, 194
conflict
how teams manage, 242
team decision-making and, 222
consensus, decision-making and, 227, 228
at expense of long-term interests,
242–243
fist of five and testing emerging,
244–245
groupthink *vs.*, 240–241
content trap, 209–212
process guardian and, 234
*The Content Trap* (Anand), 211n
Continental Airlines, 253
continuing value, 122–125
defined, 124
formula, 124n
contracts, 42
lender and, 120
managing accounts receivable and
accounts payable and, 89
contractual claims, liabilities and, 54
contribution margin, 97, 98
cooperation, leadership and culture of,
196–199, 201
cooperative behavior, leadership and
recognizing, 198–199, 201
coordination of economic activity,
143–147

corrective feedback, 163, 165, 171
cost
  of capital, 119–122, 127
  fixed, 94–97
  as lever of profitability, 23–24
  managerial contribution to, 132–134
  of revenue, 16n
  of sales, 16
  of services, 16n
  *See also* variable cost
cost of goods sold (COGS), 16n
cost structure, 93–107
  breakeven analysis, 97–99, 107
  defined, 96, 107
  economics *vs.* accounting, 94–97, 107
  profitability and, 107
  sales, predictability, and business
    models, 104–106, 107
  trade-offs between profitability, growth,
    and risk, 99–103, 107
Covid-19 pandemic
  Peloton and, 203–204
  quiet quitting and, 185–186
creditors
  claims on company, 52
  company promises to, 41
  default and, 52
  payment to, 27
crises, decision-making during, 233, 237
crisis of engagement, Gallup on, 174–178
cross-cultural communication, 157
culture, layers of meaning in
    communication and, 157
current assets, 62–63, 62n
  working capital and, 88–89
current liabilities, 62–63
  working capital and, 88–89
current portion of long-term debt, 63, 64
customer behavior, market growth and, 29
customer payments
  deferred, 82–84
  terms of, 78, 80

customers
  AT&T's balance sheet and, 64–66
  brand and, 104–105
  company promises to, 41
  company value and, 53
  paying higher price, 24–25, 26
  working capital and, 87–91, 92
customer segmentation, 25
customer value
  profitability and, 14
  quality and increased, 25
Cynefin, 215n

Dahl, Gary, 31
Dao, David, 251–252
data, decision-making and gathering,
    222–225
debt, 19–20
  AT&T's, 66–67
  on balance sheet, 58
  company value and, 51–52
  cost of capital and, 120, 120n
  current portion of long-term, 63, 64
  short-term, 63, 64
debt capital, 51–52
decision
  categorizing, 233–234, 237
  constraining through strategy, 216–220
  defined, 206
  defining the, 213, 215–226
  with longer-term impacts, 233, 237
  modeling, 208
  routine, 233, 237
decision-making
  action bias and, 210–211, 214
  automated, 216, 220–222, 251
  business games and, 206–209
  comparing decision procedures,
    233–234
  content trap and, 209–212
  during crisis, 233, 237
  defining decision, 213, 215–226

deliberating and executing (*see* deliberating and executing)
exploring options and gathering data, 222–225
as iterative process, 215
with longer-term impacts, 222
Peloton management and, 203–204
as process and outcome, 207–208
routine, 222
simple model for, 212–213
structural errors in, 214, 216
structured discussions and, 224–225, 235–236
team as unit of, 205–206
top-down, 218–219
decision point, 213
decision tree, 219
default, 52
delegation, trust and, 150–151
deliberating and executing, 213, 227–237
aligning to execute, 230–233, 237
closing mechanisms, 227–230
comparing decision procedures, 233–234
majority rule, 227, 229
process guardian, 234–236, 237
sole decider, 227, 229–230
*See also* consensus
Dell, Inc., 90
Dell, Michael, 90
demographic market growth, 29
de-motivation, 178, 187
depreciation, 17
operating cash flow and, 79–80
DESC (description, effect, solution, and conclusion) feedback model, 162, 162n
design-to-cost method, Nokia and, 24
devil's advocate, 241–245, 248
dice game, 207–208
*The Difference* (Page), 246–247

discounted cash flow (DCF) analysis, 115–117, 130
discounted future net cash flows
investor feelings and, 7–8
shareholder value and, 5, 6–8, 11
discounting, 115
discounting promise, 42
discussions, structuring, 224–225, 235. *See also* deliberating and executing
Disney+, 131
disruption, new markets and, 32, 33
disruptive behavior, addressing, 166–169
dissent, power of, 239–248
devil's advocate and, 241–245, 248
diversity and, 245–247, 248
groupthink and, 240–241, 242, 248
diverse heuristics, cognitive diversity and, 246
diverse interpretations, cognitive diversity and, 246
diverse perspectives, cognitive diversity and, 246
diverse predictive models, cognitive diversity and, 246
diversity, 245–247, 248
cognitive, 246–247, 248
identity, 247, 248
dividend, 28, 28n, 57
division of labor, 143–144
double-entry bookkeeping, 54
dumping, 96

earnings, 20n
retained, 56–63
economic activity, coordination of, 143–147
economic conditions, market growth and, 29
economics, accounting *vs.*, 94–97
Eisenhower, Dwight D., 190
employee job satisfaction, report on, 173–177

employees
  CEO as advocate for, 253–254
  communication and, 155–156
  company promises to, 41
  feedback on workplace behavior,
    166–169
  power and, 150, 189
  quiet quitting and, 185–186
  trust and, 150–151
  See also manager-employee relationship
engagement
  categorization of, 173, 174, 183, 187
  Gallup report on, 173–177
  teams and rules of, 212
  See also motivation
entertainment, Netflix and
    unpredictability of, 131–132
equipment
  on balance sheet, 55–63
  plants, property, and equipment
    (PP&E), 55n
equity, 54n
  cost of capital and, 120, 120n
  See also liabilities and equity
equity agreement, 20
equity capital, 53–63
equity investors, 120
  See also shareholder
equity value, on balance sheet, 54n, 68
execution
  aligning for, 230–233
  of decisions, 213, 218, 227
executive compensation, 38n
executives
  information shared with investors, 134
  setting expectations, 35–38
  top-down decision-making and,
    218–219
  See also CEOs; CFOs
expectations
  cross-cultural communication and
    setting, 156–157

executives setting, 35–38
  feedback and, 164–165, 170, 171
  growth, 33–38, 39
  story for investors regarding, 34–38, 39
  trust and setting, 152–155
expected value, 44–47
expenses
  defined, 14
  fixed vs. variable, 94–95
  general and administrative, 17
  increasing profitabilty by reducing, 24,
    26
  modeling future cash flow and, 118
  nonoperating, 18
  operating, 17–18
  P&L statement and, 16
  profit and, 14–15
  selling, general, and administrative, 17

factoring, 106
fairness, motivation and, 178
feedback, 159–171
  around tasks, 158
  on behavior, 166–169
  characteristics of effective, 162–166
  closing the loop and, 169–170
  core of people management and,
    160–162
  corrective, 163, 165, 171
  expectations and, 164–165, 170, 171
  good and bad, 162–166
  positive vs. negative, 165–166
  praise and, 163–164, 165, 169–170,
    171
  setting for, 164
  specificity in, 163, 171
  timeliness of, 164
feedback models, 162
feedback sandwich, 163
financial crisis of 2008, 75, 112n
financial statements
  investor examination of, 37–38

relationships among, 70, 76
*See also* balance sheet; cash flow
statement; profit and loss (P&L)
statement
financing activities, cash flow and, 71, 76
first team, 205, 206n
fist of five, 244–245
*The Five Dysfunctions of a Team*
(Lencioni), 205
fixed costs, 94–97
breakeven analysis and, 97–99
preference variable costs or, 99–103
fixed expenses, 94–95
Foley, John, 203–204, 232–233
forecasting/forecasts
aggregating private, 245
future growth, 33–38, 39
Netflix's revised, 130
forming, storming, norming, performing
model, 212
forming, team, 212
free cash flows, calculating, 118–119
free-riding, 194
future
feedback and building capacity in,
160–161, 171
past performance and, 33–34
valuation tools and orientation to,
138

Gallup, *State of the Global Workplace*,
173–177
games, 206–209
business simulations, 207–212
defined, 207
GE Aviation, 105
general and administrative expenses, 17
General Electric (GE)
incentive structures at, 195–196
theory of the firm, 145
Gervais, Ricky, 159n
gig economy, 145n

globalized world, expectation setting and,
156–157
Goedhart, Marc, 110n, 113n, 132n
*Good Morning, America* (television
program), 252
Gottman, John, 165–166
Graeber, David, 162n
Great Resignation, 186
gross margin, 22, 26
gross profit, 16, 26
groupthink, 240–241, 242, 242n, 244, 248
growth, 27–39
in accounts receivable, 85–87
increasing profit and, 27–28, 39
inorganic, 28
levers of, 28–33
organic, 28
past performance and forecasting,
33–38, 39
profitability and, 93
trade-offs between risk, profitability,
and, 99–103
value and, 9, 11
growth rate, perpetuity value and, 124n

*The Halo Effect* (Rosenzweig), 190–191
Hammond, Jan, 245
Hersey, Paul, 152
hiring process, legitimacy and, 232–233
historically underserved markets, as new
market, 31
HMD Global, 9n
Hobbes, Thomas, 151
*Högertrafikomläggningen,* 217, 220
Holcim, 178
growth forecast and, 35–37
*The Hour Between Dog and Wolf* (Coates),
51n
human factor in management, 146

identity diversity, 247, 248
impact

impact (*cont.*)
of communication, 156
feedback and, 168–169, 171
incentives
achieving alignment using, 231
leadership and, 195–196, 201
income statement, 16n
inflation, 112n
supply chain disruption and, 90–91
inflows, 71
influence, 190
information-based social dilemmas, 194
innovations
disruptive, 32, 33
sociological, 31–32
technological, 31
innovator's dilemma, 243–244
inorganic growth, 28
insurance, 106
intangible assets, 17
intent
in communication, 156
feedback and, 168–169, 171
interest, 20
loan, 54
risk-free rate, 112n, 113n
interest rate, real, 112n
interest rate policy, 112n
intrinsic motivators, 178–184, 187
achievement, 179
autonomy, 181, 181n
companionship, 179
mastery, 181
purpose, 181–182
recognition, 179–180
security, 180
status, 180
intrinsic value, 117–119, 126, 127–128
inventory
on balance sheet, 55–63
cash flow and, 82, 85
trade working capital and, 88–89

investing, neuroscience of, 51n
investments, 19
cash flow from, 71, 76
comparing, 114–115
expected value of, 44–47
modeling future cash flow and, 118
return on, 113–117
investor confidence
creating value by increasing, 47–49, 50
growth stories and, 37–38
raising, 138
United Airlines's public relations issues and, 252, 254
*See also* shareholder confidence
investor feelings, discounted future net cash flows and, 7–8
investors
defined, 19
as lenders, 120
need for, 53
risk and, 42–47
as shareholders, 120
story told to regarding future expectations, 34–38, 39
trust in executives for information, 134
iPhone, 5–6, 9–10, 243

Janis, Irving, 240, 241, 242n
Jenisch, Jan, 35–37, 178
Johnson, Lyndon B., 242n
Johnson, Spencer, 152n
Johnstone, Keith, 180n
just-in-time ordering and delivery, 89, 90–91

Kahneman, Daniel, 220–221
Kennedy, John F., 190, 242n
Keynes, John Maynard, 49
Khosrowshahi, Dara, 106
Koller, Tim, 110n, 113n, 132n
Kouzes, James, 198n

labor
    division of, 143–144
    negotiation with, 23
labor costs, profitability and, 23
LafargeHolcim, 35n
leaders, effect of known preferences on
    team, 241–242
leadership, 189–201
    authority and, 189, 190, 191
    in business, 199–200
    communicating the vision, 197, 201
    as competitive advantage, 195–196
    defining, 189–191
    incentives structures and, 195–196,
        201
    in practice, 196–199
    recognizing cooperative behavior,
        198–199, 201
    role modeling, 197–198, 201
    situational, 152
    social dilemmas, 192–194
    social dilemmas in business, 194–195
leadership behaviors, 191
The Leadership Challenge (Kouzes &
    Posner), 198n
lean manufacturing, 89
legitimacy
    achieving alignment and, 231–232,
        237
    sources of, 232
Lencioni, Patrick, 205
lending during financial crisis, 75
liabilities, 54
    current, 62–63
    limited, 43n
    noncurrent, 62–63
    other long-term, 64n, 65
liabilities and equity, on balance sheet, 55,
    57–63
life phases, work engagement and,
    175–177
limited liability, 43n

loans
    accounts payable vs., 58n
    bridge, 75
    long-term and short-term debt, 63, 64
Long-Term Capital Management, 4n
long-term debt, current portion of, 63, 64
Lucent Technologies, 86, 87

MacIntyre, Alasdair, 152, 163
macroeconomics, 112n
majority rule, 227, 229
management
    as calling, 255–256
    coordinating people and, 149–150
    division of labor and, 144
    markets vs., 144–145
    popular culture on, 146–147, 149
manager-employee relationship
    effect of feedback on, 164–166
    expectation-setting behavior and, 154
    power and, 150, 189
Managerial Dilemmas (Miller), 195n
managers
    communication and, 155–156
    contribution to value creation,
        132–134
    managing market growth, 29–30
    membership in multiple teams, 205–206
    modeling behavior and setting
        expectations, 153–155
    power and, 150, 189
    responsibility aversion and, 254–255
    Welch and stack-ranking, 195–196
managing profitability, shareholder value
    and, 23–25, 26
manipulation, 190
margin
    contribution, 97
    gross, 22, 26
    net, 22, 26
    operating, 22, 26
    profit, 22

market growth, 29–30
  increasing market share, 30
market mechanism, 144, 145n
markets
  management *vs.*, 144–145
  new, 31–32
market share
  increasing, 30–31
  mergers and acquisitions and, 31
  as zero-sum game, 30–31
Martin, Roger L., 218
Marx, Karl, 162n
mastery, as intrinsic motivator, 181
MBA degree
  as new market, 31–32
  traditional, 4
McLagan, Kate, 178n
Meier, Sid, 207
mergers and acquisitions (M&A), 31
Merton, Robert, 4n
Microsoft
  mobile devices and, 9n
  Office 365 subscription model, 66,
    105
  razor blade model and, 105
Miller, Gary J., 195n
model for decision-making, 212–213
modeling behavior and setting
    expectations, 153–155
modeling decisions, decision-making and,
    208
"model the way," 198n
moderator role, 235, 236
money, time value of, 111–117
motivation
  addressing employee, 183–184
  employee perspective on, 185–186
  fairness and, 178
  intrinsic motivators, 178–184, 187
  presence and, 184
motives, attribution of, 157, 167–168
Munoz, Oscar, 252–254

negative feedback, 165–166
negative trade working capital, 89–90, 92
negotiations, labor, 23
net cash flow, 8
Netflix
  early cash flow issues, 86–87
  pricing and, 96
  stock price and decline in subscribers,
    109
  valuation example, 129–132
net margin, 22, 26
net profit, 20, 26
new markets
  creating new need or desire, 31
  seeking, 31–32, 39
  sociological innovation and, 31
*The New One Minute Manager,* 165n
new present value (NPV), 135–136
Nokia
  design-to-cost method and, 24
  early smartphone, 33, 243
  iPhone release and, 9–10
  reinventions of, 123
  shareholder value and, 5–6
  stock price, 6, 10
nominal rate, 112n
noncurrent assets, 62–63
noncurrent liabilities, 62–63
nonoperating expenses, 18
norming, teams and, 212

Obolensky, Nick, 205n, 211
*The Office* (television program), 146, 149
Office 365 subscription model, 66, 105
*The One Minute Manager* (Blanchard &
    Johnson), 152n
operating activities, cash flow from, 71–73
operating expenses, 17–18
operating margin, 22, 26
operating profit, 17–18, 26, 56
opportunities and threats, statement of
    financial position and, 67, 68

opposition, sole decider and, 231
optionality, 112n
options, decision-making and exploring, 222–225
option values, 112n
ordered systems, complex and chaotic systems *vs.,* 215n
organic growth, 28
organizational cycles, employee engagement and, 176–177
organization size, aligning for execution and, 230
other long-term liabilities entry, 64n, 65
other people's money (OPM), 88
outcomes
    decision, 207–208, 214
    investor perspective on business, 43–47
outflows, 71
overhead, 102–103

Page, Scott, 246–247
paid-in capital, 56–63
Palantir Technologies, 52
past performance, forecasting future and, 33–38
Peloton
    decision-making at, 203–204, 205
    legitimacy in hiring at, 232–233
people management, 150–152
performance
    forecasting future and past, 33–38
    investor confidence and communication of, 48, 50
performing, teams and, 212
perpetuity value, 123–124
persuasion, 190
Pet Rock phenomenon, 31
pin factory, Smith's, 143, 144, 145–146
Pink, Daniel, 161
plants, property, and equipment (PP&E), 55n
plus/delta exercise, 239–240

policy manuals, as constraint on decision-making, 220
Porras, Jerry, 219–220
positive feedback, 165–166
Posner, Barry, 198n
power
    of dissent, 239–248
    in manager-employee relationship, 150, 189
*Pragmatics of Communication* (Watzalawick), 163n
praise
    Blanchard on, 165n
    feedback and, 163–164, 165, 169–170, 171
predictability, sales, business models, and, 104–106
presence, 184
present time, feedback and results in, 160–161, 171
present value, 115–117
    formula, 117
    net, 135–136
    total, 125–126
price
    breakeven analysis and, 97–99
    competing for market share via, 30
    dumping and, 96
    as lever of profitability, 24–25
    profit and, 13–14
    value and, 6–7
price war, 30
Prime membership, 105
principal, loan, 54
prisoner's dilemma, 192n
probabilities
    investor perspective on, 43–47
    modeling decisions and, 208
probability theory, 41n
procedural solutions to exploring options and gathering data, 224–225
procedure, legitimacy and, 232, 234, 237

process, decision-making, 207–208,
212–213
process guardian, 234–236, 237
process improvement methodologies,
profitability and, 23–24
profit
cash flow, timing issues, and, 71–73,
74–75, 76, 77
cash flow vs., 8, 69, 76
concept of, 13
defined, 14–15
gross, 16, 26
growth and increased, 27–28, 39
net, 20, 26
operating, 17–18, 26, 56
opportunity for, 13–14
as percentage of sales, 21–22
sales and expenses and, 14–15
profitability, 13–26
cost as lever of, 23–24, 26
cost structure and, 107
growth and, 93
levels of, 18
managing, 23–25
price and value perception as levers of,
24–25
profit and loss statement, 14–21, 26
profits, margins, and common-sizing,
21–22, 26
trade-offs between growth, risk, and,
99–103
value and, 8, 11
profit and loss (P&L) statement, 26, 56
accrual accounting and, 74–75
cash flow statement and, 84–85
communication performance via, 48
constructing, 14–21
defined, 16
operating cash flow and, 77–85
relationship to other financial
statements, 70, 76
sample simple, 20, 21

profit margin, 22
project evaluation, creating value and,
134–136
promises
company, 41–42, 50
discounting, 42
keeping, 10
trust and, 151, 152–153
PRWeek, Communicator of the Year
award, 252, 253
public goods, 18, 21
public relations, responsibility and,
251–254
purpose, as intrinsic motivator,
181–182
Putin, Vladimir, 242n

quality improvement, increased customer
value and, 25
quiet quitting, 185–186

Railroad Tycoon (game), 207
razor blade model, 105–106
real interest rate, 112n
recognition
of cooperative behavior, 198–199, 201
as intrinsic motivator, 179–180
redirection, 165n
Reeves, Hubert, 146
research and development (R&D), 17
creating new markets and, 31
Nokia and, 24
resources
profitability and, 13–14
valuing, 15
responsibility, 251–256
aversion to, 254–255
retained earnings, 56–63
return on investment, 111–117
revenue, 14n
risk, 41–50
balance sheet and, 59n

creating value by increasing confidence
    and, 47–49, 50
investor perspective on, 42–47, 50
return, time value of money, and,
    111–117
trade-offs between profitability, growth,
    and, 99–103
value and, 9, 11
risk-free rate, 112n, 113n
Robert, Henry Martyn, 225
Robert's Rules of Order, 225, 225n
role modeling, leadership and, 197–198,
    201
roles
    designating formal, 235
    rotating, 235
Rosenzweig, Phil, 190–191
round robin, 224–225, 239–240, 244
routine decisions, 233, 237
rules, structured discussion, 224–225
rules-based process for decision-making,
    legitimacy and, 232–234, 237
rules of engagement, teams and, 212

sales
    cost of, 16
    defined, 14, 14n
    growing, 27–28
    modeling future cash flow and, 118
    P&L statement and, 16
    predictability, business models and,
        104–106
    profit and, 14–15
    profit as percentage of, 21–22
    subscriptions smoothing, 105
    variability of, 104
Samuelson, Paul, 35n
SBI(I) (situation, behavior, impact, and
    intent) model, 168–169, 171
SBI (situation, behavior, impact) model,
    168–169
scale, fixed or variable expenses and, 95

Scholes, Myron, 4n
second team, 205, 206n
security, as intrinsic motivator, 180
selection process for decisions,
    227–230
self-similarity, in organizations, 205n
selling, general, and administrative
    expenses (SG&A), 17
setting, for feedback, 164
shareholder
    claims on company, 52
    defined, 3, 6
    growth and, 28
shareholder confidence
    debt and, 51–52
    increasing, 9
    See also investor confidence
shareholder return, 137–138
shareholder value, 3–5, 136–138
    creating, 109–110
    defined, 5
    discounted future net cash flows and,
        5, 6–8, 11
    drivers of, 11
    equity value vs., 54n, 68
    managing profitability and, 23–24, 26
    working capital management and,
        88–89
short-term debt, 63, 64
Silicon Valley, 93
simplified cash flow statement,
    constructing, 70–73
Singtel, 86
situational leadership, 152
smart phones, Nokia vs. Apple and, 5–6,
    9–10, 33
Smith, Adam, 143
sociability, as intrinsic motivator, 179
social dilemmas, 192–194
    in business, 194–195
    consensus decision-making and, 228
    information-based, 194

sociological innovation, new markets and, 31–32
software as a service (SaaS) model, 66, 105
sole decider, 227, 229–230
Sony, 105
Sports Obermeyer, 245
*Squid Game* (television program), 131
stakeholders, 3
    company promises to, 41, 50
    creating value for, 3
stakeholder value, 4, 21, 129, 136–138, 253
STAR (situation/task, action, and result) feedback model, 162, 162n
statement of financial positions, 63, 67, 68. *See also* balance sheet
*State of the Global Workplace* (Gallup), 173–177
status, as intrinsic motivator, 180
stock buybacks, 28n
stock price
    Netflix, 109, 132
    Nokia, 6, 10
    stock buybacks and, 28n
storming, teams and, 212
strategy, constraining decisions through, 216–220
strategy games, 207
structural errors in decision-making, 214, 216
structured discussions, decision-making and, 224–225
    process guardian and, 235–236
subjectivity of value, 6
subscriptions, 105
subscription services
    balance sheets and, 66
    Netflix, 86–87, 131
    Office 365, 66, 105
"success" case studies, leadership and, 191
suppliers

company promises to, 41
    operating cash flow and, 78, 80–81
    working capital and, 87–91, 92
supply chain disruptions, inflation and, 90–91
supply chain management, 89, 90–91
Sweden, switching driving sides in, 217, 220
synthetic risk-free rate, 113n

tangible assets, 17
tasks
    delegation of, 150–151
    expectation-setting behavior and, 154, 158
taxes, 18, 21
    on dividends *vs.* buybacks, 28n
team
    as basic decision-making unit, 205–206
    business simulations for, 209–212
    consensus decision-making and, 228
    development of, 212
    devil's advocate role, 241–245
    exploring options and gathering data for decisions, 222–225
    first, 205, 206n
    ideal size of, 205
    memberships in multiple, 205–206
    second, 205, 206n
    social dilemmas between, 194–195
technological innovation creating new markets, 31
*Ted Lasso* (television program), 146
terminal value, 124n
Tesla, 32
theory of the firm, 145
*Thinking, Fast and Slow* (Kahneman), 220–221
time
    balance sheet and, 62–63, 68
    P&L statement and, 18–19
timekeeper role, 234–235
timeliness, of feedback, 164

time value of money, risk, return, and, 111–117
timing
    of delivery *vs.* timing of expenses, 74, 74n
    divergence of cash flow and profit and, 74, 76, 77
    fixed or variable expenses and, 95
top-down decision-making, 218–219
trade-offs
    between drivers of value, 133–134
    of growth-oriented activities, 32–33
    increasing market share and, 30–31
    managers and responsibility aversion, 254–255
    price and value perception as, 24–25
    between profitability, growth, and risk, 99–103
trade working capital, 88–89, 91
    negative, 89–90, 92
tradition, legitimacy and, 232
tragedy of the commons, 192n
trust, 149–158
    autonomy and, 181n
    company value and, 10
    delegation and, 150–151
    do no harm to, 151, 158
    employee motivation and, 183
    globalized world and, 156–157
    at heart of value, 134
    intent and impact, 155–156
    of investors in executives, 134
    setting expectations, 152–155, 158
Tuckman, Bruce, 212
turf wars, 194–195
turnover, 14n
two-pizza rule, 205

Uber Technologies, 93, 96, 106
uncertainty, 51n
    Keynes on, 49

United Airlines, public relations disaster and, 251–254
US Federal Reserve, 112n
US Postal Service, 100
UPS, 100

*Valuation,* 132n
valuation formula, 136–137
valuation foundations, 109–128
    continuing value, 122–125
    cost of capital, 119–122, 127
    intrinsic value, 117–119, 126, 127–128
    risk, return, and the time value of money, 111–117
*Valuation: Measuring and Managing the Value of Companies* (Koller, Goedhart & Wessels), 110n, 113n
value
    of company, 4, 11
    competing for market share via, 30
    debt and, 51–52
    drivers of, 8–9
    intrinsic, 117–119, 126, 127–128
    perpetuity, 123–124
    price and, 6–7
    shareholder, 3–5, 136–138
    stakeholder, 4, 21, 129, 136–138, 253
    subjectivity of, 6
    terminal, 124n
    trust and, 10, 134
    *See also* growth; profitability; risk
value creation, 129–139
    evaluating projects, 134–136, 139
    increasing investor confidence and, 47–49, 50
    manager contribution to, 132–134
    shareholder value and stakeholder value, 136–138
    valuation example, 129–132
value perception, as lever of profitability, 24–25, 26

values, as constraints on decision-making, 219–220

variable cost, 94–97
  breakeven analysis and, 97–99
  preference for fixed costs or, 99–103

variable expenses, 94–95

*Veep* (television program), 146

vision
  as constraint on decision-making, 219
  leadership and communicating the, 197, 201

Vodafone, 86

Watzalawick, Paul, 160, 163n

*Wealth of Nations* (Smith), 143

Weber, Max, 232

*WeCrashed* (television program), 146

weighted average cost of capital (WACC), 120n

Welch, Jack, 3n, 195–196

Wessels, David, 110n, 113n, 132n

WeWork, 182n

work
  engagement at, 173–177
  social conversations on meaning of, 146–147

working capital, 87–91, 92
  modeling future cash flow and, 118
  trade, 88–89, 91

workplace
  popular culture representations of, 146–147, 149
  social conversations about, 146–147
  *State of the Global Workplace*, 173–177

workplace behavior, feedback on, 166–169

*World War Z* (film), 243

zero-sum game, market share as, 30–31